London Board of Jewish Religious Education
West Middlesex Regional Hebrew Classes
HEATHFIELD PARK CENTRE
143 Brondesbury Park, N.W.2.

𝔓𝔯𝔦𝔷𝔢

PRESENTED TO

TINA PETROOK

FOR

Good proper

_____ Hon. Superintendent

_____ Headmaster

July _____ 197 3 _____ 573 3

THE JEWISH HOME

EVELYN ROSE

THE JEWISH HOME

Vallentine, Mitchell—London

First published 1969 by
Vallentine, Mitchell & Co. Ltd.,
18, Cursitor Street
London E.C.4.

A variety of practical guides to every aspect of Jewish marriage and home life are published by the Jewish Marriage Education Council, 529b Finchley Road, London N.W.3, and readers of this book will find them most useful.

Printed and Bound in Great Britain
by Spottiswoode, Ballantyne & Co. Ltd.
London and Colchester

Contents

To my Mother . . . an inspiration in the past

And to my daughter . . . the hope for the future

Acknowledgements

Any book on homemaking must reflect the sum total of all the homes and homemakers one has known—in particular, those in one's own family circle.

So I must record the debt I owe to my mother and father, to my husband's parents, and indeed, to all the members of my immediate family. Many of my friends and fellow home economists have also been most generous with their help and advice.

For guidance on religious matters, I am indebted to Dayan I. Golditch of the Manchester Beth Din, and in particular, to the Rev. Felix F. Carlebach, M.A., who checked the entire manuscript. The final decisions on content are, however, entirely mine. I also wish to thank Harry and Jean Hyman, Gerald Somers, Lol Snowise and Issy Reece for technical advice on food; my colleague, Margaret Travis, who assisted her husband with the illustrations; Barbara Jacques and Peggy Warmisham, who have been indefatigable in transforming my illegible manuscript into "fair copy"; and my faithful Jessie, who took my place at the kitchen sink when I was too busy at the typewriter.

Above all, I must thank my husband, Myer, and my children, David, Alan and Judi, who suffered it all with hardly a murmur, and whose loyalty and faith made me see it through to the end.

Introduction

It needs both love and knowledge to make a home of one's own, and to make a *Jewish* home needs these qualities to a particularly high degree. For, in a Jewish household, the ordinary daily routine is closely involved with religious practice, and to the housewife falls the responsibility of successfully combining the two.

Fortunately, Jewish women have inherited a particularly rich tradition of homemaking, which has developed from the experience of housewives living in almost every land under the sun. Wherever they have made their home, Jewish women have always adapted for their own use the best housekeeping and cooking skills of the communities around them, and then made them part of the Jewish way of life. That is why one can go into a Jewish home any-where in the world, sit down at the dinner table, and feel immediately at home.

In the past, it was easy for a girl to absorb her family's traditional homemaking skills, for it was the custom for the unmarried girl to help her mother with the household routine. Today, however, the majority of young Jewish women are either studying or working before they are married and often live far away from their home, while the girl who stays at home to help in the house is the exception.

As there is now so little opportunity to learn homemaking by example, I have written this book in the hope that it will be possible to learn from its pages instead. Into it I have put twenty years of experience, both as a housewife and a home economist, and have tried to give you the answers to all those questions on homemaking which I wanted to ask when I was first married.

The book is concerned with the *principles* of homemaking which are as valid one year as the next, rather than with the *details*, which change with bewildering speed and are so much better learned from newspapers, magazines and television.

Much of the advice it contains is the same as you would need to run any modern home: how to set up house; plan and equip a kitchen; keep the home and its furnishings in good order; plan, cook and serve the daily meals.

But a large part of the book is specifically concerned with the running of a Jewish home; how to prepare for Shabbat and the different Festivals; how to choose and prepare kosher meat and poultry; and how to do these and many other household duties and be a working wife at the same time. In addition, there is a "Bride's Cookery Course" in which there are very detailed directions for making all those traditional and modern dishes which you are likely to need during the first few years.

As the old routines of housekeeping must constantly be revised to suit our mid-twentieth century way of life, I have not attempted to give instructions for any one infallible routine; in any case, that is something that every woman must work out to suit herself—and her husband. Instead, I have tried to give guidance on the best way of creating a "pattern" of living that will provide a comfortable background for the life of the individual family, and yet be flexible enough to modify should the need arise.

I believe that one can only keep faith with the past by creating new traditions using the materials and the skills of the present. I hope that this book will help you to do this and so enable you to create the unique, if indefinable, atmosphere of happy family living that is the indestructible possession of every Jewish home.

Shopping for Your Home and Kitchen

The kind of home in which you decide to start your married life will depend not only on the capital that is available, but also on the particular circumstances of your husband's—and probably your own—career.

Thus, you may equally well find yourself shopping to furnish a one-room flat that you have taken on a short-term lease; or a family-sized house in which you hope to live for the next decade. But when it comes to "setting up house"—transforming bare rooms into a welcoming and comfortable home—the procedure is very much the same.

The first step is to decide how much you have to spend in total, and then work out a suitable budget to cover all the predictable expenses. These will include the cost of any structural alterations and improvements, decorations (both inside and out), furnishings and household appliances. (As the kitchen needs equipment of a specialised and expensive nature, it should have a detailed budget of its own. This is discussed in detail later in the chapter.)

If your first home is to be a temporary one, you will only want to invest in absolutely essential equipment, and those furnishings which can easily be moved from one place to another, saving the bulk of your money until you have a permanent home. But no matter how much or how little you buy, make sure that everything is of the best quality that your budget will allow, for well-considered purchases will prove the best buys in the long run.

To decide what you do need, and in what order, it is a good plan to consider each room in turn, and make a list of the major items that will be needed to furnish and equip it. Then, with the help of your parents or married friends, put down an estimated minimum allowance for each item on the list. When the total sum that will be needed for all the furnishings has been worked out and compared with the amount of money that is actually available, a list of priority purchases can then be made, to ensure that the most important items are bought first from the funds available, and the less vital ones left to be purchased later. Listing the, items that you think you will require can also be most helpful as a guide to those relations and close friends who wish to avoid duplicating wedding presents, and at the same time make sure that what they do buy is to your particular taste. If you can decide on a certain range of pans, or linens or tableware, then several people can get together to give an omnibus gift which will be far more meaningful than several unrelated purchases could ever be.

Getting the Right Advice

Before you buy any permanent equipment, try and get as much information about it as you can. Many different organisations, such as the Council of Industrial Design, the Consumer Council and the Consumer Association provide excellent consumer advice. In addition many magazines will give guidance and the latest information on current models of appliances and trends in design. Several manufacturers' associations have advice centres throughout the country where a very wide range of specialised consumer goods is displayed. (See the addresses listed at the back of the book.)

Furnishing Schemes

Again it is vital to get expert advice, if only to confirm the soundness of your own ideas. This advice can be obtained most easily—if most expensively—from an interior decoration consultant. But the majority of young couples prefer to work out their own schemes, based on the advice given free by carpet, fabric, paint and wallpaper manufacturers as well as by magazines specialising in interior design. But as so much depends on factors such as the size and aspect of a particular room, as well as on individual variations in taste, the final choice must inevitably be a personal one.

However, it is always good policy to choose the floor coverings first, as they are likely to prove the single most expensive item in a house. Wall coverings and soft furnishings which are initially less expensive—and so can be replaced at more frequent intervals—can then be chosen to match.

Choose first those items of furniture that you intend to live with for some time—such as a really good mattress and base. This you can expect to last you for many years, even though the headboard of the bed may be changed from time to time to suit a particular furnishing scheme. And whether the furniture be period or modern in feeling, do examine it with care to make sure that it is solid and well finished with well fitting doors and drawers.

Before you move into your new home, mezzuzot will need to be purchased to fix on the outside of every door. The day before you move in, your parents or a close friend will arrange to leave a gift of bread and salt by the door, as a token of their hope for your future good fortune. And when you are well and truly "settled in", and your house or flat has taken on those intangible qualities that turn it into a home, you may well feel that the time has come to invite your family and friends to a "Birchat Habayit" when the minister of your local congregation will officially "bless" the first home of your married life.

1

SETTING UP THE HOME AND KITCHEN

The Kitchen

According to a survey by the Building Research Station, the average housewife is likely to spend three-quarters of her working day in her kitchen. I would put the percentage even higher in the Jewish household, because our kind of cooking—and the laws of kashrut involved in it—require a lot of attention to detail.

To keep this time to the minimum it is obvious that the kitchen must be most carefully planned. What is not so obvious—until you have actually worked in one—is just how *much* time, energy and temper this kitchen planning can save. Since my own kitchen was redesigned, I can do twice the cooking in half the time, and feel far less tired at the end of it.

What Does Planning Involve?

The planning of any kitchen must start with a decision on how it is to be used. Then follows the careful, informed choice of fittings and appliances, and their arrangement in a labour-saving sequence, surrounded by the right kind of storage. All the equipment must be at the right height, lit in the right places (with the correct degree of brightness) and with sufficient electrical points fixed conveniently near the equipment they are to serve.

The walls and floor must be covered with durable, easy-to-clean materials, and adequate ventilation provided to keep the kitchen free from cooking smells and disfiguring dirt. Above all, these different "ingredients" must be combined to create a bright, light, attractive room that will become, by choice as much as by necessity, the main focus of family living.

A lot of mumbo-jumbo is talked about kitchens, and people who will furnish their living room with confidence quail when it comes to the kitchen. It is true that there are certain proven principles in kitchen planning, but once these are known, the actual layout and the selection of the equipment require no more special knowledge than for any other room in the house.

The main point to keep in mind is that your kitchen is not for the use of some mythical magazine characters, but for you and your family, and must be planned to suit your needs and tastes. In running a Jewish household there are special needs which must be considered at each planning stage, and I shall refer to them in detail as they arise.

Any shape or size of room—providing it is large enough to hold the necessary equipment with sufficient counter space in between—can be made into a workable kitchen. This is useful to bear in mind when house hunting, as one need never reject an otherwise suitable house because the kitchen seems unpromising at first glance. In fact, once you know the basic ideas involved in labour-saving, you can interpret them to suit the needs of any kind of kitchen.

What Kind of Kitchen ?

Whether your kitchen already exists in a flat or house, or has yet to go on the drawing board of your architect, the first thing to decide is how it is to be used. Is it to be solely a working kitchen, or would you like to have a corner for eating and relaxing where, later on, the children can play ?

Your decision will be affected by such factors as the shape and size of the room—and of the rooms nearby—and of course, by how permanent you expect this home to be. Providing there is the space, it is always good policy to have somewhere to eat in the kitchen, but out of the view of the sink. In a small room, this could be provided by a pull-out table built into a unit. In a larger room, it could be a special dining corner, in which the children could play under supervision from the "business" end of the room.

On the other hand, if you prefer a "morning room" and you intend to use it in the evening as well, then it is better to be completely separated from kitchen sights and smells, albeit with the dining part nearest to the kitchen for ease in serving food.

As laundry and cookery do not mix well, it is preferable to do the washing in a separate utility room. But if there is no utility room, the washing machine is best installed near the sink, with a preparation counter above.

Once the function of the kitchen has been decided, the way

Basic Equipment

is clear to work out a basic plan and decide on the equipment that will be required.

In any convenient kitchen, a basic list of equipment will include :

(1) a sink unit (with double drainers or, alternatively, with a drainer on one side and stacking space on the other) ;

(2) a cooker (either split-level, or free-standing) ;

(3) a refrigerator for perishable foods, with some type of frozen-food compartment.

These first three appliances form the "eternal triangle" of kitchen planning, round which all the other equipment must be arranged :

(4) a larder or ventilated storage cupboard (for semi-perishable foods and those foods which are better not refrigerated) ;

(5) storage cupboards for canned and dry goods not in frequent use (these may be incorporated in the larder or larder cupboard) ;

(6) working tops and counters, with one counter at least 42 inches long as a main food preparation centre. These will link up the different appliances, and be fitted with cupboards and drawers for the storage of cutlery, cooking utensils and table china.

Of less urgent need, but useful to bear in mind when planning a layout that can be adapted for future as well as present needs :

(7) a washing machine and drier ;

(8) a dishwasher ;

(9) a deep-freeze cabinet (which may well be part of the refrigerator).

To this list must be added the extra furnishings that your particular kind of kitchen requires.

Now that the basic function of your kitchen has been decided, and you have worked out a priority list of equipment, the first steps can be taken in planning the layout. This first rough plan will help you determine what size and design of equipment can be fitted in, and where.

Now is the time to make a preliminary shopping trip and collect leaflets on the different appliances; from them you can gain some idea of the basic dimensions of the equipment to be included in your plan. (You will find that there is very little variation in overall size between appliances of similar performance and capacity.)

It is at this stage, when your basic requirements are clear, that you can call in the professional kitchen designer. He may be from the Gas or Electricity Board, an architect or a kitchen contractor. You give him a plan of your kitchen, showing the position of doors and windows (or he comes and draws one for himself), a list of the equipment you would like to include, and leave the rest to him. His plan may not suit you in every detail, but because it will be based on sound planning principles, it can provide an excellent foundation on which to base the final plan.

Alternatively, once you have decided on the make of kitchen units you prefer, you can send the same information to the makers, who will send you their detailed plan, based, of course, on the units in their range. You may, however, enjoy working out the layout yourself

Perhaps the easiest way, once you have decided on the sequence you would like, is to draw a scale plan of the room on squared graph paper, make scale cardboard cut-outs of the various pieces of equipment, and juggle them about until you find the best arrangement. We did this, even when we called in a professional designer, for once we knew where we wanted everything to be, his trained eye enabled him to combine the different elements in such a way, that the kitchen was as efficient in use as it was in appearance.

To plan a good working order for any kitchen, one must first analyse the main job to be done there—the preparation of food. This always follows a definite sequence: The food which is brought in at the back door is first stored, then in turn prepared, cooked, served and eaten. Finally the dirty dishes are stacked, then washed and stored away. The more closely the arrangement of the appliances follows this sequence, the more labour-saving it will prove to be.

In practice this means that, ideally, one should take the food from the refrigerator or larder and prepare it on the

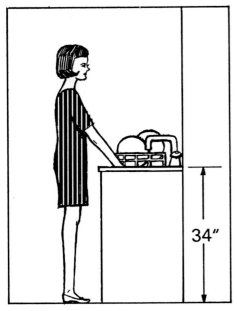

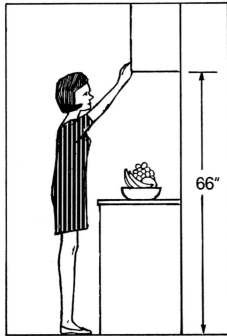

adjoining counter, next to the cooker. Once it is cooked, it should be placed ready for service on a counter convenient to the dining room. Finally, used dishes should be stacked on one side of the sink, washed, dried and put away in storage cupboards placed nearby.

At the same time, as no cooking job is ever done in a straight line, but involves constantly moving between one appliance and another, the more compact the arrangement and the less floor space involved, the better it will be.

The kingpin of the kitchen is the cooker, and this should be the first appliance to be placed. It should be sited if possible, in a good natural light, convenient for food service, and with ample counter space on either side. This counter should connect it directly with the sink, which should itself have drainers or counters on both sides. The position of the plumbing must be taken into account when positioning the sink; but it is wiser to put the sink in the most suitable place and pay for the extra piping, than to suffer for years the inconvenience of a badly situated sink.

The main preparation counter should be at least 42 inches long, and is ideally sited at one side of the cooker. The oven of a split-level cooker can be sited away from the hob, but needs a counter at least 21 inches long—and preferably of heat-proof material—at the side. Counter space must also be allowed for the storage of small appliances in frequent use, such as the toaster, the coffee grinder and the mixer, and for the stacking of food and crockery before and after service.

A plan that satisfies the basic requirements I have mentioned can be devised to suit the idiosyncrasies of any shape or size of room.

For instance:

(1) *In a square room,* a double-drainer sink unit can run the length of the window wall, flanked, on the two adjoining walls by the cooker and refrigerator.

(2) *In an L-shaped room,* the cooker and refrigerator can be placed on one wall, with the sink on the other.

(3) *In a long, narrow room,* all three pieces of equipment can be lined up on one wall, with the cooker in the middle.

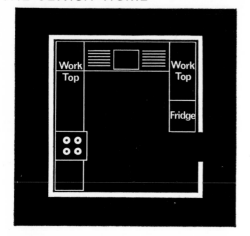

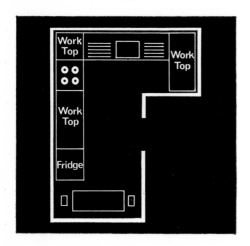

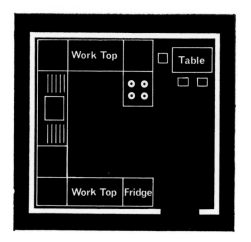

(4) *In a rectangular room*, a peninsula unit, built out from one wall, and housing either the sink or cooker hob, can act as a divider between the working and dining areas, or make a more compact arrangement in an over-large kitchen.

In each case, the length of counter dividing each appliance will vary with the size of the room.

My own kitchen follows the fourth plan. The peninsula housing the sink unit is built out parallel with the wall containing the cooker and refrigerator, with the main preparation counter bridging the two. It is effective, because sufficient floor space to enable two people to work comfortably back to back divides the cooker from the sink. This peninsula has created a third wall in the working kitchen, providing in a very limited floor space, enough room to include a split-level cooker, an under-counter refrigerator, and a dishwasher built in under the drainer.

And by backing the sink with a counter-topped range of cupboards, standing 9 inches above it, the unit itself is masked from the dining area beyond. The problem of standing at the sink in one's own light has been overcome by positioning lights directly over the sink unit itself.

The height of kitchen equipment is of vital importance, as stooping and stretching are major causes of kitchen fatigue. Most women work best at a counter height of 34 inches from the floor. They can easily reach a shelf 70 inches high (66 inches if it is set back above a counter), but will have to do a minimum of bending and stretching to

9

reach storage between 2 and 5 feet high, the level at which the most frequently used materials should be kept.

Before buying any kitchen equipment it is wise to stand at it, and "try it for size". This applies especially to sink units for, while the draining board height may be right, the sink itself may be too deep for comfort. A slightly lower counter is useful for pastry-making, but if this cannot be included, the whole counter should be set at the best average height. This, depending on the height of the user, will be between 34 and 36 inches from the floor.

To test the practicality of a paper plan, it is a good idea mentally to prepare a meal in the kind of kitchen the plan proposes, rehearsing in one's mind all the steps it will be necessary to take. How many steps are there from cooker to sink . . . and where is the refrigerator? Where will the hot dishes be put down before they are served, and where will the dirty ones be stacked? Do this with the help of an experienced housewife, and if the arrangement seems to cover all the points I have made, then the kitchen plan is likely to work.

Shopping for Equipment

Before the *final* kitchen plan can be drawn, specific models of appliances and makes of equipment must have been selected, so that their exact dimensions are known, and their precise position decided.

Either because of financial limitations or restricted floor space, at some point during this selection the need for compromise will surely arise. Before you start to shop, it is good policy to decide exactly how much money you intend to spend, then work out a budget based on your priority shopping list.

With a limited sum to spend, it is better to buy only the essential equipment at first, but of a quality and capacity to meet your probable needs for a decade, than to try and equip the entire kitchen for a shorter period in one fell swoop. Storage space, in particular, needs to be planned and bought with the next ten years in mind, for it is better to have room to spare now, than to be frustrated and handicapped by the lack of it later.

Where floor space is limited, one may need to make a choice between two equally desirable pieces of equipment—perhaps between a split-level cooker and a double

Real Value for Money

drainer for the sink. Only you can decide which will have to go, keeping in mind the pros and cons of selection set out below.

In everything you buy, look for intrinsic quality rather than fancy finish. Do not be misled by the surface glitter of gadgets and chrome, but (aesthetic considerations apart) base your decision on the manufacturer's specification giving details of construction. In this way you may well find that you can get equal quality, performance and convenience from a cheaper, if less elaborate, model.

Cleanability and Durability

Be they cupboards, counters, floors, walls or appliances, the cleaning of kitchen surfaces is a daily chore. The materials of which these surfaces are made must therefore be impervious to kitchen grease and dirt, easily cleaned by wiping down and, above all, sturdy enough to withstand the friction that this constant cleaning must involve.

Servicing Arrangements

If an appliance is powered by electricity or gas, make sure that it can be serviced easily, quickly and by locally based men. Indeed, for appliances in constant use, the ideal is a service contract, under which the appliance is overhauled at regular intervals while in working order, rather than repaired in an emergency when it has broken down.

Expert Advice

Before the final choice is made, there is much expert advice on which to call. In the magazine, *Which?*, there are detailed reports comparing and contrasting the performance of similar models, and also giving full details of capacity and price. (The magazine is published by the Consumers' Association for subscribers only, but back copies can be consulted at the local library.)

In the Design Index, there are full details and illustrations of a very wide range of British-made goods of first-class design. The Index—and a constantly changing display of goods from its lists—can be consulted in Manchester and London in the Design Centres run by the Council of Industrial Design.

Magazines and newspapers also constantly report on the latest and the best, while a well-informed and experienced salesman, with his bird's-eye view of the entire market, can be of inestimable help. As you sift and sort the opinions from all these different points of view, you will suddenly find that certain makers will stand out as the best, and it is from their ranges that you can then confidently choose the models that most satisfy your personal requirements of price, size and design.

The Sink Unit

The kitchen sink is in more constant daily use than any other part of the kitchen equipment, so it must be convenient to work at, and made of a hard-wearing material that is easy to maintain. It is usually bought as part of a complete cupboard and drawer unit, though for a non-standard length it may be more convenient to buy the sink alone and have the lower unit custom-built to fit. Despite the initial cost, the most satisfactory material for the sink itself is heavy-gauge stainless steel, for it withstands scratching, heat and abrasion better than other materials, and is most easily cleaned.

A single sink bowl with extra-long drainers is ideal for the Jewish kitchen, where dishes are washed in a plastic bowl rather than put directly into the sink. A sink of useful size measures approximately 19 inches × 15 inches × 7½ inches deep, and a drainer to hold a family size plate rack with room for larger dishes at the side will be about 32 inches long. Under a drainer of this length, it is possible to accommodate a dishwasher of average size, and even if this appliance is not to be bought for a while, it is worth trying to make provision for its eventual installation near the sink, and even to arrange for the preliminary plumbing to be laid on.

The single sink arrangement I suggest is as efficient as a double sink and far less expensive in floor space and money. Indeed, dishes can be more easily rinsed right in the dish drainer by a built-in hot-water spray, which may be bought as part of the tap unit. If there is the space, however, a second, smaller sink bowl, complete with waste disposer and fitted chopping-board cover, can be installed in the working top, for the preparation of fruit and vegetables.

Though a washing-up sink set directly into laminated plastic looks smarter, it is far less efficient than one surrounded by drainers of stainless steel. Hastily set-down pans will scratch the plastic surface, and stove-hot ones may scorch it. And because it is set level rather than at an angle, it will be constantly waterlogged. If, however, the sink itself is set on one side, at right angles to a work counter, it is quite convenient to use this top for dishes, providing there is a lengthy stainless steel drainer on the "business" side.

Whether set in the main or vegetable sink, a waste disposer is a great convenience, and providing it is used as instructed, should prove quite trouble-free. Present models cannot digest large bones, paper and cans, but disposable paper bags for this kind of kitchen waste can easily be fitted to the inner sink unit door.

The Cooker

Though the styling of a cooker is the first thing to catch the eye, the decision to buy must be based on its convenience, capacity and cleanability.

On your personal preference will depend the choice between electricity and gas, as both kinds of cooker are now so well designed that there is little to choose between them from any point of view. Both are made in split-level as well as conventional models, both have features like auto-timers and spits, and both incorporate really efficient grills. Your choice may well depend on the kind of cooker you have used in the past, or which fuel is laid on in your new home.

I like the flexibility of gas on the top, but prefer an electric oven because of its all-over even heat. One can now buy a stove using both fuels, but I have a separate gas hot-plate and a built-in electric oven, which I find ideal.

Though undoubtedly costly, a split-level cooker has a great deal to offer. The oven can be inset at a comfortable (and child-proof) height, so that heavy dishes can be slid without strain from shelf to drop-down door to counter; and, because it can be sited quite independently of the top, it need not be put in the main preparation part of the kitchen. The separate hob can be slotted right into the preparation counter, the light on it unobscured by cooker back or grill, and with a large and convenient pan cupboard below.

Some cookers have twin ovens, which allow one to cook at different temperatures at the same time. This can prove of particular use when preparing meals in advance for Yom-tov and Shabbat.

But no matter what style you may choose, the key to convenience in a cooker lies in its size. The oven should hold two 7-inch sandwich tins on one shelf without crowding, and be deep enough to roast efficiently a 15-lb. turkey. The hob should have four hot-plates or burners and be wide enough to accommodate an 11-inch frying pan and a ½-gallon chicken pan (not necessarily, of course, at the same time). The grill should hold eight chops at once, though the bigger it can be the better.

Features worth paying extra for include an auto-timer, a glass-fronted oven, a warming drawer or large-size plate rack, and a thermoguard on one of the burners to keep the contents of a pan at a constant temperature. This is a great help when frying fish or chips, as well as when simmering soup.

The cleanability of a cooker cannot be considered apart from its durability. For cleaning causes wear, and cooker parts must not only be easily detachable for cleaning, but also come up like new after each session in the sink. Enamel must be of a heavy gauge, and metal parts well finished and sturdy, without dirt-catching indentations and curves. Control knobs should be detachable for cleaning, and placed where they are easily seen. And the spillage trays of a gas cooker must be smooth and deep, preferably sealed to the cooker top at the sides to prevent liquid from flowing where it cannot be removed.

All metal parts of the oven should be detachable for cleaning, and a removable door is a particular help. And be it electric or gas, unless it is built in, a cooker should slide forward from the wall for cleaning.

But in making the final choice, let experience be your guide. Take along a housewife of discernment and ask her opinion. Stand at the cooker yourself and "try it out", and make as sure as you can before you buy that you will be able to go through the routine of cooking and cleaning up with the minimum of effort and strain.

The Refrigerator

When shopping for a refrigerator, you must first decide on what size you are likely to need—and are able to fit into your kitchen. Then, having narrowed the field down to models of this size, you should take a long and careful look at such features as the star rating of the frozen food compartment, the layout of the cabinet, the system of defrosting and the floor space requirements of the different makes. Remember that if you choose with care, this appliance will last you for at least ten years.

The Size

A spacious refrigerator is an absolute necessity in a Jewish household, where quantities of food for Shabbat and Yomtov often have to be stored (in both a raw and a cooked state) for several days at a time. Providing there is room for it in the kitchen and your budget will allow, I consider a 7 cubic foot model to be the optimum size.

Of course, it will be too big for your needs at first. But too large a refrigerator is both more convenient in use and more efficient in operation than one that is "just right" or too small. Food is put away more quickly when there is no struggle to fit it in, while the freer circulation of air in an uncrowded refrigerator allows the temperature to stay constant at an economical setting. But if, for any reason, an appliance of this size is out of the question, do not despair. A 5 cubic foot model that fits under the working counter will certainly meet your needs for the first five years; but it is worth rearranging the rest of the kitchen to fit in the largest possible size of refrigerator, for you will save both money and time in the long run.

When I needed additional refrigerator space, and was planning a new kitchen layout, I bought an under-counter refrigerator for the kitchen, and moved the original one into the adjoining utility room. Here I keep bulkier items and cooked foods that may not be needed immediately, while in the smaller refrigerator in the kitchen are all the everyday supplies of dairy foods, left-overs and "cooking" vegetables and herbs. The system works to perfection.

The Star Rating

The number of stars (from one to three) marked on the door of a British-made refrigerator, indicate just how long commercially frozen foods can be safely stored. Unless one lives miles away from the shops, a two-star rating (in which food keeps safely for a month) is quite high enough.

In a three-star refrigerator, the temperature in the frozen

food compartment is low enough to freeze and store fresh and home-cooked food. But the extra cost of this star is only worthwhile if the freezer compartment itself is of a useful size. Anything less than 2½ cubic feet is really too small to be practical. If you intend to home-freeze food in any quantity, then it is more economical to buy a separate deep-freeze cabinet.

Inside the Cabinet

Depending on the way the interior is designed, refrigerators of the same cubic capacity may well differ in the amount of actual *shelf* space they provide, and it is worth checking up on this in the descriptive brochure. The shelves themselves should be adjustable, so that it is easy to store containers of differing sizes. For example, to store a pan of chicken soup, you will need a shelf that is at least 8 inches high. There should be a large vegetable crisper with a snug-fitting lid, extending ideally, the entire width of a shelf, with room on another for a meat container about half its size, and 6 inches deep.

In the door (where the temperature is just right for dairy foods), there should be storage space for two dozen eggs, four or five ½-lb. packets of butter and five bottles of milk, with 12 inches of "headroom" above one of the shelves for wine bottle storage. I have found an enamel lining to be more durable than a plastic one (which tends to crack), but I would not reject an otherwise suitable model for this reason.

The Defrosting System

The faster this works, the better, for it then becomes unnecessary to remove food from the frozen food compartment. The best system of all is fully automatic and requires no attention. When defrosting becomes necessary, the refrigeration unit automatically cuts out, and cuts in again when the job is completed. The water produced by defrosting is evaporated by the heat generated in the compressor. The semi-automatic method involves pressing a button to stop the unit, but it does cut in again automatically when defrosting is complete. With this method, however, the water collects in the drip tray during defrosting, and has to be removed at the end.

Fitting into a Floor Plan

How much room the refrigerator will take up depends not only on the area of the base, but also on how far the

16

appliance itself will need to be sited from the wall. Some models have "works" that project at the back. Others have to be brought forward to allow the door to open to its full width, unimpeded by the unit beside it. This usually means that all the equipment on that wall of the kitchen has to be lined up with the hinges of the fridge door, rather than with its front, and allowance will need to be made for this when calculating the depth of the counters covering them.

Guarantees and Maintenance

Refrigerators rarely go wrong, but it can be a costly and inconvenient business when they do. It is vital to ensure that the appliance is adequately covered by a guarantee (usually one year for the cabinet and five for the unit), and that repairs and spare parts can be speedily secured. This matter of spares should be investigated with especial care if the refrigerator is of foreign manufacture.

Storage Units

You will probably spend more on storage fitments than on all the other kitchen equipment put together. But if you choose sturdily constructed, well-finished units, carefully tailored to fit the storage requirements of the kitchen, they should still be in useful working order in twenty years' time.

Fitments made of well-seasoned wood or heavy gauge steel are equally durable, providing the construction itself is good. *Doors* should have well-fitting catches that close at a touch. *Drawers* should be made with close-fitting joints (dovetailed, if wood), and move easily, whether empty or full. *Shelves* should be adjustable to different heights and be available (if the fitments are ready-made) in different widths to suit their contents and their siting in the kitchen (see below).

The outer finish of the units, whether laminated plastic, wood or paint, should be resistant to damp and grease, and need no more complicated maintenance than a wipe with a damp window-leather or cloth.

The inner finish ideally, should be laminated plastic, but if this is too expensive, well-finished paint will do.

Factory-made units that meet these specifications are generally cheaper than custom-built units of comparable quality, and it is usually possible to find a wide enough

variety of units in at least one manufacturer's range to meet almost any requirements of shape or size. However, in an awkwardly shaped kitchen, it may be preferable to have all, or at least some, of the cupboards made to measure.

Assessing Your Needs

Just as you made a rough floor plan of the kitchen, so it is worthwhile to make a *storage plan* before you begin to shop, so that you will have a good idea of what storage accommodation you will need and where it might be placed.

To make this plan you will need to know *what* you have to store, *where* it will be most convenient, and *how.*

Start by dividing the kitchen into *storage centres* for baking, cooking, food preparation, washing up, etc., with each centre based on the appliance or equipment with which it is concerned. Next, list every single item of food and equipment that needs to be within arm's reach of each centre. Then, on graph paper, draw out in turn the walls that house each centre and its appliance, so that you can work out how much shelf and drawer space will be required to put away everything on the list.

Of course it will not work out to perfection, and many infrequently used or awkwardly shaped pieces of equipment will not fit in where they should. But it will still be an invaluable help when you go shopping.

SETTING UP THE HOME AND KITCHEN

In estimating your storage requirements, you will need to keep in mind the special needs of a Jewish kitchen. These include room for the separate storage of meat and milk dishes and utensils, shelf space for a great variety of large-diameter frying pans and soup pans, and cupboards for Passover pots and pans.

Be sure to leave as much room as possible for expansion, because, as the family grows, so, too, will the size of the cooking equipment and the shelf space it requires.

To be convenient in use, stores and equipment must not only be kept in the right *part* of the kitchen, but also in the right *kind* of cupboard, set at the right height.

On the counter, close to a power point, keep small appliances ready for use (the coffee grinder, electric toaster, electric mixer, wall can-opener).

Above the counter, in the most accessible cupboards, set approximately at eye level, keep stores which are in constant daily use. On the back of the counter and in the drawers just below it, keep cooking cutlery and small gadgets in frequent use. Everything else will be stored in cupboards above and below this centre "band".

The depth and height of cupboards must be carefully considered in relation to their position and contents.

Depth

Cupboards should never be more than eighteen inches in depth, or it will be difficult to reach the back of the shelves. In fact, it is better if the majority of things are stored in a single row.

The depth of cupboards should be approximately:

Nine inches at eye level (for the storage of canisters and small packets of food);
Twelve inches for hanging cupboards and china cupboards;
Eighteen inches for below-counter cupboards (for pans, casseroles, mixing bowls, etc., which can, if necessary, be conveniently stored in two rows).

In addition, extra shelves can easily be fitted in, where necessary, to hold plates, jars and containers of very narrow diameter.

Height

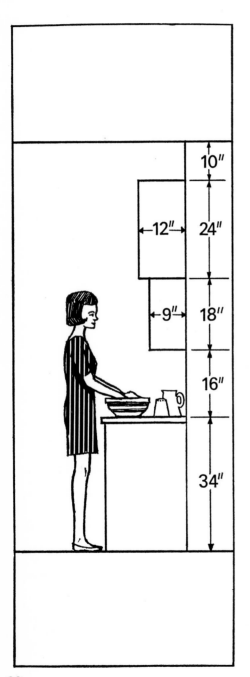

10"

←12"→ 24"

←9"→ 18"

16"

34"

The position of lower cupboards is decided by the height (or absence) of a counter. Cupboards above a counter must be set low enough for as many of their shelves as possible to be within easy reach, yet high enough for outward swinging doors to open clear of one's head. Cupboards immediately above the counter must be set up and back, so that they are well out of the way when you are working there. The most suitable position depends on your height and reach.

As a guide, I have given below the height and arrangement of the cupboards positioned above and beneath my main preparation counter, which is 36 inches high.

Immediately above the counter, there is a shallow bank of cupboards, divided into three units, each 42 inches wide, set back 12 inches from the front of the counter, and hung 16 inches above it. Each unit has sliding doors. The cupboards are 18 inches high and 9 inches deep, with the upper shelf only 7 inches from back to front.

Directly above these cupboards and projecting $2\frac{1}{2}$ inches forward, is a further bank, of the same width, but 24 inches high and 12 inches deep. These cupboards stop 10 inches short of the ceiling, to avoid a boxed-in look. The bottom shelf of this bank, which is 68 inches from the floor, is low enough to be reached without stool-steps, yet high enough to allow the door to swing open clear of my head. Each unit has two doors which open away from each other, so that the contents of the shelves can be seen at a glance, and large equipment easily removed.

Below the counter, there is a row of shallow drawers, with cupboards 18 inches deep beneath them.

On the other walls there are cupboards and drawers, each tailored for their contents.

Special storage units. The right *kind* of storage for a particular food or piece of equipment greatly adds to the efficient running of the kitchen. Often, a simple adaptation of a standard fitment is all that is necessary. Here are some storage ideas for foods and equipment with special requirements.

Bread. Line a 6-inch deep drawer with laminated plastic, and keep the bread in plastic bags.

Baking and roasting tins. Fit an 18-inch deep lower cupboard with divisions made from two rows of ½-inch dowelling, so that the different tins can be "filed" in separate divisions.

Breakfast stores. Keep jams on four-inch wide shelves, and breakfast cereals in a cupboard near the boiler or other warm, dry spot.

Tinned goods. Keep stocks on narrow shelves so that tins stand no more than two deep.

Casseroles. Heavy iron casseroles should be kept below the counter, or at waist height, as it is dangerous to attempt to lift them from above shoulder height.

China. Keep on narrow shelves, ideally a step from the dish-washer or drainer. Special china racks are very saving of space. Hanging cups by the handles weakens them and should be avoided.

Cooking tools. Knives are best kept on a magnetic rack at the back of the counter. Frequently used tools should be kept on racks in the same place. More specialised tools and gadgets are best kept in cutlery racks in a drawer.

Cleaning equipment. Keep in a specially fitted cupboard with plenty of shelves, hooks and holders for different brushes and stores. Keep this cupboard away from the preparation centre; perhaps, if space is limited, under the stairs.

Dry stores (cereals, pulses, pasta, dried fruits, etc.). Buy an assortment of glass jars with ground, airtight stoppers, in ½-lb., 1-lb. and 2-lb. sizes. They are convenient, attractive and cheap. Keep them in the above-counter cupboard, or on a ledge at the back of the counter itself.

Herbs and spices. You are sure to be given some kind of jars as a present. Unlabelled glass jars with airtight stoppers are ideal. Label them yourself. I use butterfly-"killing" bottles, which are decorative and effective. Simple wood shelves can be bought to hold them. Keep herbs and savoury spices near the cooker, sweet spices in your baking centre.

Frying and cooking oil. Keep in an airtight plastic container, on a tile or small tray, in a cupboard away from the light. Keep oil for daily cooking in a decorative wine bottle at the side of the stove.

Frying pans. These are best hung from hooks under a counter or tiled slab. Otherwise, stack them on a shelf lined with laminated plastic (in case they are warm when put away).

Pans. Keep these out of sight, side by side on shelves. There is no harm in keeping the lids on, providing the pans are quite dry when put away.

Vegetables and fruit. Keep potatoes and onions on special plastic-coated racks, with non-perishable fruit such as oranges, grapefruit and baking apples. All other fruits and vegetables should be kept under refrigeration to conserve their food value.

Washing-up equipment. Special fitments can be bought for the inside of the sink unit door to keep all kinds of detergents, pan scourers and brushes conveniently out of sight. Dish drainers are best hung from a hook on the inside of the cupboard, with meat and milk washing-up bowls on separate shelves.

Items for Which You Will Need to Allow Storage Space in the Kitchen or Dining Area

For Cooking

    Pans (meat, milk, soup, frying) ;
    Casseroles and roasting dishes ;
    Covered glass casseroles and pudding dishes ;
    Herbs, spices, salt, pepper and seasonings ;
    Kitchen tools on rack ;
    Cooking cutlery and knives (meat and milk) ;
    Mincer, koshering bucket and draining board ;
    Small gadgets (apple corer, knife sharpener, lemon-squeezer, etc.) ;
    Chopping board and chopper.

For Baking

    Mixer, rolling pin and board ;
    Baking gadgets (cutters, piping tubes and bag, etc.) ;
    Flour bin and flour sifter ;
    Baking stores (sugar, dried fruit, nuts, flour) ;
    Mixing bowls ;
    Tins (flat and deep), pie plates, cooling trays ;
    Kitchen stationery (foil, greaseproof paper, paper cases, etc.) ;
    Bread board, chopping-board.

Stores

Breakfast cereals, cheeses, pasta, preserves, soup cereals and pulses (peas, beans, lentils) ;
Vinegar, salad oils, condiment sauces, sweet and savoury biscuits, cakes ;
Cooking oil, fish oil in use ;
Tea, coffee, sugar canisters ;
Fruit and vegetables in rack, current stock of canned goods.

Washing-up and Cleaning

Bowls, drainers, brushes, detergents, pot scourers ;
Laundry basket, iron, ironing board, powder, flakes, clothes airer ;
Vacuum cleaner, brushes, cleaning materials, dusters, mops ;
Tea towels (meat and milk) ;
Shoe cleaning equipment.

Small Appliances

Coffee grinder and maker, wall can-opener, toaster.

Tableware

Everyday china and glassware, cutlery ; ⎫
Special china and glassware, cutlery ; ⎬ Meat and milk
Carving and serving dishes ; ⎭
Cloths or place mats, table napkins, salt and pepper sets ;
Passover pots and pans.

Miscellaneous

First aid equipment and disinfectant ;
Sewing supplies ;
Kitchen refuse (wet and dry) ;
Letter rack and notice-board ;
Bread bin or drawer.

Counter Tops and Backs

For the main preparation counters, laminated plastic is the most serviceable material. It is quiet to work on, resistant to moderate heat, and easily maintained with a detergent wipe down. The inevitable scratching that comes with wear shows less on a matt than on a glossy finish, and on marbled patterns less than plain. For the counter backs, ceramic tiles and laminated plastic are equally practical, though near the cooker, tiles are better, as they are less affected by grease and heat.

At the side of a wall oven and next to the cooker hob, a stainless steel counter is more practical than plastic, as it will stand up better to prolonged heat from an oven dish or pan, but as it is rather noisy in use and clinical in appearance, I do not recommend its use for the main counter top. It is better to have a separate wood chopping-board rather than a wood section let in to the counter, as this tends to discolour and shrink with daily use. If you intend to bake a lot—and have the space for it—a section of marble counter is superb for pastry making.

The Washing Machine

A washing machine cannot be considered a necessity for a family of two. Indeed, if you are at work all day, it is wiser to save your time and energy for the more creative home-making jobs, and send the washing to the laundry.

But when the family expands, and you are ready to buy a machine, it is well worth the extra cost to invest in an automatic. This type of machine not only takes all the labour and guesswork out of clothes-washing, but leaves one completely free to do another job while it is in operation. Handling is reduced to the minimum, and washing and rinsing are scientifically controlled.

Some automatic models have more efficient washing and spinning actions than others, but unless one has had experience of the comparative performance of similar machines, it is difficult to assess this merely from a demonstration. One must rely to a great extent on the results of tests such as those published in *Which?* magazine, and on the advice and experience of friends who already possess a machine.

It is important that the machine you choose should have a washing "programme" to cover all kinds of modern materials, woollens and delicate fabrics, that it should handle a small load as efficiently and economically as a large one, and that it should leave the minimum of moisture in the clothes after they have been spun.

Drying Equipment

All clothes are softer and sweeter when they are dried outside, but if this is impractical (either because of weather or housing conditions), some kind of indoor drying equipment will be needed. If the house is centrally heated, this can be as simple as a telescopic airer or a retractable, wall-mounted airing rack on which clothes can be left to dry overnight.

When more intense heat is needed—for instance to dry nappies and bed-linen—then a separate tumbler drier (which can be mounted above the washing machine) is the best solution. Some washing machines have driers built into the tub, but as no more clothes can be washed until the first load has been dried, it is not a practical solution in the household with a large and varied wash. Before you buy any kind of drier, make sure you know how long it takes for different fabrics, how much electricity it uses, and how crumpled the clothes are likely to be when they emerge.

The Dish-washer

Though the perfect pan- and dish-washer has not yet been invented, at least in this country, the ones already on the market are saving enough of time and labour to make their purchase a good proposition, even for a small family. Dishes can be stacked in the machine as they are used (so that the kitchen sink is always tidy) and the machine turned on only when it is full. With my household of seven, this means that the machine is only in operation twice a day during the week, while a smaller family might accumulate a complete load once a day only.

As yet, no machine tested by the London Beth Din has proved acceptable to them for use with both meat and milk dishes. But as the actual washing procedure and the temperature of the water (the crucial factors) vary from one machine to another, it is worth asking the Beth Din for a ruling on a particular model. Indeed, it may well be that future machines made to new specifications will prove more readily acceptable for the requirements of kashrut.

In choosing a machine, one must first consider where it is to be installed and its size. The ideal position is at the side of the sink (into which the dishes can be scraped before stacking in the machine), and it is now possible to buy sink units tailored to fit specific models. A permanently plumbed machine is preferable to a portable one, as it operates completely independently from the sink taps which are thus left free for the washing up of pans and wiping down of counter tops.

There is usually just time to wash up large cooking dishes

and wipe down the cooker and counter before the dish-washer has completed its cycle and the dishes are ready to be removed. However, if permanent plumbing cannot be arranged, the machine can be connected to the sink taps after the kitchen has been tidied, turned on as you leave the kitchen, and the dishes removed from the machine later in the day.

It is advisable to buy the largest machine that the budget and floor space will allow, but in any event, no machine that holds less than six place-settings is worthwhile. Make sure that the dishes and cutlery can be stacked quickly and without back strain, and that the trays are designed to take a wide variety of differing shapes and sizes. In a house with a constant hot water supply, it is more economical to have a machine that operates from the hot tap than to buy one that works from the cold.

The smaller the machine, the more vital the time factor (reloading may well be necessary in the middle of a dinner party), so it is important to compare both the washing and drying times of different machines. It is worth noting that dish-washers which dry their loads with residual heat rather than by using a heated drying cycle (they also use the hottest water), can be opened as soon as the washing cycle itself is complete, and the dishes "flash dried" in a couple of minutes, by evaporation.

But, whichever machine seems best suited to your needs *on paper*, must also be proved so in practice—by washing a complete load of dirty dishes before you buy. Also, since even the best dish-washers can prove temperamental in use, you must be assured of a speedy repair service whenever it may be needed.

The Deep-Freeze

A domestic deep-freeze cabinet is of especial value in three situations: Where there is home-grown food to be frozen; where there is a large family (and their circle of friends) to be fed; and where the mother has a job outside the home and wishes to rationalise her cooking times.

The first case applies to very few households, and when it does, a freezer of commercial size—about 10 cubic feet—will certainly be needed. Until either of the other two situations arises, the freezer compartment of an ordinary two- or three-star refrigerator will be quite adequate for the storage of commercially frozen foods and the freezing of small quantities of home-prepared ones.

When the family circle does grow, however, and it becomes more convenient to concentrate food preparation activities into one or more longer periods, rather than spread them over numerous short periods throughout the week, a deep-freeze can be a tremendous help. Adequate supplies of commercially frozen foods can always be on hand to meet any sudden need; seasonal fruits (even if bought at retail prices from the greengrocer) can be frozen at half the cost of the commercial packets; small portions of cooked foods can be kept for hungry teenagers or unexpected guests; staples such as stock, gravy, and pastry can always be on hand, and pies, cakes, soups and casseroles can be prepared on easy days, for use when time and energy are short.

I find it especially useful to be able to spread the cooking for Shabbat and Yomtov over several days, so that all my baking can be done at the beginning of the week, leaving the days immediately before the holiday for the preparation of those foods that are best served freshly made.

Before buying any freezer it is wise to read all the literature available on domestic deep-freezing, for it will give you a good idea of the kind of freezer your household is likely to require. For use in the ordinary household, where the only foods to be stored for more than a couple of months are out-of-season fruits and, possibly, raw meat, I recommend a freezer of not less than 5 cubic foot capacity. I have a 6 cubic foot cabinet model which, I find, gives me adequate room for both long- and short-term storage.

If, however, you have the space, it may be worthwhile to buy a larger commercial model which, because it is free of purchase tax, is hardly more expensive than a much smaller domestic model, or even to buy a combined commercial freezer and refrigerator. At the other end of the scale, it is often possible to buy reconditioned ice-cream chests which, though less easy to fill and empty than upright cabinet models, are so ridiculously cheap as to outweigh any possible inconvenience.

Floorings

Kitchen flooring must be comfortable to walk on, resistant to grease and easy to maintain without polish. Terrazzo and tiling are the most easy to maintain, but they are hard to work on ; linoleum is comfortable, but must be polished. Probably the best all-purpose material is vinyl, cushioned with a backing that makes it springy underfoot. Vinyl can be bought in a huge range of qualities ; buy the best that your budget will allow, and make sure that it is fitted by experts who leave you with complete instructions for its maintenance.

Walls and Ceilings

These must be finished in some material that is non-porous, resistant to both grease and moisture, and easily wiped down. For skirting boards, doors and ceilings an eggshell paint finish is ideal. On the walls (except near the cooker) a vinyl-coated paper is a good choice, as it is both practicable in use and attractive in appearance. Near the cooker, however, where paper will be ruined by steam, grease and heat, the wall is best gloss painted, panelled in metal or plastic, or tiled. Even with an effective ventilator, you must be prepared to redecorate the kitchen more frequently than any other room in the house.

Ventilation

This is essential if the kitchen is to be comfortable to work in, and cooking odours and grease are not to be wafted through the house, especially during a fish-frying session. The best form of ventilation is provided by a hood slightly wider than the cooker top and set no more than 30 inches above it. With this method, oil fumes and cooking smells are trapped as they arise and instantly sucked outside by a fan.

A ducted hood is best of all, but if this is impossible to fit, then one with a charcoal filter may be used. This is effective against grease, smoke and smells, but, unlike the ducted hoods, it does not reduce the heat and moisture in the kitchen. If neither type can be used (if, for instance, they would obscure the light), then an exhaust fan can be set in the window or wall, though in a large and busy kitchen, it is nowhere near as effective as a hood.

Lighting and Power Points

Every work spot in the kitchen needs its own source of light. Strip lights can be built into the cooker hood to light the cooker, or countersunk into hanging cupboards to light the counter. Other lights can be sunk into the ceiling or suspended from it to give a shadowless light on a peninsula unit or other working area.

Power Point.
Dishwasher, Waste disposer

Power
Point.
Kettle

Pendant
Lights

Strip
Light

Power
Point
for
Fridge

Power
Point.
Cooker

Power
Point.
Coffee
Grinder,
Toaster

SETTING UP THE HOME AND KITCHEN

Of equal importance is a generous supply of power points, set into the back of the counter for small appliances such as the mixer, the coffee grinder and the toaster. The positioning of these points must be determined before counter backs are fitted, so it is worth making a careful lighting and power plan to give to your electrician.

2

FOOD PREPARATION—THE TOOLS FOR THE JOB

Food preparation— the tools for the job

Once upon a time, the Jewish bride bought her kitchen equipment as she did her bed-linen and furniture—as part of a trousseau that was expected to last a lifetime. She would start her cooking career with two sets of pans, from minute to monster, that between them covered almost every conceivable cooking need. With the addition of various earthenware casseroles, enamel pie plates and baking dishes, a selection of cooking knives and tools the list was complete—and she was stuck with it for years.

Today, I believe this policy to be out of date. While every kitchen should have the basic equipment, the "etceteras" are far better left to be purchased when the need arises. This gives an opportunity for special preferences to be developed—one person may find she loves to bake, while another prefers to concoct interesting casseroled dishes. Then, each year new materials are developed for kitchenware, which may outdate yesterday's pots and pans, long before they are worn out. So it is wisest to buy the minimum, but the best; to buy the larger pan rather than the smaller, bearing in mind the probable needs of the family in five years' time. For, while it is perfectly satisfactory to cook for two in a pan made for six, the reverse is never the case.

The basic list must allow for every cooking situation likely to be met in the first year. "Making do" with inadequate tools is no economy, particularly if you are working and housekeeping, for the job will take twice as long and be less well done. Before you buy any "gadget" or tool that will do only one job, make sure there is not another tool that can do that job just as well—and another one besides. That is why your first purchases should be of those utensils and tools that have stood the test of time, and shopping for the "gimmicks" left till later.

Buying for the Jewish kitchen involves two special considerations. First, there is the need to keep separate tools and utensils for meat and milk dishes. But this is not as expensive or cumbersome as it seems, for in *any* kitchen certain equipment must be kept for a special job or process.

In my suggested lists I have indicated duplicates only where identical equipment is used for both meat and milk cooking. Obviously it is only necessary to buy one milk pan, one fish-frying pan, or one chicken casserole. Then there are the dishes dictated by the kind of food usually cooked in a Jewish kitchen. You will need a large variety of frying pans, more and bigger soup pans, more utensils for braising rather than dry roasting, and oven-to-table casseroles which can be used on a direct flame. And you are sure to want many pie plates and cake tins.

But whatever you decide to buy, let it be suitable for *you and your way of life*. And if you are in doubt, *do not* buy until you are sure that what you are buying is what you need. Below I give guidance on the selection of utensils and the materials from which they are likely to be made, but the final choice must be yours.

Where to Buy

For basic, long-lasting equipment, it is best to go to a specialist hardware shop or to the hardware department of a large store. In many towns there are also "kitchen boutiques", run by enthusiastic amateur cooks who stock their shelves with equipment that is practical and easy to maintain. These good hardware shops will be able to advise you on makes, sizes, and materials, and goods will have been chosen for their utility as well as for their appearance. Fancy goods departments, though useful for unusual dishes, should only be visited later, when you know exactly what special equipment you require.

First Principles

Before you buy any article, make sure it fulfils these requirements:

(a) it has been designed to do its job efficiently and with flexibility;

(b) it is made from materials which will stand up to reasonable daily use. In this regard, look carefully at any decorations that are not part of the basic design. It must be easy to keep clean and free of "dirt and grease traps" that a washing up brush cannot reach;

(c) its shape and appearance are pleasing in a way that will not appear out of date five years hence; and in the case of oven-to-table ware, it should look good as a background to food.

A Guide to Selection

(1) Stove and Ovenware

It is very helpful, in the case of British-made goods, to check with the Design Index of the Council of Industrial Design. Nothing is included in this index unless its performance and appearance are equally good.

There are six main categories:

Today there is no sharp division between utensils which are used on top of the stove, in the oven, or direct from either to the table. In fact the more dual-purpose dishes you can buy the better, for they avoid the need to transfer food at any stage of cooking from one dish to another, and greatly reduce washing up. Particularly useful are dishes in which food can first be browned, then casseroled, and finally brought to the table.

Cooking utensils are now made in many and varied materials, each of which has specific advantages. These materials include: aluminium, enamelled iron or steel, toughened ceramic, glass, heatproof porcelain, stoneware, pottery and copper.

Of these *aluminium* is still the "bread and butter" material from which most basic equipment is made. For a moderate price, one can buy utensils of good design, incorporating such features as heat-resistant handles, anodised coloured lids, ground bases which sit evenly on either gas or electric hotplates (an essential for speedy cooking and fuel economy), lips that pour well and shapes that make for quick and efficient cleaning.

On the debit side, aluminium is easily marked by alkaline foods and hard water (though the staining can be removed by boiling with a dilute acid); the surface will pit if the pan is stored damp; and some of the gaily-coloured handles crack and discolour if exposed to great heat—as in a frying pan.

Buy the best you can afford, but in any event, avoid very cheap grades which may look good but feel light in the hand and have thin bases which are sure to buckle and heat unevenly. Choose *non-stick* aluminium for milk and small frying pans, but avoid its use for those utensils that are likely to be scratched by heavy wear, unless a heavy duty coating has been used.

Aluminium is suitable for: Basic soup and vegetable pans; frying pans and deep-frying pans; baking equipment.

Enamelware, once an easily chippable "Cinderella" material, is now used for utensils which are particularly practical in the Jewish kitchen. Fused onto cast iron or steel, the highly glazed surface makes it resistant to staining from both food and hard water deposits and, because grease and odours cannot penetrate the surface, it is easy to clean. But the surface, being made by a glass-like process, is not as tough as aluminium . . . it will flake if left dry over heat, plunged into cold water when hot, or cleaned with scratchy or harsh cleaning materials.

But its big advantage is that, providing it has a ground base, it can be used both for the browning of foods over direct heat, and for their final cooking in the oven. And because designs and colours are good, the same dish can also go on the table. The best enamelware is comparable in price to aluminium, though imported utensils are often dearer. A cheaper gauge (without a ground base) is used for self-basting roasters, but this grade is not as easy to keep clean, because the surface is less impervious and more easily scratched.

Enamelware is suitable for: All kinds of oven-to-table casseroles (choose domed ones for meat and fowl cookery; more shallow ones for braising steaks and meat-balls; small-based, deep ones for stews and long-cooking casserole dishes such as tsimmes; shallow open ones for grilling or baking fish and baked puddings); soup pans which can double as family soup tureens; fish grilling dishes.

Glass is the cheapest of all the materials that can stand up to heat, though it is more expensive in flame-proof grades. It is also the most expendable. Remember that when glass utensils are used for serving they are considered parev, but once heat is used on them, separate dishes must be used for meat and milk.

Heatproof glass combines the virtues of an enamel-hard, impervious surface with lightness, low cost and attractive design, and it makes excellent dual-purpose dishes that are equally suitable for both oven and table. But it does crack easily with heat or careless handling, and the colours change with constant heating.

Heatproof glass is suitable for: Pie plates and dishes; pudding and casserole dishes; mixing bowls; measuring jugs; coffee makers; serving platters. It is cheap enough to be replaced by more expensive materials as tastes and interests crystallise, so it makes a good basic material for first purchases.

A glass-like substance originally developed for use in the nose-cones of missiles is also being made into top-of-stove and oven dishes. Porcelain-like in appearance, with an unscratchable, unburnable surface, it cannot be damaged by extremes of either heat or cold, and it cannot crack, but it will break if dropped on a hard surface. It heats slowly, but retains heat longer than most other materials, and should be used on a lower heat—and in a 25-degree cooler oven. It is useful for all kinds of stove-to-table cooking, particularly frozen vegetables, milk soups, meat casseroles, sauces, and the heating of liquids that can also be served in it, such as cocoa, coffee and milk. It is more expensive than most conventional materials.

Toughened ceramic, heatproof porcelain, stoneware and pottery are materials which are used more for their appearance than for their durability. None of them will stand up to fierce and direct dry heat, careless handling or extremes of temperature, but used with care, they make the most attractive of all stove-to-table dishes. However, while the main surfaces have a high glaze, the inner rims are often left unglazed and do discolour with oven heat.

They are suitable for: Casserole cookery that does not involve initial browning; au gratin dishes; fish cooked in, or coated with sauce; and, in the case of the toughened ceramics, stove-to-table cookery of frozen vegetables. Stoneware and ovenproof pottery heat slowly and evenly, browning and deepening the flavour of a dish; so they are useful for cooking such dishes as tsimmes and holishkes.

While most dishes made from these materials tend to be expensive, the undecorated, brown glazed, heatproof French porcelain is moderate in price and ideal for baking eggs, cooking soufflés, rendering chicken fat, and any household use where a simple, heatproof dish is required.

Copper is the material used by chefs, for it makes pans which are heavy and conduct heat evenly. But it is expensive and heavy for domestic use, and the inside needs annual retinning, the outside constant cleaning (chefs have someone to do the job for them). However, copper pans are decorative, and a frying pan made of this material is pleasant to have for "flambé" dishes in the dining room. As a copper pan gets extremely hot, make sure the handle is well insulated.

Stainless steel pans are often made with copper bottoms. But though the interior of such pans is extremely easy to clean, the copper needs buffing after every use. Because they conduct the heat quickly, these pans are speedy for vegetable cookery, where liquid is involved. But they are less suitable for frying pans, as the foods tends to burn easily.

Perhaps the ideal metal pan has a copper layer sandwiched between a steel interior and an aluminium base. Such a combination incorporates the ease of cleaning of the aluminium, the speed and spread of heating of the copper and the impervious surface of the steel. Of course it is expensive—but very easy to wash up. Stainless steel is increasingly used for serving dishes, and is one material which comes out of a dish-washer as gleaming as when it went in.

To sum up the choice

For basic pans, aluminium is durable, easily cleaned and moderate in price. Aluminium-clad stainless steel with a copper core is dearer, quicker heating, and even easier to keep clean.

For casseroles, oven-to-table ware and serving dishes, enamel on steel or cast iron are reasonably durable, easily cleaned, and flexible in use. Thinner-gauge enamel is cheaper, more difficult to clean, but useful for self-basting roasters. Ovenproof glass is cheap, light, easily cleaned and easily broken. Undecorated porcelain and pottery cooks evenly, but is expendable.

For special occasion casseroles and serving dishes, toughened ceramic, ovenproof porcelain, stoneware and pottery are attractive, good to cook in, but tend to be expensive and (on top heat) easily cracked. Toughened glass-like materials are extremely durable, but initially expensive. Copper is expensive but attractive, and cooks well.

(2) Knives and Kitchen Cutlery

While specialised gadgets can be extremely useful, a set of well-sharpened knives is *indispensable*. Most British-made household knives are of hollow-ground stainless steel, ideal for cutting bread and fruit. But for the majority of cooking jobs, the tapered, French-type knives are best. Traditionally, they are made of high-grade carbon steel, which extends right up into the handle, giving the knife great strength, and the handle itself is shaped to give good balance. Carbon steel is not stainless, but you can get these knives in stainless steel as well. The only prerequisite is that it must be possible to sharpen them at home.

Do not buy knives by the set, unless you are sure it includes exactly what you need. Buy them singly, to fill a special need. The same policy should apply to cooking tools, for made-up sets often contain useless tools. It is better to buy the rack and stock it with your own choice of utensils, which will differ for your meat and milk cookery. For kitchen cooking cutlery, invest at the start in meat and milk sets in stainless steel, and they will last you a lifetime.

(3) Baking Equipment

This should be of the very best quality, made from heavy-gauge aluminium that will brown cakes and biscuits evenly. Do not buy too much at the start, or you will find yourself with a clutter of unused and unsuitable cake tins.

(4) Specialised Equipment and Gadgets

None of these should be included in the initial kitchen equipment. First, they are not essential, and secondly, their selection takes a great deal of time and comparison of different models. The particular virtues of different equipment will only become apparent when you know your special requirements. But when you do buy, again, buy the best.

(5) Storage Containers

For dry goods in frequent use, choose glass. It is the cheapest, most durable and most easily cleaned, and when equipped with a ground-glass stopper, the most airtight.

For refrigerator and freezer storage, airtight plastic containers are ideal. They are made in angular, space-saving shapes, and are light, cheap and easy to clean. But they do absorb odours and attract dust and grease when exposed to the kitchen atmosphere. So for open shelves or top of the counter storage of dry goods such as coffee, tea, sugar and flour, use pottery jars with inset rubber lids.

Washing up. Whatever equipment you buy will need to be in duplicate for meat and milk dishes. Choose washing-up brushes and cloths of synthetic materials which can be sterilised by soaking in bleach rather than by tedious and unpleasant boiling. Buy detergent-filled wire-wool pads for hard-surfaced pans, spun nylon ones for softer surfaces. And be sure to buy the correct cleaner for stainless steel and copper.

The Kitchen Shopping List

Under each heading is listed, first, essential equipment, and then those items which are useful, but not strictly necessary, and which, in any event, are best purchased only when a specific need arises. Where duplicate sets are needed for meat and milk, the abbreviation word "dup." appears after the item. (Keep your meat and milk items separate by choosing a basic colour for each that can be carried through in pan lids or handles, plastic material, and tea towel trims.)

(1) Pots and Pans

(Diameters are always measured across the *base* of equipment)

Kettle (electric or gas)

1-pint non-stick milk pan with pouring lip

Set of 6-inch, 8-inch and (if possible) 9-inch diameter lidded saucepans (dup.)

Egg-boiling pan

6-inch omelette pan with rounded sides

10-inch diam. frying pan with lid (for meat cookery)

10-inch diam. extra-heavy base frying pan with deep sides (for frying fish)

Twin-lugged soup pan (approximately 6-pint capacity)

Oval enamelled casserole (preferably with ground base for stove-top use) large enough to hold a fowl or a 4-lb. joint

To buy later

Pressure cooker (for cooking children's lunches, making stock, etc.)

Steamer (to fit 8-inch saucepan)

Double saucepan (for lemon curd, delicate sauces and fillings)

Deep fryer and basket (the larger the better)

Lidded frying pan (about 8 inches in diameter) for poaching fish and fruit

Assorted "cook and serve" casseroles which can double as pans (for frozen vegetables, tinned and packeted soups and stewed fruits), tsimmes, lokshen pudding, etc.

(2) Cooking and Baking Equipment

Six-inch rounded metal strainer with handle (dup.)

Colander (dup.)

Roasting tin and rack

Rectangular tin for roasting potatoes (approximately 8 inches × 10 inches × 1 inch)

Set of fireproof glass lidded casseroles of 6-inch diameter but varying depths

Nest of glass mixing or pudding basins (dup.)

Meat preparation board (wood)

Vegetable chopping board (wood)

Bread board

Mincer

Funnel (for oil)

Shallow pie plate (8-inch diameter)

Deeper pie plate (8-inch diameter × $1\frac{1}{2}$ inches deep)

Two oval pie dishes for baked puddings (1- and $1\frac{1}{2}$-pint capacity)

Pair of oven trays for baking biscuits ⎫

Set of loose-bottomed round cake tins (6-inch, 7-inch and 9-inch diameter)

Pair of loose-bottomed sandwich tins (7-inch diameter × $1\frac{1}{2}$-inches deep) ⎬ Non-stick

Set of twelve patty tins (for little cakes and tartlets) ⎭

Wire cooling tray

Pint glass measuring jug

Flour dredger

41

To Buy Later
Salad-drying basket
Icing sugar dredger
2-lb. loaf tin
Yorkshire pudding tin
Rectangular baking tin (12 inches × 8 inches × 2 inches)
Sponge flan tin
Pair of flan tins with loose bases for sweet and savoury flans (8-inch and 10-inch diameter)
Moule à manqué (slanting-sided tin) for iced cakes and gateaux
Six each tartlet, boat mould and cream-horn tins
Hinged "spring form" tin with fluted centre insert (for ring cakes, cheese cakes)
Shallow oval or rectangular gratin dish (for puddings, creamed vegetables and sauced fish dishes) (dup.)
Jelly moulds
China soufflé dish (5½ × 3½ inches deep) for sweet and savoury soufflés (dup.)

(3) Kitchen Cutlery and Special Tools

(*Note:* Buy a duplicate rack for meat and milk utensils, but buy the tools separately. A magnetic knife rack is safe and practical.)

Bread knife. Scissors
Two French cook's knives (6 and 8 inches long) (dup.)
Serrated-edge fruit knife
Grapefruit knife
Stainless steel tablespoon, teaspoon, round-bladed knife and fork (dup.)
Knife sharpener
Short- and long-handled wooden spoon (dup.)
Rolling pin (dup.)
Slotted draining spoon (dup.)
Soup ladle (dup.)
Long spatula (meat)
Wooden spatula (milk)
Trowel-shaped spatula (milk)
Stainless steel hand egg whisk
Hand chopper (for herrings, etc.)
Hand can opener
Bottle opener
Plastic measuring spoons and cups (B.S.I. specification) (dup.)

Small wire sauce whisk (dup.)
Pastry brush (dup.)
Rubber or plastic spatula (dup.)
Lemon squeezer
Stainless steel egg-slicer
Stainless steel grater

To buy later
Set of assorted diameter biscuit cutters (metal, plain and fluted)
Large nylon piping bag and assorted tubes
Garlic press
Melon-ball cutter
Stainless steel apple corer
Cherry and plum stoner
Food mill (for sieving soups and purées)
Plastic pepper mill
Oil thermometer
Sugar thermometer
"Pinger" timer (if not built in to cooker)

(4) Small Appliances

Toaster

To buy later
Electric or hand coffee mill
Coffee maker (drip, vacuum, filter or percolator)
Hand-held mixer
Large electric mixer with blender and attachments
Electric mincer (either free-standing or attached to mixer)
Electric or manual wall can opener.

(5) Storage Containers

Set of six airtight plastic containers of varying size, shape and depth for refrigerator use (dup.)
Two of each size of glass airtight jars for dried fruits, nuts, etc. (2-lb., 1-lb., ½-lb. capacity)
Two of each size of plastic containers for pulses and other dry stores (2-lb. and 1-lb. capacity)
4-lb. plastic container for caster sugar
3-lb. flour tin
Airtight storage canisters for granulated sugar, tea and coffee
Cake storage tin
Biscuit storage tin
Salt box

Quart plastic container for used fish oil
Dry rubbish bin

To buy later
Additional glass, pottery, stainless steel and plastic containers as the specific needs arise
Spice jars and rack
Dispenser for foil, paper towelling and greaseproof paper
Storage fitment for washing-up supplies

(6) Koshering Equipment

Enamel bucket
Draining grid
Wire grid for liver
Plastic cleaning cloth

(7) Washing-Up Equipment
(All in duplicate)

Heavy plastic bowl to fit sink
Plastic-coated wire dish drainer (largest available)
Long-handled nylon washing-up brush
Dozen meat tea towels
Dozen milk tea towels
Hand towels for kitchen use (roller towels ideal)
(Buy detergents and other expendable supplies as needed)

3

RUNNING YOUR HOME

RUNNING YOUR HOME

The very first job you will have to undertake as a new housewife is to plan the smooth and efficient running of your home. This will mean blending all the essential jobs involved in keeping house into one workable, flexible routine. Once this has been done, you will feel more free, both mentally and physically, to start building your new life with your husband, secure in the knowledge that you have the "mechanics" of your joint way of life well under control.

It is not an easy job ; and in many ways, it is less easy than it used to be. Unlike the Jewish women of a generation ago, few modern girls have time before marriage to be "apprenticed" to their mothers, with the result that household routines are largely strange and unfamiliar. After marriage, most young wives expect to work outside their home for at least part of their time.

Even when children arrive, few women are content to devote their entire life to housekeeping, and rightly expect to use part of their energies outside their primary role of wife and mother. On the other hand, there is an ever increasing battery of mechanised home aids which were simply not available even twenty years ago, to assist a working housewife to run her home pleasantly and well.

The very first step in planning the running of any home is to decide precisely what jobs are likely to be involved, then to arrange them in order of importance and decide how often they need to be done.

From the feminine point of view, the weekly routine of homemaking revolves round the need to keep the home and its contents clean and tidy, and the family healthy and well-fed. From these basic daily needs stem all the other activities of the housewife. In addition, there are other jobs, perhaps less vital, but equally important for a rich family life, for which time must be allowed. Under this heading, come such activities as arranging the flowers, personal and household sewing, entertaining, communal activity, indeed, all the multifarious jobs that inspire the saying, "A woman's work is never done".

It is a great help, when trying to decide where to fit in each job, to consider the rhythm of activity that holds sway in every Jewish home. First, there is the daily one, into which one must fit the routines of everyday life. Next, there is the weekly one, which builds up to its climax on Erev Shabbat, when every Jewish housewife worthy of the name likes to feel her week's work is done, her silver shining, her table ready, and her larder well-stocked for Friday night and Shabbat. Finally, there is the yearly one, punctuated in a very satisfying way by the major and minor Festivals and by the family preparations that must precede them.

The priority to be given to a job, how often it must be done and when, must be taken into consideration when planning the actual household routine. Now, it would be easy (as some textbooks set out to do) if one could work out a daily, weekly, and yearly routine to include every possible task and the needs of every household where it is to be carried out. However, I believe this to be impossible. A routine that means freedom for one woman spells prison to another. Then, some people enjoy sticking to a rigid time-table, while others can only work to a flexible one.

Most women feel restricted by the thought that their week has been planned in minute detail before it has even begun. But they do enjoy the sense of security that a *flexible* routine provides, as well as the saving of time that allows them both to run their home for the good of their family, and still to keep a finger on the pulse of the world outside. Above all, they value any system which helps them to get through tedious jobs quickly and then enjoy the luxury of lingering over more congenial ones, without feeling guilty.

The ideas given below for setting up these flexible routines have been developed in twenty years of looking after a husband and family of three, while, at the same time, pursuing a career in home economics. I think their main virtues are speed, efficiency and flexibility, while room is left for them to be varied according to personal whim and preference. Above all, I believe they can help you to create that unique and indefinable atmosphere that we call "a Jewish home".

Keeping the Home Clean

A home that is kept neat and clean is more comfortable and pleasant to live in—as well as being more healthy—than one that is grubby and untidy, while furnishings that are well cared for and maintained not only look more attractive, but also have a longer useful life.

But the importance of the effort needed to keep them this way—and the time spent in doing so—should not be exaggerated at the expense of the other jobs involved in running a home. Once upon a time, it is true, keeping a house clean took up much of a housewife's day. Today, we have been freed from this bondage by mechanised home aids and modern cleaning agents. Housework is just another, albeit vital, job to be dovetailed into the daily routine, and there is certainly no need to feel a sense of guilt or inadequacy if it is the least favourite. It is true that some women really enjoy doing housework, but for the majority, once the novelty of looking after their own possessions has worn off, it proves one of the less satisfying household chores, and the best policy is to do it with efficiency and speed and then move on to a more congenial job.

The work involved in keeping a home clean can be made more simple and less time-consuming in several ways.

(1) Furnishings and fittings should be selected with their cleanability well in mind—a factor which, fortunately, is usually allied to good design. As much of the furniture as is practicable should be built in or cantilevered off the floor, while heavy pieces like beds should be fitted with large castors so that they can be moved without effort from one part of the room to another. Finishes should be resistant to marks and need the minimum of polishing to maintain their shine.

Walls, whether painted or papered, should be easily wipable, and uncarpeted floors should be of tough-surfaced materials which can be mopped clean rather than polished. Soft furnishings in daily use should be washable or easily shampooed at home, and as many wall, cupboard and counter surfaces as possible should be finished in tiling or laminated plastic.

(2) From the beginning, resolve to have a place for everything—and keep everything in its place, for a tidy house looks cared for, even when there has been no time to give

it a thorough clean. If every item in the house has its allotted storage place, it can be tidied away without a thought, and quickly found again when it is needed.

To keep drawers and shelves tidy, use shallow rather than deep ones, and narrow rather than wide ones. And label every drawer and cupboard with its contents. Train yourself to tidy up the kitchen as you cook, rinsing used utensils and leaving them to drain as you go along. And make it a "house rule" to straighten up the living room before you go to bed at night. Most men find tidiness a bore, although they like the sense of order it brings. Make it easy for your husband to put things away, and you will be sure of his co-operation.

(3) Buy the minimum of cleaning equipment, but buy the best, making sure that each appliance is flexible in use and can be easily serviced and cleaned. Choose multi-purpose detergents, rather than a different one for each job ; and be guided in your choice by more experienced housewives.

(4) Keep dirt under control by making "little but often" the housecleaning rule. If you are limited for time, particularly if you are out at work each day, make sure that every single item in your home has a little attention at regular intervals, rather than leave some things for the unattainable day when you will have plenty of time. And for the regular care of articles that are in constant use, it is good policy to have some paid help if you can secure it.

Cleaning Routines

When a home and its contents are new, very little effort is needed to keep them clean. Once they start to wear, they not only look less attractive, but they soil more easily and it takes longer to get them clean ; so the aim of any cleaning method must be to keep them in new condition as long as possible.

While a dust and a wipe will do for daily care, it is important to give regular and thorough cleaning *from the outset* to those surfaces and appliances that are exposed to hard and constant wear—for example, kitchen equipment—and not wait until they start to lose their newness before beginning a regular cleaning routine.

Just when and how you fit in your housework is for you alone to decide, preferably with the help of your mother or a married friend. Much will depend on whether and when you work, and where you live—a home in the country will need far less daily care than one in a town. Work out an experimental routine and put it down on paper. Then try it out in practice and amend it as you go along. Never clean anything because you think you should, but only because it really needs attention.

As a general rule, the rooms you are using will need to be tidied and dusted daily, and the carpet swept or the floor mopped. This regular care will stop dust being changed into dirt by atmospheric damp, and will prevent grit and soil being tracked through the house. Tidy and wipe down the bathroom and toilet fixtures ; wipe the kitchen counters and appliances, and sweep the floor after every meal.

This is the minimum of daily care a home demands, for which you will need to find the time. In addition, different furnishings and equipment need more thorough, if less frequent attention. Until recently, this extra attention was given when a room was "turned out"—cleaned from top to bottom on an ordained day of the week. But today it is considered more efficient to clean all the items in a particular category right through the house at the same time, fitting the job in with the usual daily routine.

Thus, one day all the upstairs windows will be cleaned, all the downstairs windows on another. All the silver will be cleaned at one time, or all the carpets vacuumed through-out the house. The advantage of this system is that the other rooms are given their routine care daily, so that, if the special job has to be postponed, the whole house will still be reasonably clean and tidy.

It is impossible to lay down dogmatic rules as to when and how often anything should be deep-cleaned, but as a rule of thumb, clean weekly those things that get heavy and regular wear. Those exposed to atmospheric dirt can be cleaned only at intervals of two or three weeks. Clean seasonally (once or twice a year) things which are difficult to dismantle (such as light fittings), or soil very slowly.

Which days are selected for particular jobs is a matter of choice. However, most women find it convenient to get the bulk of the laundry and special cleaning of bedrooms and bathrooms done towards the beginning of the week, giving more attention to the living room towards the week-end, and making the kitchen the last cleaning job of all, after all the week-end cooking has been done. Seasonal cleaning is most conveniently done before the main Festivals—especially in the spring (before Passover) and the autumn (before Rosh Hashanah), so that the necessary preparations for these Festivals can be combined with the regular house-cleaning routine.

Below are listed the main items in the home which need special care, and suggestions as to how often and in what way they can best be maintained. It is worth noting that, while most men loathe the "dust and wipe" of the daily routine, they quite enjoy cleaning of a more demanding nature, particularly if some sort of mechanical appliance, like a vacuum cleaner or carpet shampooer, is involved.

(1) Beds and Bed-Linen

Turn the beds back to air before breakfast, and make them afterwards. It is only necessary to strip them completely once a week, on the day you change at least one of the pillow-cases and sheets. At the same time, move the position of the bed slightly, so that the castors do not make a permanent mark on the carpet. Once a month, turn the mattress head to toe, to equalise the wear. Always keep the mattress and pillow in an under case, for once the cover becomes soiled, they will need to be recovered. Twice a year, thoroughly vacuum both the mattress and the base. Have the blankets cleaned only when they begin to look dingy, and if possible by a firm recommended by the manufacturers. While man-made fibre blankets wash to perfection at home, wool blankets stay clean and new longer if commercially cleaned.

(2) Carpets

Sweep carpets daily and start to vacuum new carpets after the first three months. This will give the backing time to settle, and allow some of the loose wool left in during manufacture to become embedded in it. Then vacuum once weekly, but do it thoroughly, so that the grit that the daily carpet sweeping cannot remove can be sucked away. When a stain is made, treat it at once. If it is a grease mark, use a dry cleaner; for any other stain use a foaming shampoo. Shampoo the whole carpet when it begins to look dingy, usually twice a year if you live in a town. Follow the shampooing instructions to the letter, and wet only the surface of the carpet, never the back. Have fitted stair carpets moved yearly to equalise the wear on the "nose" and the "tread". And turn carpet squares and rugs round regularly for the same reason.

(3) Chairs and Settees

These should be brushed or vacuumed weekly to remove surface dust, and shampooed regularly before they become too soiled to get clean. Just sitting in a chair causes soiling, so if you want light coloured upholstery, make sure that it can be safely shampooed at home. Polish chair legs at the same time as the other furniture, and have heavy chairs fitted with castors or domes to spread the pressure on the carpet. Vinyl upholstery, especially in a light colour, needs an occasional clean with a special detergent.

(4) Curtains and Loose Covers

These should be washed before they begin to look noticeably dirty, for ingrained dirt can weaken the fibres. Twice a year should be sufficient, though nylon or glass material will need washing more often. Curtains made from heavier fabrics which must be dry-cleaned, should be well shaken weekly and brushed or vacuumed monthly (especially near the top) to prevent dust and atmospheric grease from settling into the fabric.

(5) Enamelled Doors

Refrigerators, washing machines and other appliances should be wiped over with a cloth wrung out in a weak detergent solution, whenever marks are seen. Once a week, wash over thoroughly in the same way, rinse with clear water and allow to dry. Then, polish with a little silicone cream, using a soft duster to bring up the shine. Never use polish on the enamelled parts of a cooker; merely wash well and rub dry.

(6) Laminated Plastic Surfaces

These should be wiped down daily with a dilute detergent on a soft sponge or cloth. If the counter surface becomes stained with fruit or vegetable juice, add a drop of bleach to the detergent mixture. For "stuck on" bits (such as pastry in the kitchen, or plasticine in the nursery) rub gently with a woven nylon scrubber, and as laminated surfaces scratch easily, use a paste or powder cleaner only when everything else has failed.

(7) Light Fittings and Radiators

Where these are awkwardly shaped or situated, they are best dusted weekly with an old fashioned feather duster, or a flexible attachment from the vacuum cleaner. To be effectively cleaned, light fittings need dismantling and washing at the sink, probably no more than twice a year.

(8) Paintwork

On skirting boards and window frames, paintwork is best dusted every other day, and treated fortnightly with a silicone cream polish that protects and cleans at the same time. Once or twice a year it can be washed down with a mild detergent, then polished again in the same way. Painted doors should not have polish applied, as this causes finger marks. Once a fortnight, wipe over with a wash-leather wrung out in clear water. When dry, rub up with a soft, clean duster. Window frames should be leathered at the same time as the windows, and occasionally polished with the same cream as the skirting boards.

(9) Polished Wooden Furniture

Whatever the finish, the minimum of polish should be applied, for unless it is thoroughly rubbed in, it tends to attract dust and dirt. Dust wooden furniture daily and rub it over once a fortnight with a damp chamois leather, allow to dry and give a very light application of aerosol wax polish, then rub up again.

Antique furniture needs regular applications of a solid wax polish, which feeds the wood at the same time as it burnishes it. But very modern furniture may need no polish at all, for it may have a polyurethane lacquer applied during the manufacture. *Teak* furniture needs a special oil applied only once a year; in between times it is dusted weekly, and any marks removed with a special furniture *stainer*. But if you suspect that your furniture has any special kind of finish, be sure and get precise maintenance instructions from the manufacturer.

(10) Silver

Keep silver in airtight cupboards (casement doors are better in this respect than sliding doors) or be prepared to polish it frequently. Treated with a long-lasting silver polish, silver behind doors will need repolishing only two or three times a year, providing it is rinsed in boiling water and rubbed up with a duster after use. If you keep your candlesticks and teaset on display, you will need to repolish them every few weeks in winter, but less frequently in summer. Always dry the inside of a silver teaset thoroughly after use to keep it sweet and clean, and remove the salt from a silver salt cellar, or it may discolour and pit the surface of the metal.

Highly chased pieces may occasionally be returned to the silversmith for professional repolishing.

Rub all table silver or plate with a duster after use, and repolish it only when it looks dull—probably once a month. Keep rarely used table silver in tarnish-proof bags which are specially made to keep out the air. If these are not available, use heavy gauge polythene bags, tightly sealed with plastic closures (the kind used for freezer storage).

(11) Stainless Steel

This needs the minimum of maintenance and is ideal for use with a dish-washer, unlike silver, since it is not dis-coloured by the dish-washing detergent. Flat pieces, such as cake trays and dishes, benefit from an occasional rub with a stainless steel paste cleaner, which is also ideal for sink tops and cooker rims.

(12) Tiles

Whether on walls or floors, tiles need only gentle though regular treatment. Wall tiles and vitrolite should be dusted every few days, leathered once a fortnight and given a good mopping down with mild detergent once or twice a year. Floor tiles and terrazzo should be mopped down daily, or weekly, in the case of an entrance way or porch. For terrazzo tiling, a combined cleaner and floor polish gives a pleasing finish.

(13) Vinyl and Other Plastic Floor Coverings

These are made in so many varieties that it is essential to get the right maintenance instructions for the particular floor. The object of any cleaning method must be to preserve the surface finish, so that dirt can be easily mopped away. In downstairs rooms where there is a lot of traffic, the floor is best mopped daily, but in upstairs rooms such as bathrooms or children's rooms, a water-based liquid polish applied monthly will give an excellent finish, which can be freshened weekly with clear water and dry mopped in between if necessary.

(14) Walls

No matter what their covering, walls need regular brushing down, either with a special long-handled bristle wall-brush or with a mop covered with a tied-on duster. This regular care is especially important in a centrally heated home, or where the wall covering is textured in some way, and if done every fortnight, it greatly lessens the need for redecoration.

Washable wallpapers should be wiped down monthly in the kitchen and lightly mopped with a "squeezy" mop in hall and passageways once or twice a year. Painted walls should never be allowed to get very dirty, so that only mild detergents will suffice to get them clean. Painted walls in the kitchen should be wiped over monthly, and in the bathroom and toilet two or three times a year. Mop over with a mild detergent, leave for a few minutes, then wipe down with a cloth or mop wrung out in clear water.

(15) Washbasins, Bowls and Baths

If these are wiped down daily with dilute detergent applied with a woven nylon pad or lintless duster, no stronger cleaner will be needed and the use of powder cleaners, which tend eventually to destroy the surface, can be avoided. Every fortnight, pay special attention to the pedestals of washbasins and toilets, and every week leave a lavatory bleach in the toilet bowl overnight.

(16) Windows and Mirrors

These are best cleaned with a wash leather wrung out in warm water, to which a spot of detergent can be added for the more greasy windows of the kitchen. Once a month, rub over mirrors with a cloth damped with methylated spirits. Glass covers of sills, tables and furniture tops should be treated like windows. Do kitchen windows once a week, all other glass in rotation, once a fortnight.

(17) Wood Floors

Have these professionally sealed as soon as they are put down, and they will then only need to be dry mopped weekly. Again, it is important to get precise maintenance instructions from your contractors, particularly as to the correct procedure for removing scuffs and heel marks. If you insist on wax polishing the floor, you will need to invest in an electric floor polisher and be prepared to remove the old polish completely with wire wool and white spirit, once a year.

Basic Cleaning Equipment

To buy now
Vacuum cleaner with attachments
Carpet sweeper
Soft sweeping brush ; firm outdoor sweeping brush
Shovel and two dustpans (one kept upstairs)

Firm hand brush for stairs, soft for upholstery
Stool steps
Squeeze mop and plastic bucket
Nylon lavatory brush and holder
Woven nylon and foam bath and wash-basin cleaner
Two small plastic buckets (for round-the-house work)
Two first-quality wash leathers
Twelve best-quality polishing dusters and plastic box to hold them
(The soft "rag" type of duster so useful for so many jobs can only be got from a sympathetic relative or friend!)

Wash polishing dusters regularly (as impregnated dust will scratch).

To maintain chamois leathers: after each use, squeeze gently in soap flakes, then rinse in cold water. Squeeze in fresh suds, but do not rinse; then squeeze out excess moisture and hang up to dry. Treated in this way, a leather will not crack or go slimy, but will stay supple and soft for months.

To buy later
Oil-impregnated dry mop for floors
Wall mop or brush for wallpaper
Feather dusters (for behind central heating radiators, etc.)
Electric floor polisher/carpet shampooer (or manual shampooing appliance).

Cleaning Materials

One all-purpose detergent, such as Teepol (bought by the gallon) for floors, walls, counters and windows; specialised cleaners for silver, chrome, copper, stainless steel; mild paste cleaner and scouring powder for sinks; spray-on oven cleaner; jelly cleaner for "disasters"; aerosol furniture polish; soft silicone cream for woodwork.

Disinfectant; bleach; aerosol sprays for protection against moths, flies and household smells.

4

FEEDING THE FAMILY

FEEDING THE FAMILY

Because the ability to enjoy life to the full depends to such a great extent upon eating nutritious, well-cooked and easily digested meals at reasonably regular hours, it is no exaggeration to say that the correct feeding of her family is the single most important job for any woman.

To the new housewife, the prospect may seem daunting, but if the job of cooking for two is tackled in a logical and methodical way, it soon settles into a regular routine, which is easy to adapt to the needs of a larger family as the years go by.

Feeding a family can be divided into three phases: Deciding what to cook; shopping for the ingredients; then preparing and serving the food.

Deciding What to Cook

The first thing to consider is what *kinds* of food need to be eaten every day to provide a balanced diet, their approximate amount, and the best way to cook them to conserve their goodness. Then it is not difficult to plan meals which include these foods in dishes suiting both your personal tastes and your budget.

Foods Which Should be Eaten Every Day

Meat, poultry, fish. One or more servings daily.

Eggs. One a day, or at least three a week.

Fruit. One serving of any fruit, whether fresh, dried, canned or frozen; in addition, one serving of citrus fruit (orange, grapefruit, lemon) or tomato, whether fresh or canned.

Vegetables. One serving of a yellow or green vegetable; one serving of a potato or root vegetable; one serving of any raw vegetable, usually in a salad.

Milk and cheese. One pint of milk for adults, more for children. This can be served as a drink, or included in the cooking. From a nutritional point of view, an ounce of cheese is equivalent to half a pint of milk.

Fats. Approximately 1 ounce of butter daily, as well as margarine and other fats and oils used in cooking.

Bread and cereals. Two or more servings of bread, whole grain cereal (such as porridge and breakfast foods) and

MEAT
POULTRY
FISH

EGGS

FRUITS

VEGETABLES

MILK &
CHEESE

FATS

BREAD &
CEREALS

WATER

pasta, including lokshen. (Bread is quite a good source of body-building food and the B vitamins.)

In addition drink plenty of water.

Once these basic needs have been satisfied, one can eat whatever else one pleases—a gain in weight will soon show when one has been eating too much! Of course, most people do eat rather more than their basic requirements, but this is all to the good, provided these extras are made up of body-building foods such as meat, fish, poultry and dairy products, and foods which are rich in vitamins and minerals—such as fruit, vegetables and whole grain cereals.

Extra amounts of such foods are, in fact, vital to nursing and expectant mothers, as well as to growing children, whose appetites must be satisfied with essential foods before they are allowed to eat sweet foods. Once they reach adolescence, it is important that their naturally large appetites should not be appeased with a constant supply of sugary or starchy "snacks". Instead, green vegetables, eggs and liver in particular, should be provided in as large quantities as they can eat.

Of course, a good diet must be a flexible one, allowing for the mood of the moment, and for variations from the normal routine; but if the *ideal* daily diet is always kept in mind, then the good habits started at the beginning will safeguard the health of the family at every stage of their lives.

To be nutritious, meals need not be expensive, for there is as much food value in a "cheap" but prime food, as in a similar one in the luxury class. Braising steak, for example, contains the same nutrients as *entrecôte*, while herrings have as much food value as salmon. In fact, all food is at its best when it is cheapest—at the very height of the season.

The actual food value of the *cooked dishes* you put on the table greatly depends on how the *raw ingredients* have been stored and prepared.

The vitamin content in particular is easily destroyed. To protect it, all leafy green vegetables should be kept away from the light, which tends to yellow their leaves and diminish their content of Vitamin C. Dairy products should also be protected from light, and as much fresh food as possible should be stored in the refrigerator.

Many of the vitamins in food are destroyed by heat, and others are soluble in water. Green vegetables should, therefore, be cooked as quickly as possible, and the cooking liquor then used in soups and sauces. However, it is a mistake to assume that vegetables are always better eaten raw for, in practice, so much more can be digested in a cooked rather than a raw state, that when the total of Vitamin C absorbed by the body is calculated, it will be found to be about the same for cooked as for raw vegetables!

In fact, when planning a healthy diet, moderation is always best, and a little of a variety of foods more sensible than a slavish adherence to a specialised régime.

When fresh foods are scarce, preserved ones, whether they be canned, frozen or dried, can add a very welcome out-of-season variety to the menu. Of course, their flavour and food value cannot compare with truly garden-fresh food, but because of the care and speed used when they are processed, they are often superior in every way to many so-called "fresh" foods bought from a shop.

The risk of food poisoning from raw animal foods is greatly reduced by the laws of Kashrut governing the selection of meat, fish and fowl. But dangers can still arise in the kitchen. Once meat, poultry and fish have been exposed to heat, they should be cooked completely, or the raising of the internal temperature of the food may encourage the growth of bacteria instead of being high enough to destroy them. All cooked foods which are not going to be used at once, or are left over from a meal, should be rapidly cooled, then covered and refrigerated to prevent contamination. The reheating of food is not harmful, but should be done quickly, so that the food is not actually recooked, which would make it become hard to digest.

The menus you build round the daily dietary needs will depend on the money and time you are prepared to spend, as well as on the kind of food that you and your husband enjoy. You will also have to work out the kind of dishes that can be prepared in advance for Shabbat.

Money For Food

A food budget is useful not only in keeping expenditure down to a specific amount, but also in helping to ensure that money is spent in the right proportion and on the most essential foods, no matter how much or how little you may have to spend. Without such a plan, it is easy for food bills to rise without any obvious extra enjoyment being gained.

Because of the extra cost of Kashrut and the special foods prepared at different seasons, food bills are always high in the Jewish household. However, I cannot suggest a minimum sum you should spend. Much will depend on how often you eat out and how many convenience foods must be bought to save a working wife's time.

Start off with an experimental sum that strikes a balance between what your husband thinks your general budget will stand, and what, from discreet enquiries among your contemporaries, you calculate you may need. Then, for the next six months, keep a scrupulous record of your expenditure in every category of food. After a few weeks, you will find that for each kind of food there is a basic minimum you will *have* to spend, plus extras which, though not strictly necessary, are very pleasant to buy.

In addition, it is wise to put by a regular sum to prevent heavy expenditure one week from ruining the budget for the next. Extras to be allowed for in this "fund" would include extra food needed for entertaining, the purchase of seasonal fruit for jam making and freezing, and the extra costs involved in catering for a festival.

But however tight your final budget may have to be, do not think it means that your meals need be dull, for when your spending is planned, you may well cater far better than the disorganised impulse shopper, who never has all the right ingredients in the house at one time and must rely on cooking with dull and expensive convenience foods.

Budgeting Your Time

Long after the purse-strings have become loosened, time and energy may still need conserving, so that a careful balance must always be kept between the saving of money and time. When you are at work, it pays to save *time* with prepared foods rather than to save *money* by laboriously making them from scratch at home, particularly if they can be made as well in a factory. Such foods include frozen and dehydrated vegetables, canned, bottled and dehydrated soups, chicken and beef bouillon cubes, ready prepared raw pastry, bread, cakes and biscuits, pickled meats and delicatessen. However, the majority of these foods should not be regarded as complete in themselves, but only as *ingredients* for a dish, or as extras to enliven a meal, and except in an emergency, the actual assembling and cooking of a main course should always be done at home. For, while no one ever tires of a home-cooked dish, a similar one made commercially soon becomes an unwelcome bore.

Much time can be saved in the kitchen by dovetailing the cooking for several meals by preparing larger quantities of similar foods at one time. For example, pastry for two pies can be made as quickly as for one ; and meat cooked in one casserole can be used for both a stew and a pie ; sufficient rice for a vegetable and a main dish can be cooked at the same time, while one pressure cookerful of vegetables and bones will provide enough jellied stock to make a week's supply of soups.

Planning Menus

Only one main meal a day during the week and perhaps two at the week-end will need to be planned in any detail, for week-day lunches will probably be eaten away from home or be a snack at the most, while breakfast tends to follow a standard routine, according to the habits of the household. To cater for it, one need only make sure that a good variety of suitable foods such as fruit juices, breakfast cereals, eggs, cheese, bread, butter, milk, coffee and tea are always in stock.

At the beginning, you will find it far easier to plan both the shopping and the cooking if the menus for each week are actually written down in a book. After a few months, when meal planning has settled into a fairly regular pattern, you may feel that you can just as easily carry the details in your head. But whenever there are any special meals to be planned, it is always wiser to revert to the original pen and paper routine.

As dinner on Friday night should be the highlight of the week, it is a good idea to decide what to serve at that meal and for lunch on Saturday, and then plan the remainder of the week's meals.

If the menus are planned in this way, by the week rather than by the day, you will find it much easier to ensure that they are varied and well-balanced from the point of view of food value and flavour, and that their cost is kept within the bounds of your budget.

The main dish for each meal should be decided on first, and then the rest of the menu planned round it. The *kind* of dish, be it meat or milk, roast, braise or grill, can be planned on Monday or Tuesday, but the *details* should be left until you know what meat and fish are prime that particular week. Depending on what is available, you can then decide whether the roast shall be beef or lamb, and whether, for example, it will be better to fry plaice or hake.

Try and balance the main dish for each day with those on the menu for the rest of the week. If you have a high-priced grill one day, have an economical casserole of mincemeat the next. Ensure that a complicated recipe is reserved for the day you come home early, and a "quickie" for the day you know you will be late.

Try also to balance each *meal* within itself by choosing dishes that provide contrasts in texture, flavour and colour. With a bland, creamy soup serve a brown crunchy loaf; precede a savoury casserole with a mildly flavoured fruit cup; follow a hearty roast with a light dessert; and never serve many highly seasoned dishes at the same meal, or the subtleties of flavouring may be submerged.

Traditional Jewish dishes such as tsimmes or strudel, which are so delicious to eat, tend to include a high proportion of fat and starch. These "fuel" foods provided a useful form of "internal central heating" in the colder climates where they originated. But when such a rich dish is included in the menu today, it should be counterbalanced by the serving of lighter, less fattening foods (such as fresh fruit and salads) in the rest of the meal.

In planning the menus, make the most of seasonal "best buys", using one food that is plentiful in a variety of ways in the same week. At the height of their season, for example, tomatoes might be served on three different days—in a salad, a soup, and a braise. Take advantage of the saving on a larger size can or packet than you would normally need by using the contents more than once, but in dishes of a different kind—a can of blackcurrants might be used as a basis of a fruit salad one day, and the remainder folded into a half-set jelly for serving the next. Effect a saving in *fuel* by loading the oven to the full with dishes that require the same temperature, but are to be served on different days. Casserole a fowl for the week-end while you braise steak in wine sauce for today. Effect a saving in *time* by preparing the dessert for tomorrow while waiting to serve the roast you have just cooked for today.

At first you will be wise to choose dishes for your menus with which you and your husband are familiar from your own family backgrounds, and which you already have a good idea how to cook. Once you become more confident in the kitchen, however, you will want to try out new recipes—and you will want to develop new tastes together. But never plan to cook more than one experimental dish at a time, or the whole meal may well end in disaster! And to make serving more simple, arrange to have at least one of the courses served cold.

When the main meals for each day have been planned and you are satisfied that, taken together with breakfast and lunch, they will provide a satisfactory diet, you can then check which of the necessary ingredients you already have in stock and which will have to be specially bought.

Shopping

Shopping for food is an art which it is absolutely essential to acquire, in order to keep a good table with the minimum of work and expense.

Until the invention of the telephone and the refrigerator, it was necessary to go shopping in person almost every day of the week. Today, one can order most foods by telephone with complete confidence. Better home-storage facilities make it possible to buy staple foods far less frequently than in the past, and in far greater bulk, and only the most perishable of foods need to be bought on the day they are to be served.

However, it is still wise to shop in person on occasion, and also to resist the temptation of turning one's larder into a storeroom for bulk supplies which might be more conveniently kept on the shelves of a shop! Indeed, unless one lives away from a Jewish district, it is not necessary to carry more than a month's supply of any food in everyday use. The foods that must be bought for a household come into three categories:

(1) *Basic foods* that should always be in stock, for they are essential no matter what the menu or the time of the year. These include groceries of all kinds, as well as dairy products. Because they are standardised in price and

quality, foods of this kind can be re-ordered automatically, and there is no real need to go shopping for them in person, once you have decided on the brands you prefer. If it is not convenient to have groceries delivered at home, it is best to select them weekly at a high-class supermarket or family grocers.

(2) *Basic foods with seasonal variations,* depending on the supply available at different times of the year. These include meat, fish, and fowl, as well as everyday vegetables and fruit. To get consistent quality and price throughout the year, it is advisable to give a regular weekly order for each kind of food to one particular retailer. Because he values your regular custom, he will advise you of "best buys" without prompting, and always give you satisfaction if you should have cause to complain.

Whenever possible, however, it is best to consult him in person, even if the goods you select are afterwards delivered to your home. Of course, you will rarely get the bargains from him that can be found by "shopping around", but you will also never be landed with an unreturnable "dud".

(3) *Speciality foods,* of which you do not need a regular supply. They include exotic fruits and vegetables, unusual canned and pre-packed foods and seasonings, special bakery goods and delicatessen. The more special the food, the more specialised must be the supplier, for only in his shop will the turnover be large enough to guarantee a constantly fresh supply. For example, buy nuts and dried fruit from a health food shop, pasta from an Italian food shop, spices from a large chemist or Indian food shop, soup cereals and delicatessen from a Jewish grocer.

Order no more of any one food at one time than you can reasonably expect to make use of while it is still in the peak of condition.

Order a Month's Supply at a Time

Canned goods of all kinds; frozen foods; sugar; tea; flour; drinking chocolate and cocoa; breakfast cereals; dried and candied fruits; rice, pulses and soup cereals; sauces and salad dressings; lokshen and other pasta; cooking, table and koshering salt; seasonings and herbs; oil and cooking fats; dried vegetables; bottled delicatessen (such as olives and gherkins) ; packeted foods other than biscuits ; sweet and savoury spices.

Order a Week's Supply at a Time

Butter and margarine ; eggs ; packeted and processed cheese ; instant coffee and coffee beans ; packeted sweet and savoury biscuits ; vorsht and prepacked sausages ; durable vegetables such as potatoes, carrots, leeks and parsley, onions and green peppers ; fruits such as oranges, lemons, grapefruit, apples, bananas, tomatoes.

Order a Three Days' Supply at a Time

Meat and poultry (unless it is to be frozen after koshering) ; perishable fruits and vegetables such as pears, stone fruits, cauliflowers, peas, cabbage, sprouts and aubergines, as well as those that are best ripened at home, such as melons and avocados ; Gouda cheese ; cooking cream cheese ; yoghurt, soured cream and smetana ; enriched bread, such as challah.

Buy Fresh Each Day

(As needed, though they can be stored in a refrigerator overnight.) Milk ; double-cream cheese ; soft fruits and berries ; grapes ; fresh corn ; cakes, kuchen, bread and rolls ; all fresh delicatessen (including salads, cooked meats and smoked fish) ; fresh cream ; liver ; raw mince-meat.

In practice, this means giving a weekly order to the grocer, greengrocer, fishmonger, butcher and poulterer, supplemented by the occasional mid-week purchase as it is needed ; having bread delivered or purchased three times a week, buying speciality bread on the day it is needed ; having dairy products delivered daily ; and buying cakes when they are required.

Of course, with a freezer, perishable foods can be bought less frequently if that is more convenient ; but it is always better to use food fresh from the earth, river or field, rather than one that has been kept for some period in "suspended animation".

A Guide to Food Selection

Learning to recognise and judge quality and good value in food is very difficult from a book, since it is so closely involved with the senses of smell, taste, touch and sight. Although these senses can only be educated by experience, the process can be greatly shortened with the aid of specialist information like that contained in the booklet, *About Buying Food and Drink* (which is published by the Consumer Council). This booklet tells one what the wording on labels actually means and what trade expressions signify; what the rights of the consumer are when purchasing food, and what are the protective food laws which help to enforce these rights. For the new Jewish housewife, however, there are extra pitfallls, different requirements and specialised tastes to be considered when shopping for food. It is from this point of view that this guide to food selection is written.

(1) Meat

First choose your butcher, either by personal inspection or recommendation. Look for the one who keeps his meat in refrigerated counters in an immaculate shop, and knows how to make the most of the limited kosher cuts by cutting and dressing them with skill. Although it may be more convenient to order the meat by telephone, it is essential at first to buy in person at least once a month, in order to become familiar with the different cuts.

All kosher meat has passed rigorous inspection for signs of disease, but the quality of the meat does vary according to the butcher—and the time of the year. You are most likely to get the best that is available if you know how to judge the quality for yourself.

Young beef has creamy fat and pinky-red flesh; older and tougher beasts have yellower fat and an abundance of gristle, especially between the rib bone and the flesh. *Baby beef* is a cross between veal and beef—light brown in colour, tender to eat, but relatively tasteless. *Baby lamb* has pinky flesh with a purple-tinged bone and is sweet to eat. When the bone looks flinty white and the flesh brownish red, the meat is well on its way to becoming stronger-tasting mutton. Veal is usually so dear, that it is worth buying when it is milk-fed and choice, with dead-white fat and rather pink flesh. Calves' liver should be pale and tender, and have a delicate smell. The colour darkens, the flesh becomes more springy, and the smell more pronounced as the beast matures.

Though it looks more attractive when it is freshly killed, meat is far more tender when it is about ten days old. To keep meat for this length of time, it must first be koshered in the usual way, then either hung by the butcher in his cold store at a temperature of about 30° F, or well wrapped and stored in a domestic freezer. This tenderising period is of special importance if the meat is to be roasted or grilled.

Even the finest quality meat "on the hoof" needs skilful dressing by the butcher to be seen at its best on the table. A roasting or braising joint should have a compact shape, without unwieldy pieces of flesh or unnecessary projecting bone; braising steak should be evenly sliced and free of too high a proportion of wasteful connective tissue; ready-minced meat should be only faintly speckled with fat and virtually free of gristle; and to be tender when cooked, both roasts and grills must be lightly dappled with fat, for the leaner the meat, the more moisture it will need to become tender.

(2) Poultry

Most birds now come ready-koshered, scalded and neatly trussed, so the selection must be of the poulterer rather than of his birds. Poulterers tend to run in families even more than butchers do, and you will probably get the finest birds if you give your custom to the one who runs in yours! The most popular bird for the kosher table—for which it is specially bred—is about twelve months old, mature enough to make excellent soup, yet still young enough to be tender and flavoursome en casserole. A top quality bird should have a full, round breast and white skin, and if it is to be braised, be free of excessive sub-cutaneous fat. However, the slow cooking in liquid needed to make soup will tenderise even an over-fat grandmother hen. Hens should weigh between 5 and 6 lb., ready-dressed.

Roasting chicken should have pliable breastbones and weigh between 3 and 4½ lb. for a young roaster to 6 lb. dressed weight for a capon. *Frying chickens* should have full, compact bodies and breasts and weigh between 1 and 3½ lb., while birds for grilling should weigh no more than 2½ lb. and are then usually split by the butcher to make two portions. *Turkeys* should be "double-breasted" and almost square. Specially bred "miniatures" of 8 lb. dressed weight make an excellent choice for a Yomtov meal for eight; but for a larger family or to make more than one meal, a 15-pounder is to be preferred.

(3) Fish

Fish must be chosen with the nose as well as the eyes. Fresh fish looks moist and firm, with a glistening skin, bright eyes and markings, and bright red gills. It should smell of the river or the sea, but never of ammonia. Many varieties—such as herrings, smoked fish, mackerel and salmon—vary in quality according to the season and the fishing grounds where they were caught, so the fishmonger's advice should always be sought as to the right time to buy. Indeed, it is never wise to go to the fishmonger's with too firm an order in mind. It is better to follow his guidance on which fish is prime on that particular day.

In deciding which fish shop is likely to give you the "best buy", the relationship between price, variety of fish and quality must be understood from the start. A difference in price between two kinds of fish in the same shop usually means that one is more popular with customers than the other—halibut, for instance, is always much dearer than haddock of the same quality. However, if haddock is dearer in one shop than it is in another in the same neighbourhood, you can be almost certain that the difference in price reflects a difference in quality. (Of course, you must expect to pay more in the shop that dresses the fish with care or delivers it to your door.) The seemingly cheaper fish may well cost you dearer in the end, for if it is of second quality, it is likely to be undersized or stale.

The fishmonger who already has a proportion of Jewish customers is the one most likely to sell the variety and quality of fish that you will require, for he will know by experience what kind of fish is most popular in a Jewish household, and how to prepare it correctly for the different dishes. He can also help the inexperienced cook to choose the right fish for a particular dish. He will know, for instance, which size of fish is best for frying and how to steak it, or which mixture of fish in a particular week is likely to prove the most tasty and economical for chopping. Fish should always be bought on the day it is to be cooked, but as the fishmonger also buys daily, it is good sense to place your order the day before it is required.

(4) Groceries

Today, an ever-increasing variety of foods leave the factory in individual packets instead of in large containers from which they are weighed out in the grocer's shop. Although the prepacking of food does make it slightly more costly than the same product bought loose, it also ensures that handling is reduced to the minimum, as is the risk of contamination either by airborne dirt, or by non-kosher material. The freshness and quality of the food is also guaranteed to a very large extent by the fact that there is a trade name—and address—on the packet. However, it is still more economical to buy in bulk those foods, such as soup cereals, and dried fruits, used in quantity in the Jewish kitchen.

To help assess the quality of prepacked and canned food, it is well worth learning to "read" labels and know how to decipher the jargon of the food trade—consumer booklets like *About Buying Food and Drink* can be particularly helpful in this regard. Imported foods, such as canned fruit, often have different gradings from those produced in Britain, and a family grocer can be most helpful in guiding you in your choice, at least until you have learned your way around the cans.

Unless you buy all your prepacked foods from a grocer under Beth Din supervision, it is sometimes difficult to know which foods, other than those labelled as prepared under supervision, can be safely used in a kosher kitchen. All prepacked foods are required by law to have their main ingredients listed on the packet, but as this does not indicate their method of manufacture (some savoury biscuits, for instance, are fried in animal fat), it is best to consult the local Beth Din, who keep an up-to-date list of chosen foods which they consider acceptable.

It is important to buy the right variety, as well as the right quality, of food for a particular dish. Firm, long-grained or "Patna" rice should be bought for savoury dishes, the rounder and softer "Carolina" rice for puddings. The more expensive "patent" flour (either plain or self-raising) makes the best rich cakes, sponges and biscuits, whilst the cheaper "household" flour is perfectly adequate for scones and pastry. For bread, especially challah, and for puff, flaky and other rich pastries, a specially milled "strong" bread flour should always be bought.

(5) Butter, Fats and Oils

Although many margarines state that they contain no animal fats, they may contain some milk solids or butter, and cannot be considered as "pareve" unless they carry a "kosher and pareve" seal. Even the best-quality white cooking fats are sometimes blended with animal fats, so only the approved ones should ever be used. All packeted butter is untouched by hand from the cow to the consumer, and the stainless steel dairy equipment is kept clean with soapless detergent. One can, however, buy Dutch butter with a rabbinical seal on the packet, though it should always be used soon after purchase as it is salt-free, and so does not keep for as long as salted butter.

All vegetable oils can be used freely in the Jewish kitchen, except at Passover, when corn oil should not be used. Oil is very much more economical when bought by the gallon rather than by the pint, and as it keeps indefinitely, bulk buying is a proposition for even the small household. Corn oil is a good all-purpose oil, equally suitable for frying and for salad dressings, though a good-quality olive oil makes the finest salad dressing and mayonnaise of all.

(6) Cheese

Cheese is a particularly perishable commodity, and should only be bought at a shop with refrigerated storage counters, and a large enough turnover to ensure a constantly fresh supply.

For a particular cheese to be considered truly kosher, the rennet used in its manufacture must have come from the stomachs of kosher cows—being a secretion rather than an actual body tissue, rennet itself is considered to be pareve. Thus, the variety of kosher cheese available really depends upon the cheesemaker. The range on sale in Britain is restricted to Gouda, processed Gruyère, and cheese spreads, as well as the many varieties of cream cheese that can be made without rennet.

You may well find different kosher cheeses abroad, and more might be imported into this country if there were sufficient demand. The price of soft cream cheese depends mainly on the amount of cream used in its manufacture. For cooking and baking, the cheaper single and curd cheeses are best, as they contain less liquid, while the softer and richer double-cream cheeses are most delicious for eating as spreads or dips.

Though soft and mild in flavour when fresh, Gouda cheese matures in flavour and becomes hard enough to grate, if it is left loosely wrapped in a cool, dry larder, or at the bottom of the refrigerator.

(7) Bread

There is a tremendous variety of bread, and it is worth shopping around to find the baker who bakes the kind you like. Here are some of the kinds available :

A French stick has a crisp crust and a fluffy "crumb", but goes stale in a day. Always put it in a 300° F (gas No. 1) oven for four minutes, then allow it to cool before cutting it for the table.

A Vienna roll is baked in a special oven which gives it a characteristic crisp and flaky crust. The dough is enriched with milk.

A Scotch farl is a brown, yeasty loaf with a crunchy topping of cracked wheat.

A rye loaf may be brown or "black" and usually has caraway seeds on top. It is best eaten the day it is made, though the stale loaf is delicious when toasted and thickly buttered.

An American enriched loaf is the best sliced bread for sandwiches, as it has a fine texture and keeps its freshness for several days.

A milk plait is soft and cakey and keeps well. It makes excellent melba toast and rusks.

A challah dough is enriched with egg and oil, which gives it a soft and spongy texture. As it is mixed with water rather than milk, it can be used for both meat and milk meals. A challah varies its shape with the season, being plaited or tin-shaped during the year, and round at Yomtov.

Wheatmeal, wholemeal and "Hovis" breads have more of the wheat germ and bran left in than have white breads, and because this means that they are especially rich in Vitamin B1, they are very good for children of all ages.

Bread rolls are made in infinite variety, but can be divided into two main types—the "cob" type made with French bread mixture, and the enriched rolls, such as croissants and brioches. Baigels are in a class by themselves, as they are first boiled and then baked to give them their inimitable flavour and crust.

All rolls should be eaten the day they are purchased. All kinds of bread and rolls can be frozen, and taste freshly baked when they are thawed out again.

Jewish bakers make perhaps the tastiest bread of all, though the best bread maker is not necessarily the best cake baker. Many Jewish bakers, however, specialise in the baking of yeast cakes, sponges, cheese cakes and continental gateaux.

But note that, only if the bakery is under the supervision of the Beth Din, can you be sure that all the ingredients used are strictly kosher.

(8) Milk and Cream

As far as quality and cost are concerned, it matters little from whom you buy your milk, as the "richness" or percentage of milk fat in the different grades of milk, as well as the price to be charged, are strictly controlled by law. With the exception of a small amount of farm-bottled T.T. (tuberculin tested) milk, almost all milk is heat-treated to ensure that it is free from infection. The most common method is pasteurisation, which does not affect the taste of the milk, as does sterilisation, which takes place at a higher temperature. Pasteurised milk is the best all-purpose grade for family use, though a small family might find it worth a little extra for Channel Islands milk and using the extra cream in their coffee. Homogenised milk has the cream evenly distributed, but the extra it costs is not really justified for domestic use. Kosher milk is available in certain parts of the country.

Single cream, which contains not less than 18% milk fat, is excellent for using with coffee and fruit, and mixing with an equal quantity of double or thick cream for whipping, but it will not whip by itself. Double cream is nearly three times as rich (it contains 48% milk fat), and can be whisked with single cream, top of milk, or unbeaten egg whites (one to each $\frac{1}{4}$ pint), to make a whipped cream that is lighter and less buttery than when it is whipped alone. Jersey cream costs more than ordinary double cream, but as it is so much richer and tastier and seems to keep longer, I think it is well worth the extra cost. Sterilised cream is mid-way in richness between single and double cream, but as it has the same boiled taste as sterilised milk, it is really only worth using in an emergency.

(9) Ice-Cream

The only ice-cream that must by law contain only milk fat, is that labelled "dairy ice-cream", "dairy cream ice" or "cream ice". All the others may, and often do, contain fats of animal origin. Even dairy ice-cream sometimes contains gelatine, so one must either buy kosher pareve ice-cream (which contains 10% of vegetable fat and no milk products), or write and enquire about ingredients from the manufacturers concerned.

Soured cream and yoghurt are both "cultured" products that have been set with a lactic-acid bacillus to give them their characteristic thick, smooth consistency. Which brand you choose is a matter of personal taste, and while they are freely available in supermarkets and grocer's, most milkmen will now deliver them to the door. As they have a refrigerator life of up to seven days, it is not necessary to buy them fresh daily like milk and fresh cream, but if they have been kept in stock for too long, the contents will shrink in volume and the taste will become bitter.

(10) Eggs

The freshness of an egg depends on how speedily it can be delivered from the hen to the kitchen, so the freshest eggs often come from dairies with their own packing station, which handles eggs gathered from specially selected farms. However, many grocers also buy direct from the packing station, so the best and freshest source of supply in the neighbourhood can only be discovered by experiment.

The yolk of a fresh egg stays plump and separate when the egg is broken into a cup, while the yolk of a stale egg flattens and spreads into the surrounding white. Eggs with a "blood spot" on the yolk are considered treife and must be discarded.

Eggs are graded by weight, ranging from small to medium, standard and large, and the price varies accordingly, but as the price of each size also fluctuates according to the seasonal supply, it is very difficult to work out which grade of egg (weight for weight) gives the best value in any particular week. As there is usually only a difference of a few pence between one grade and another, it is more convenient to buy large eggs only for cooking and baking, a policy which ensures at the same time that the family

(11) Delicatessen

gets as much food value as possible from this very valuable food.

Delicatessen are now widely available in supermarkets, as well as speciality shops, so the choice of shop must depend on the quality of the food, the frequency of the turnover, and perhaps above all, the adequacy of refrigerated storage facilities. While it is obvious that foods such as potato salad and chopped herring are highly perishable, it is not so evident that (even when they are refrigerated) smoked fish and meats also have a limited "shelf life", and must be bought during the short period when they are at their peak.

Pickled meats and sausages are made in so infinite a variety that it is difficult to assess their comparative value, except on the basis of *taste*, but as a general rule, the higher the price, the greater the meat content in the sausage or vorsht, and the choicer the cut of pickled meat. Pickled "brisket", for example, is always dearer—and tastier—than simple pickled "meat". Yet, while frying vorsht is cheaper, if less meaty, than salami, most people would consider it equally delicious to eat! *Scotch* smoked salmon, though it costs more, is always more delicious than salmon smoked in the identical fashion which has been caught elsewhere. Frozen smoked salmon is an excellent emergency supply, but cannot compare either in taste or texture with the original food!

Though pickled cucumbers, olives and similar delicatessen are dearer than the same foods bought loose, they may prove a more economical buy, as any leftovers will keep for another time in the pickling brine. Large olives are more economical than small, as pound for pound they have a higher proportion of edible flesh to stone. The finest black olive is the Greek Calamata, which is imported in the late autumn, and canned in an olive oil sauce.

Schmaltz (matjes) and salt (milt) herrings have their allotted season, and should only be bought when the time is right. Many delicatessen shops now sell ready-filleted schmaltz herrings or excellent canned Icelandic fillets. There are also ready-cooked foods such as chopped liver, gefilte and fried fish and roast chicken which, though more expensive than home-made, can be most useful when time and energy are in short supply.

(12) Fruit and Vegetables

As it is often impossible for the new housewife to select the best-flavoured fruit and vegetables by appearance alone, the guidance of a knowledgeable greengrocer is essential. This can be obtained by patronising a specialist shop, or by shopping at a chain store which has a reputation for stocking only those foods that are at the peak of their season in a particular week. The external appearance of fruit and vegetables can, however, be a useful guide to quality. The colour should be intense, the skin firm and unblemished, the texture crisp or smooth, according to type, but never soggy or spongy. Root crops should be free of spade marks and bruises, and soft fruit should look dry and show no sign of staining on the underside of the carton. Mushrooms of all sizes should have firm white caps and pinky-brown gills; aubergines and peppers should be fat, glossy and unbruised, while citrus fruits should feel heavy for their size, and all fruit with cores, stones or pips will prove a better buy when purchased in a larger rather than a smaller size.

Frozen fruit and vegetables depend for their flavour as much on the way they are stored in a shop as on the quality of the raw food that goes into the packet. For this reason, it is essential to buy frozen foods only from a freezer that is kept in good condition and shows no sign of undue icing up round the sides, and where the packets of food are stored below the "freezing" line clearly marked on the inside. The danger of frozen foods partially defrosting while in stock is greatly reduced when they are displayed in shelf, rather than chest-type freezers.

Herbs and Spices

Herbs and spices quickly lose their flavour if they become stale, so it is essential to buy them in small amounts from a shop with a constant turnover. Dried herbs are usually freshest at a health food or whole food shop, spices at a larger chemist or specialist in Oriental and Middle East foods. Buy only one ounce of any one variety of a herb or spice at one time.

Condiments

Salt for koshering meat must be especially coarse, and should be bought from a Jewish butcher or grocer; fine cooking salt is best bought in a tin, though if you have a salt mill, the Maldon or sea-salt crystals are the tastiest. Table salt is slightly finer than the koshering grade, and is usefully bought in a 3 lb. bag. Black pepper is best bought as peppercorns and coarsely ground in a mill at the table or cooker, but white pepper, which needs to be finer, can be bought ready-ground in a drum.

How to Store Food

Every kind of food, whether it is cooked or raw, must be stored under the correct conditions if it is to be kept safe, fresh-looking and flavoursome until it is needed. These conditions vary with different foods, but in every case, they must include protection from light, heat and disease-carrying insects.

Highly perishable foods, especially cooked foods, left-overs and foods of animal origin, such as raw fish, meat, poultry, manufactured meat products and dairy foods, must be stored in a refrigerator if they are to be safe to eat the next day. At the normal refrigerator temperature of between 38° F and 45° F, the growth of the bacteria and moulds which cause food to go bad is inhibited for a period that may vary from two to twenty-eight days, depending on the nature of the food and how fresh it was when it was put into the refrigerator. In a freezer, the safe storage period can vary between a week and a year, again depending on the type of food, but also on the internal temperature of the freezer.

The Refrigerator

A refrigerator is basically a food cupboard in which the temperature is kept down by the constant circulation of cold air. So that this air can flow freely, the shelves should never be overcrowded with food. The coldest part of the refrigerator is directly under the freezing unit, and it is here that the most perishable foods should be stored.

Before it is put into the refrigerator, food must be covered, or put in a container of some kind, so that it does not shrivel up or become discoloured in the cold dry air, and also so that it does not absorb flavours and smells from the foods around it. Airtight plastic containers are ideal for this purpose, for they are light to handle, relatively cheap, and can be bought in a wide variety of shapes and sizes. The square-sided ones are particularly compact. Aluminium foil is also useful to wrap round bulky or awkwardly shaped food—a plate pie or the remains of a roast, for example—while plastic bags are excellent for storing fruit and vegetables.

Like any other food cupboard, the inside of the refrigerator and its shelves need to be washed out weekly. Use a little mild-smelling detergent in hot water, adding a tablespoonful of bicarbonate of soda if there should be a strong odour of food. The outside enamel should also be washed weekly and then protected from fingermarks with a light application of silicone cream. In many new models, defrosting is done automatically, but where this is not the case, the refrigerator should be defrosted when the ice on the unit has reached a thickness of a quarter of an inch.

Below, I give a guide to the refrigerator life expectation of various foods, and how and where they are best stored on the shelves. Whether the food will remain edible for the minimum or maximum periods given will depend on how fresh it was at the start. Common sense must be the ultimate guide. Any food that looks or smells even slightly unappetising or peculiar should always be thrown away. The contents of the refrigerator should be reviewed daily, so that any left-overs can be used up quickly, and fresh foods enjoyed while they are still at their peak.

(1) *Butter and margarine,* which easily absorb "foreign" smells and tastes, should be kept in their original wrapping in the special compartment in the door. Stocks should be renewed weekly. Cooking butter can be kept in a covered plastic container, so that it does not need to be rewrapped each time it is used. Enough butter for each day can be kept out in a butter dish in the kitchen, but it should be protected from the light, as this may diminish its food value. Chicken fat and meat drippings can be kept on a separate shelf in the door, and will stay fresh for a month or more. White cooking fats do not go "off" as they are made from oils, so they can be kept either in the refrigerator or the larder.

(2) *Cream* (unless it is whipped) goes "grainy" if it is frozen, so it is best stored in the door. Sweet cream and any dishes or cakes that contain it will keep for three to four days before going sour, but sour cream, smetana, cultured cream and yoghurt will keep for seven to ten days, after which they may become bitter.

To store any dish with a whipped cream topping, cover it with a large upturned pudding basin, to protect it without squashing it. Left-over whipped cream can be put into a

container and frozen until it is needed again. Pasteurised milk will keep for up to three days in the door rack, but it is better ordered fresh daily.

(3) *Cheese* will keep its flavour and texture better for a short period if it is kept covered in a cool larder. If this is not possible, or if it is to be kept for more than twenty-four hours, it should be stored in its own container in the bottom of the refrigerator. To prevent the surface from drying out, each piece of cheese should be in its own plastic bag or foil wrapping.

Grated cheese will keep in a container for two weeks. Cottage and cream cheeses are far more perishable, and they should be eaten within four or five days. Over-chilling ruins their flavour, so they should be kept near the bottom of the refrigerator. All cheeses have a better taste and texture if they are removed from the refrigerator at least one hour before they are eaten.

(4) *Eggs* in the shell will keep for up to ten days in the door rack or in their original boxes. Egg yolks will keep for up to two days, either in a tiny plastic container just big enough to hold them without air space, or covered with a film of cold water in a larger airtight container. (This water is thrown away before the yolk is used.)

Egg whites can be kept in any airtight container, and will keep for at least a week—they are fit to use as long as they have no smell. Strangely enough, stale egg whites make the best meringues! Hard-boiled eggs (which should be marked as such on the shell) will keep for a week. Stuffed eggs and any egg salads should be refrigerated as soon as they are made, and then used not more than four hours later.

(5) *Fresh fish* tastes better if it is used the same day it is bought, but it *will* keep for twenty-four hours if it is first loosely wrapped in damp greaseproof paper and then stored on the bottom shelf. Gefulte fish, halibut in lemon sauce, and other cooked fish dishes will keep for three days in a covered container. (Gefulte fish actually improves in flavour after forty-eight hours.)

Fried fish does, however, tend to lose its crispness and, if it must be refrigerated, it should be only loosely wrapped and then taken out an hour before it is to be served. Chopped herring should be used up in three days, as it tends to develop "off" flavours. *Smoked fish* should be *tightly* foil-wrapped and stored under the freezer. Sliced smoked salmon will keep in this way for up to three days (it is nicer, of course, used the day it is cut) while kippers and finnan haddock will keep for up to ten days, depending on how highly they have been smoked.

Pickled fish in jars (such as herrings) will keep for two months once they have been opened, but they do tend to become more acid the longer they are kept. Potted herrings keep extremely well, for the vinegar acts as a preservative and keeps them fresh for up to a week.

(6) *Meat,* once it has been koshered, should be stored in a *loosely* covered container directly under the freezing unit, and then used within three days, or it may begin to smell. (If this is impossible or inconvenient, it should be *tightly* wrapped in foil as soon as it has been koshered, and then stored in the freezing compartment.)

Fresh liver and mincemeat should be used within two days. Any kind of cooked meat, whether it is roasted, braised, stewed or in a pie, should be tightly wrapped or covered and used within two or three days—casseroles that have a tomato sauce keep the best because of their acidity. Pickled meats, tongue and most kinds of salami and sausage will keep for two to six days, but the sooner they are used the better. (Some kinds of vorsht can be hung up in a cool larder, but should be refrigerated once they have been cut—ask the grocer when you buy them.)

Freshly koshered poultry should be loosely wrapped in plastic or foil and cooked within two days, but a frozen bird can be left to defrost in the refrigerator and will keep for two days after it has been thawed. Cooked poultry should have the stuffing removed and wrapped in a separate parcel, and both stuffing and bird should then be used within two to three days. A chicken pie or casserole should be used within twenty-four hours, and a chicken salad refrigerated the moment it is made, and served no more than four hours later.

However, you will have no difficulty in knowing when you have kept any kind of meat, fish or poultry for too long. You can tell by the smell!

(7) *Soups* will keep for at least two days, and then taste better than when they were first made. If you want to keep

them for longer than forty-eight hours, bring them to the boil, cool and refrigerate them again for another twenty-four hours. If you wish to keep soup *stock* for more than a day, strain out any starchy vegetables, such as carrot and potato, before you refrigerate it, as these go sour very quickly.

(8) *Fruit.* All fruit should be kept towards the bottom of the refrigerator, well away from the freezing unit.

Apples and pears. Although it is not necessary to refrigerate them if they are to be kept for only a few days, apples and pears *taste* better if they are served chilled, though pears should be left at room temperature for half an hour before they are eaten. Neither fruit needs covering, but both should be stored on the bottom shelf. They will then keep for ten days before they start to shrivel.

Stone fruit—peaches, plums, etc.—should be lightly washed, then stored in an airtight container, and used within three or four days.

Oranges and grapefruit need only be refrigerated if they are to be kept for more than a week, but lemons soon shrivel in the larder, so they should be kept in the vegetable or fruit container at the bottom of the refrigerator. They keep for weeks. If half-lemons have their cut surface tightly covered with foil, they will stay juicy for another three or four days at least.

Melon and pineapple are both ruined if they are over-chilled, so they should only be refrigerated either to keep them from spoiling once they have been ripened in the larder, or when they have been cut. Whole fruit should be stored uncovered at the bottom of the refrigerator. Cut fruit, however, should have the surface tightly covered with foil—it will then keep for up to four days. (Slices of sugared melon can be left uncovered for half an hour to chill before they are served.)

Grapes should only be refrigerated if they are to be kept for more than three days, and then they should be put unwashed into an airtight container and used within a week. This treatment does not affect the hardier grapes used in fruit salads, but will take the bloom off the hot-house varieties.

Soft fruit. Currants and berries are at their best the day they are bought or, even better, picked. But they will keep for forty-eight hours if they are first lightly rinsed then sugared and put in an airtight container—a delicious syrup will develop from the natural juices and the sugar. However, they will *not* taste the same as when they are sugared at the table, as they lose their fresh texture when soaked in juices.

Stewed fruit and fresh fruit salad should always be tightly covered and used within twenty-four hours, or the fruit will go soggy and lose its fresh flavour.

Bananas should never be refrigerated, as the texture is ruined and the fruit may go black. They should always be added to a fruit salad just before it is served.

(9) *Vegetables* (with the exception of potatoes and onions) keep fresh longer if they can be stored in the bottom of the refrigerator. (Even cut onion will keep for several days, if it is covered with foil like a cut lemon.) The vegetables are easiest to handle if each kind is kept in its own plastic bag, and all the bags then kept in the large vegetable container on the bottom shelf. More delicate vegetables and salads should, however, be kept in a separate container to prevent them from getting bruised. These include green peppers, tomatoes, aubergines and courgettes.

The keeping quality of vegetables, in particular, varies according to their freshness when they are first stored, but good-quality produce should keep in excellent condition from one week to the next, and root vegetables will keep for up to a fortnight. Mushrooms are the exception. They should be used the day they are bought, and certainly no longer than twenty-four hours later.

Salads and fresh herbs (such as parsley) will keep crisp and sweet for several days, either in a large airtight plastic container or, even better, an aluminium pan. Once they have been washed and dried, they will become crisp in two or three hours, if covered, but should then be used within the next twenty-four. Any kind of vegetable salad with dressing should also be used within a day.

Cucumber bought with a plastic "skin" will keep in the refrigerator for a week, but if it is not protected in this way or has been cut, it should be used within three days, or it goes soft and mushy. It should *never* be frozen. This applies also to pickled cucumber, which will, however, keep for a month in the pickling liquid, providing it is stored in an airtight jar or container.

(10) *Sandwiches* will keep in the refrigerator for twenty-four hours, but they must be foil-wrapped, because greaseproof is not sufficiently airtight. Put them in the middle of the refrigerator.

(11) *Uncooked pastry* made with water will keep for a week wrapped in foil, but if it has been mixed with egg, it should be used within seventy-two hours. Cooked pastry will keep as long as its filling, but it should always be used within seventy-two hours. The whole pie dish should be covered with foil, or the pastry will soon go crumbly and stale.

(12) *Canned foods* (except where recommended on the label) do not need refrigerating until they are opened. Then, with the exception of fruit and fruit juices (which are best kept in plastic or glass), the can makes the best container, for it has been thoroughly sterilised during processing. This applies in particular to baby foods, which can be safely kept covered in their cans from one day to the next.

(13) *Home-made mayonnaise* should be kept covered and away from the freezer, and will then stay fresh for two or three weeks. Bought mayonnaise contains preservative, and can be kept in the larder.

(14) *Beer, lager and white wine, as well as soft drinks,* taste better when chilled, but do not actually need to be refrigerated all the time. However, left-over wine will keep satisfactorily in the door of the refrigerator for a fortnight, though it is then better for cooking purposes than for drinking.

(15) *Commercial and home-frozen foods* should be kept in the freezer before use for only as long as the manufacturers of the refrigerator recommend. They should be put away as soon as they are brought into the house, and never refrozen once they have been thawed out. In a separate freezer, both home-cooked and frozen foods can be stored for a much longer time, but again, the advice of the manufacturer must be strictly followed if the food is still to be wholesome when it is removed.

For the storage of less-perishable foods, a cool, dry, well-ventilated larder or food cupboard is ideal. Here, canned foods and jams, as well as dried vegetables and packeted soups, will keep for up to a year if necessary, though all stocks should normally be used up before the next season. Here, on pull-out racks, is the best place to keep potatoes and onions, baking apples, bananas, under-ripe melons, pineapple, pears and avocados, as well as the weekly supply of grapefruit and oranges. Fresh oil, as well as the fish and chip oil in current use, should also be kept in the larder rather than in the refrigerator, for too low a temperature may cause it to solidify and become difficult to pour. Certain *cooked* foods can be kept in the larder overnight, providing the temperature is not over 50° F (this can be checked with the small thermometer which should always be kept clipped onto a shelf in the refrigerator). These cooked foods include those that are high in acid, such as stewed fruit and pies, as well as roast meats and poultry, the harder varieties of cheese, and fried fish of all kinds.

Those foods that require dry rather than cold storage conditions are best stored in ordinary non-ventilated kitchen cupboards, or in racks on the walls or counter. Foods that are in regular use are best decanted into airtight glass jars as soon as they are bought (reserve stock should be kept in the orignal packets). These include staples such as dried fruit, rice, soup cereals, matzo meal, coating crumbs, herbs and spices, and dry ingredients for baking, like flour, sugar, baking powder, spices, drinking chocolate, cocoa and nuts. Bulky foods, such as pasta and breakfast cereals, are best left in the original packet, which should be carefully re-closed to keep the contents airtight, each time it is used.

Koshering salt should be kept in a plastic bag in a cupboard. Table salt should be kept in its tin, and the salt cellar refilled as required. Cooking salt is most conveniently kept in a salt box or "kit" near the cooker. Salt will keep indefinitely, providing it is kept dry.

Sweet and savoury shop biscuits should be kept in separate airtight tins once the packet has been opened. Homemade biscuits should be stored in a tin as soon as they are quite cold. Chocolate biscuits should be stored well away from air vents or chimney breasts, as warm air causes their coating to melt.

All cakes that are to be kept overnight should be put in a tin; and if they contain fruit, cream, or butter icing, the cake tin should then be refrigerated. Fruit cakes and ginger cakes will keep fresh for days if they are completely wrapped in foil before they are put in a tin. Yeast cakes, such as kuchen, should not be put in an airtight tin, as this makes them go mouldy, but are better wrapped loosely in a plastic bag and then kept with the bread.

Bread should always be wrapped in a plastic bag before it is put away. If a loaf is expected to last for more than forty-eight hours, it is better refrigerated, but for normal family use, a bread tin or a plastic-lined bread drawer is ideal. Bread and rolls do, however, freeze extremely well, so a reserve stock of several varieties is worth keeping in the freezer, or even in the freezing compartment of the refrigerator. When shopping is difficult, enough bread for a week can be frozen at once, and then taken out and thawed as it is needed. (To thaw the bread, open the plastic bag and leave the loaf at kitchen temperature for one hour, or if it is crisp-crusted, put it in a cold oven, turn on at gas No. 1 (300° F), then take out after five minutes and leave until it is soft enough to slice.)

Tea, sugar and coffee, which will be used several times a day, are best kept in canisters near the cooker. While tea will keep in the packet for weeks, coffee soon loses its flavour once it has been roasted. It should, therefore, be kept in a really airtight tin, and whether it is ground, instant or beans, it is best to use it up within a fortnight of purchase.

Candles for Shabbat should be kept in a dry cupboard, either in the kitchen or the dining room. The triangular ones are the easiest to fit into a candlestick, and it is convenient to buy three 1-lb. packets at a time. If these are put into a tall, airtight tin, they will keep in perfect condition until they are needed. For summer use, when Shabbat comes in very late, special short candles can be bought.

In Store for the Unexpected

As an insurance against the unexpected—such as the day you arrive home tired or late, or when unexpected guests suddenly appear—it is useful to have a stock of those kinds of food from which a complete meal—or at least one course—can be quickly concocted.

In the larder keep a variety of canned and packeted soups and bouillon cubes, packets of quick-cooking soup cereals, fruit juices, canned tomatoes; canned salmon and tuna (for casseroles, quiches, soufflés and fish cakes); main course canned vegetables like new potatoes and *petits pois,* and "salad" vegetables, such as artichoke hearts, sliced green beans, corn and asparagus tips. Canned fruit is always useful for adding to flans and jellies, and pineapple titbits are especially tasty for sparking up an otherwise dull fresh fruit salad.

One should also keep in stock several varieties of pasta—vermicelli, egg noodles and spaghetti—as well as a packet of Patna rice, for these foods are the best of all insurances against the arrival of an unexpected dinner guest. In the cake tins there should if possible always be one "cut and come again" type of cake, such as fruit cake, madeira or ginger, and you should have a separate tinful of home-made biscuits.

In the refrigerator keep the "makings" of an *hors-d'œuvre* such as olives, gherkins and bottled herrings of various kinds. Besides a constant stock of root vegetables and fresh parsley for using in soups and stews, keep an un-washed lettuce; a few tomatoes; several hard-boiled eggs; some vorsht; a tube of tomato purée and a con-tainer of gravy (for use in pasta dishes and casseroles); a ball of raw pastry, and a couple of lemons. Also, keep a container of ready-grated cheese, for folding into omelettes, sprinkling over casseroles and piling on to toast, as well as foil-wrapped cream cheese to use for sandwiches and dips.

In the freezing compartment of the refrigerator keep puff pastry; concentrated orange juice; fish fillets and whole trout, and a small selection of packeted fruit and vege-tables. If you have a *separate freezer,* you can add to the list such home-made and bulky foods as pastry and sponge flan cases; a selection of bought or home-made cakes; pies and bread; a raw fowl and half a cooked one, and a container of bolognese or Spanish rice meat sauce.

In the drinks cupboard, it is good policy to keep supplies of crisps, nuts and savoury biscuits for the day your husband "just happens" to bring home a friend.

5

*PREPARATIONS FOR THE SHABBAT
AND FESTIVALS*

Preparing for Shabbat

To ensure that Shabbat is truly a day of rest from house-hold tasks, careful preparations must be made in advance. Before the Eve of the Sabbath (Erev Shabbat), sufficient food must be prepared to last the family from Friday evening to Saturday night, the house must be cleaned and polished with especial care, fresh flowers arranged to give a Shabbat atmosphere, and preparations made for the different family ceremonies, such as Kiddush and Havdalah.

Details of the religious customs and laws associated with Shabbat can be found in any book of Jewish practice. Guidance on specific points of law (particularly those relating to food preparation on Shabbat) should be sought from the Rabbi of your congregation, for new rulings must constantly be made as new cooking appliances appear on the market.

Preparing Food for Shabbat

There is no one cut-and-dried routine that can possibly meet the differing circumstances of every household. To-day, in fact, many women find that even the way their own mothers prepared for Shabbat does not suit their more modern way of life. For example, the "double-duty" working housewife will not have time for a concentrated preparation period just before Shabbat, but will have to spread her cooking over a greater part of the week, and delegate the less essential jobs to paid help.

Fortunately, new foods and new appliances can lessen a great deal of the labour associated with "making Shabbat" for so many generations. Few women, for instance, need scald and kosher a fowl themselves, as they can buy a pre-packed bird from almost any kosher butcher; many fish-mongers sell ready-minced fish; and with a modern refrigerator and freezer, it is possible to do the "week-end" baking at the most convenient time during the earlier part of the week.

But, however you arrange to do your week-end cooking, you will find that (with the exception of cakes and bread, which are best bought fresh on Friday), it is convenient to have all the supplies you need in the house by Thursday afternoon. This allows plenty of time for meat and poultry to be koshered, fish to be prepared, soups and casseroles to be cooked and refrigerated, and the week-end stocks of fruits and vegetables to be properly stored away.

On most week-ends, the meals will be found to follow a fairly predictable pattern, for of necessity, they must be composed of dishes which can be safely kept from one day to the next.

Over the years, Jewish housewives have built up a wide repertoire of suitable dishes, many of which actually improve in flavour when refrigerated overnight. In addition, there are foods like "tsimmes" and "cholent", which can be left to cook in a low oven, or over an electric hot plate or shielded gas flame, from Friday afternoon until Saturday lunch. Many of these recipes have their origins deep in the past, but there are other more "modern" ones which can be used with equal success. A list of both traditional and "modern" recipe suggestions is given at the end of this section.

All the preparations for the week-end's food should be completed by early Friday afternoon, for once the candles have been lit at the commencement of Shabbat, no further cooking should be done until after Havdalah on Saturday night.

Additional Preparations

When making up the week-end shopping list, check that there are sufficient kosher wine and candles in the house for both Kiddush and Havdalah. On Friday night and for Saturday lunch, there should be two complete "loaves" on the table, over which a blessing is made. In a large house-hold, three challahs should be ordered for the week-end, but for the smaller family, only one full-size challah need be bought, and miniature challahs, rolls, or even unbroken matzos substituted for large loaves when the blessing is said.

On Friday afternoon, when all the cooking has been com-pleted, the dining table should be set with a freshly laundered cloth. The two loaves (symbolising the double portion of manna that appeared in the wilderness on Erev Shabbat) are set on a breadboard, and covered with a special cloth (called a "challah decke"). Beside them should be set a salt container into which the bread is dipped before it is handed round the table. The Kiddush wine should be set on a tray, with the special goblet or "becher" ready for Kiddush to be made when the head of the household returns from the Friday evening synagogue service. Kiddush is preceded by the lighting of the Shabbat candles, and the saying of the blessing over them. Although there is no limit to the number that can be used, most women light two and, if women guests are present at the time, provide them also with candles to light.

The meal served on a Friday night has a special quality of its own. In part, this is because of the choice foods it is customary to serve on this occasion; in part, to the unique atmosphere that pervades the house itself and which lasts throughout the whole of Shabbat, especially when family and friends gather for afternoon tea.

Then, when three stars appear, the ceremony of Havdalah is performed. The prayer is said over a plaited candle, each of whose seven strands represents the hope for a good day in the coming week. The spice box is smelt, the wine is drunk, and it is time to start thinking of the week ahead.

Suitable Foods to Prepare for Shabbat

Below are some suggestions for foods which are particularly suitable for serving on Shabbat. Whether they be traditional or modern, these dishes have one factor in common—they can all be made one day to serve on the next. In some cases, they actually improve in flavour overnight! Some of the dishes can be served hot on Friday night, and cold for lunch the next day.

(1) Hors-d'œuvres and Appetisers

Traditional
Chopped egg and onion;* chopped herring;* pickled and schmalz herring hors-d'œuvre;* chopped liver.*

Modern
Ratatouille (served hot or cold); chatzilim (Israeli aubergine hors-d'œuvre); artichoke or avocado vinaigrette; Guacamole (Mexican avocado hors-d'œuvre); egg mayonnaise; grapefruit half; citrus fruit cocktail; melon.*

* Denotes recipe in Bride's Cookery Course.

95

(2) Soups

Traditional
Chicken ; * tomato rice ; * barley ; * hobene gropen ; * lentil. *

Modern
Borscht on the rocks * (iced) ; minestrone ; Vichyssoise (cold cream soup) ; chilled avocado soup ; Gazpacho (chilled tomato soup).

(3) Soup Garnishes

Traditional
Helzel * (stuffed neck) ; mandelen * (soup nuts) ; lokshen * (noodles) ; knaidlach * (matzo meal dumplings).

Modern
Baked or fried croutons (bread squares) ; sour cream (for milchik soups).

(4) Casseroles

Traditional
Cholent * (bean, meat and potato) ; tsimmes * (sweet carrot casserole).

(5) Main Dishes

Traditional
Fowl, boiled and served cold, * or browned after boiling, * or stuffed and casseroled ; * corner of bola ; * braised brisket. *

Modern
Roast chicken ; * fried chicken joints ; casseroles such as chicken cacciatora (with wine and peppers) ; coq au vin (with wine and mushrooms) ; meat loaf. *

(6) Fish Dishes

Traditional
Gefulte fish ; * chopped fried fish ; * fried steaks or fillets of fish ; * halibut in egg and lemon sauce. *

Modern
Gefulte fish in savoury tomato sauce ; poached salmon. *

(7) Pickles and Salads

Traditional
Sweet and sour cucumbers ; dill cucumbers ; chrane (horseradish and beetroot relish) ; stuffed Queen and black olives ; radishes ; mixed green salad ; potato salad.

Modern
Coleslaw ; other salads such as corn ; tomato and pepper ; cucumbers in sour cream ; tartare ; * mayonnaise ; * mustard sauces (for fish).

* Denotes recipe in Bride's Cookery Course.

(8) Desserts and Cakes

Traditional

Sweet lokshen kugel* (noodle and raisin pudding) ; fruit pies ;* fresh fruit salad ;* apfel strudel ;* fruited strudel ;* kichlach* (biscuits) ; fruit kuchen ;* streusel kuchen ;* cut-and-come-again cake ;* traditional cheese cake. *

Modern

Pareve chocolate mousse ; liqueur fruit salad ;* flans, such as lemon meringue and raspberry chiffon ; apple crisp ;* trifle ;* wine cake ;* golden button biscuits ;* chocolate cake ;* Jodekager* (Danish biscuits) ; American cheese cake ;* chiffon sponge cake. *

* Denotes recipe in Bride's Cookery Course.

Preparing for Festivals

To prepare the house and table for each successive Yomtov during the year is one of the most important—and pleasurable—responsibilities involved in running a Jewish home.

Although each Festival has its own special religious and historical significance, all of them depend for their proper enjoyment on the very special atmosphere that each individual housewife creates in her own family circle. This atmosphere cannot be easily analysed, for it is an amalgam of so many things—the scent of flowers, the smell of fruit, the glow of a well-polished home, the rich flavour of lovingly cooked food.

Of course, it takes much time and effort to give the house this special shine and to cook food with a flavour unique to each Festival in the calendar. But with the help of modern appliances and convenience foods, it is far easier to do today than in the past, and any extra work—and expense—that may be involved is more than compensated for by the happiness these occasions always bring to one's family and friends.

While the detailed preparations differ for each Festival—depending on the particular customs and traditions associated with it—the general preparations follow a very similar routine, modified, of course, according to the season. Thus, to give the house a special look, one may redecorate it at Passover (which occurs in the spring), and fill it with flowers on the Eve of Rosh Hashanah, which coincides with early autumn. Of course, every family has its own traditions, which you will certainly want to carry on in your own home, but in most households the general preparations before a Festival or Fast are similar to the ones suggested below.

Although the English date on which the different Festivals and Fasts are celebrated changes each year, the sequence is always the same :

PREPARATIONS FOR THE SHABBAT AND FESTIVALS

Purim comes in February/March
Pesach comes in March/April
Shavuot comes in May/June
Rosh Hashanah comes in September/October
Yom Kippur comes in September/October
Succot (including Shemini Atseret and Simchat Torah) comes in September/October
Chanucah comes in December

General Preparations

About two weeks before a Festival (four weeks in the case of Passover), it is time to sit down and decide exactly what needs to be done.

This is a good time to do household renovations and repairs, and to send carpets and soft furnishings to be cleaned. Wardrobes will need to be checked, so that clothes can be got ready for the new season. Nearer the date, silver and linen will need to be inspected to make sure that they are in good order and cleaned, ready for Yomtov entertaining.

Then the main meals for the holiday will have to be planned so that the shopping—and the cooking—can be done in good time. This is especially important if you are at work during the day, for you will have to fit all the extra preparations into a very limited space of time.

To allow time for special Yomtov cooking, make use of as many convenience foods as you can for the basic dishes. Bouillon cubes and packeted soup mixes, frozen pastry and vegetables, savoury sauces and bottled hors-d'œuvres, pre-packed poultry and ready-minced fish should all be given priority on your shopping list.

You can also save cooking time by making full use of the electrical appliances you have in the kitchen. For example, an electric mixer can be used to make pastry as well as cakes, and it can also be used to stir a family-sized quantity of gefulte fish far more quickly than the human hand.

A freezer can be stocked in advance with pies and cakes, and in particular with special delicacies, such as blintzes or holishkes, which you may not find time to make in the last hurried days.

In any case, plan to bake a week beforehand. Rich butter cakes and biscuits will keep for at least a week in airtight tins, while pastry can be made and refrigerated one week, and then rolled and baked the next.

Although one is allowed to cook on most Yomtovs, most women prefer to have all the main dishes cooked or partly prepared in advance, so that they can go to the synagogue with the rest of the family, with a free mind.

Plan to complete all this cooking by lunchtime on the eve of the Festival, so that the afternoon is left free for the final preparations. There will be flowers and fruit to arrange and the table to be laid with special care, the candles set ready in their gleaming candlesticks, the challahs covered with their newly laundered cloth. Then it is time to relax and give oneself a personal Yomtov "shine".

Rosh Hashanah (New Year—1st and 2nd Tishri)

As this is the first Festival in a cycle that lasts for a month, there is much to be done in preparation. As Rosh Hashanah falls in the autumn, this is the time to get the household ready for the winter season. All the winter clothes should be looked over, so that alterations can be made and replacements bought where necessary. It is traditional, in any case, to buy at least one new garment to wear in honour of the occasion.

Carpets and soft furnishings may need to be shampooed after the summer holidays, and small items, such as lampshades and covers, may have to be renewed.

Most people like to send New Year cards to their families and friends, and exchange gifts of fruit and flowers with their immediate family. It is the vases of autumn flowers and the bowls of choice fruit that above all give a home its special New Year "look".

Ever since the return from Babylon, Jewish housewives have made all kinds of sweet foods at this Festival, as a symbol of the sweetness they hope for in the New Year ahead.

You will need to order honey, sugar and syrup to make such traditional delicacies as honey cake (lekach), honey teiglach, and carrot tsimmes.

While all kinds of fruit are served at Rosh Hashanah, the apple is the symbolic fruit of the season, expressing in its shape and sweetness our hopes for a good and sweet New Year. Besides being used in all kinds of pies, cakes and strudels, it is also served in slices spread with honey, after Kiddush has been made on the Eve of the Festival. On the second night, it is usual to serve an additional fruit—such as pineapple—to justify the recitation of the Shehecheyanu blessing. Even the familiar challah takes on a new shape at this season, for it is baked in a round shape instead of a plait, and its dough is enriched with extra eggs and oil. If

101

you have the time, this is the occasion to bake some challahs of your own.

Suggested Menu for Eve of the New Year

Melon *
Gefulte fish * with horseradish sauce
Roast, stuffed chicken ; * roast potatoes ; * peas * and corn
Apple pie ; * fresh fruit salad ; * honey cake *
Coffee

Suggested Menu for Lunch at the New Year

Grapefruit cocktail
Carrot tsimmes *
Braised bola ; * roast potatoes ; * cauliflower *
Apple crisp *
Fresh fruit
Lemon tea

* Denotes recipe in Bride's Cookery Course.

Yom Kippur (The Day of Atonement—10th Tishri)

Although Yom Kippur is a Fast Day, the main preparations from the housewife's point of view are concerned with making two special meals—the one before the Fast and the one eaten twenty-five hours later, when it has ended.

On the Eve of the Fast it is important to serve a meal that is sustaining without provoking thirst. *After* the Fast, the meal should be light and easily digested after a day of abstinence from food.

Before the Fast

Dinner often starts with a meat or chicken soup garnished with kreplach, matzo balls or savoury lokshen kugel. Poultry makes a lighter main course than meat, and the meal may be finished with a fruit sponge pudding or fruit salad, followed by large glasses of lemon tea. The food should be prepared in good time, as the meal must be eaten earlier than usual (between 5 p.m. and 6 p.m. according to the calendar), for the family will need to leave at once for the synagogue and the Kol Nidre service. After the meal, the table is cleared, and then reset with the cloth and candles. A special "yahrzeit" candle is lit if either husband or wife has lost a parent, and then the wife lights the Festival candles, and the Fast has commenced.

After the Fast

Most people prefer to break the fast with a glass of wine followed by tea, a slice of sponge or buttered kuchen.

As the meal has to be prepared the day before, a fish main course is the most convenient to serve. This may be preceded by a tray of mixed hors-d'œuvres, traditionally known as "vorspeise". Although no food has been eaten for more than a day, most people find that, once their thirst has been satisfied by a cup of tea, and their hunger assuaged with a slice of cake, a light, easily digested meal is more welcome than a heavy or rich one.

103

THE JEWISH HOME

Suggested Menu Before the Fast

Melon *
Chicken soup * with meat kreplach, * or savoury lokshen kugel * or knaidlach *
Braised stuffed fowl ; * rice pilaff ; * green vegetables *
Stewed fruit or fruit salad * or apple sponge *
Lemon tea

Suggested Menu for After the Fast

Chiffon sponge, * or marble cake, * with tea
Tray of mixed hors-d'œuvres, including smoked salmon or other smoked fish *
Cream of vegetable soup *
Platter of assorted fried fish ; * gefulte fish ; * assorted salads *
Buttered challah *
Fruit mousse or ice-cream
More tea, or coffee

* Denotes recipe in Bride's Cookery Course.

Succot (15thTishri)

Succot is the autumn harvest Festival which commemorates the years that the Jews had to wander in the Wilderness, living out their days in makeshift huts. It is a happy Festival, however, when families make their own Succah, where they eat their meals, and every house is fragrant with fruit and flowers, while vegetables of every kind appear on the menu.

After the termination of Yom Kippur, it is customary to decorate the Succah of the synagogue. This is a joint occasion for both husbands and wives, for the men hang up the decorations, while their wives string the fruit and vegetables, and make up baskets of fruit for those members who may be ill or housebound. In many congregations, the women also arrange the flowers in the synagogue, and bake cakes and biscuits to serve at Kiddushim in the Succah.

To symbolise the richness of the harvest, all kinds of stuffed foods are prepared as both savouries and sweets.

Cabbages, vine leaves, tomatoes, aubergines and peppers are stuffed with mincemeat and braised in a sweet and sour tomato or meat sauce. Holishkes and gevikelte kraut (the stuffed cabbage, respectively, of the Sephardi and Ashkenazi Jews) are the most popular in the West, but in Israel, stuffed aubergines (chatzilim) and peppers (pilpel mimulad) are in a newer tradition.

For dessert, strudels are stuffed with apples and dried fruit, and melons of all kinds are served in the Succah.

It is well to buy several melons at the beginning of Succot, so that the less ripe can be allowed to mature in the larder, in time for any Simchat Torah entertaining at the conclusion of the Festival.

THE JEWISH HOME
Suggested Menu for Succot

Ogen melon halves * filled with black grapes
Holishkes * or gevikelte kraut *
Roast turkey with cranberry sauce ; corn and peas
Apfel or cherry strudel *
Pomegranates
Black coffee

* Denotes recipe in Bride's Cookery Course.

Chanucah (The Feast of Lights—25th Kislev)

The famous defeat of the Greeks by Judas Maccabaeus and his followers is celebrated during the eight days of Chanucah with parties and presents—particularly for the children. This is the season for potato latkes eaten hot from the pan, and for rich puddings and cakes, such as trifle, fruit cake and pudding with wine sauce.

The pudding and the fruit cake should be made a month beforehand, then left to mature in a cool cupboard. A week beforehand, the Chanucah candles, either coloured or white, should be bought. Coloured candles are prettiest, but plain white Chanucah candles will do just as well. (Left-over candles can be stored in a dry cupboard from one year to the next.) The menorah itself will need to be cleaned if it has been in store since the previous year.

(Silver menorah will not tarnish if they are wrapped in a special tarnish-proof cloth that can be purchased at a silversmith's.)

During the eight days of Chanucah, the menorah is kept on display. In many families, it is the custom to let an additional member of the family light the extra candle each night, before everyone joins in singing the Chanucah song, "Maoz Tsur".

Suggested Menu for a Night during Chanucah

Avocado vinaigrette *
Lentil, pea, barley and bean soup *
Stuffed capon;* saveloys; potato latkes;* carrots and peas *
Chanucah pudding * with wine sauce
Fresh fruit
Black coffee

* Denotes recipe in Bride's Cookery Course.

Purim (The Feast of Lots—14th Adar)

Purim occurs exactly one month before Pesach—on the 14th of Adar (which usually falls in March). As it commemorates the downfall of Haman, the vizier of King Ahasuerus, who tried to exterminate the Jews of Persia, most of the traditional foods have some connection with his name. There are Hamantaschen (Haman's purses) and kreplach, both of which are three cornered like his hat, as well as Haman's Ears (sugared fritters) and "Little Dutch Hamans" —special gingerbread biscuits cut in the shape of a man.

Older members of the family often exchange gifts of cakes and pastries, and both children and adults hold parties, plays and dances to celebrate the occasion.

A few days before Purim, it is wise to order Hamantaschen from the baker. His Hamantaschen are made with yeast, and are difficult for the inexperienced home cook to make. But it is quite easy to make Hamantaschen at home using a kichel or short-pastry dough, stuffed with a poppyseed or fruit filling. Both versions can be made a week or so beforehand, and kept in an air-tight tin.

Suggested Menu for Purim

Jaffa grapefruit half
Barley soup *
Grilled lamb chops;* new potatoes; minted peas; red-currant jelly
Tossed green salad with French dressing *
Wine and walnut Hamantaschen *
Stewed apricots
Black coffee or lemon tea

* Denotes recipe in Bride's Cookery Course.

Preparing for Pesach (Passover—15th of Nissan)

Each spring, during the Passover week which commemorates the liberation of the Jews from slavery in Egypt, more than 3,500 years ago, the Jewish household takes on an appearance quite different from the one it presents during the rest of the year, or indeed, during any other Festival.

In the kitchen, unfamiliar pots and pans stand on the cooker top and counters; in the larder, matzot, matzo meal and other Passover foods are stacked on the newly covered shelves, and there is no trace of either bread or flour; while in the dining room, dishes are served that do not appear on the table at any other season.

To effect this transformation, preparations must be carried out in a particularly thorough and methodical way. To the newly wed couple, these preparations may seem rather complicated, and indeed, many young couples prefer to celebrate the Festival with their parents—at least for the first few years. But even if one does not conduct a Seder service at home until one has children to share in the pleasure of this unique meal, it is not as difficult as it might seem to create a true Passover atmosphere from the very beginning of married life, and the pleasure and satisfaction it brings more than compensate for the effort involved. It is important, however, to start the preparations in good time, and leave only the last minute "changeover" of foods and utensils till the day before the Festival begins. These preparations can be divided into several distinct phases:

    (1) The general cleaning of the whole house
    (2) The planning of the Passover food order
    (3) The special cleaning of the kitchen and larder
    (4) The baking and cooking
    (5) The preparation of the Seder table and its contents.

(1) The General Cleaning of the Home

Immediately after Purim (that is, a month before Passover), it is time to start putting the house in order; to redecorate where necessary, and to spring-clean each room in its turn. Now is the time to do those "twice-a-year" jobs, such as shampooing carpets and upholstery, cleaning or washing curtains and other soft furnishings, and repairing or repolishing furniture and fittings. Mattresses should be vacuumed and, if necessary, the blankets should be sent to the cleaners or laundered at home. Clothes will also need to be looked over after the winter, and cupboards and drawers cleaned and tidied. Any chocolates, sweets or drinks that will need to be used up before Pesach should be stored in one cupboard, which can then be cleaned out at the last minute. The dining room, kitchen and larder can be generally spring-cleaned, but most of the cupboards will have to be left to the last day or so, when the everyday utensils and supplies are locked away, and the shelves made ready for the Passover ones that are put in their place.

(2) Planning the Food Order

Shopping for perishable foods such as fish, meat and greengrocery can be done, as usual, a few days beforehand, but the basic Passover supplies, including matzot, baking ingredients, dry goods and bottled delicatessen, are best ordered about a fortnight in advance, though they should not be delivered until they are needed, usually three or four days beforehand. Most Jewish grocers will give one a printed list as a guide to the foods that are available, though almost any food (other than those containing leaven), can now be bought in a "Kosher le-Pesach" pack. If you are not having a Seder at home, the main additions to your normal shopping list, in addition to "Kosher le-Pesach" packs of standard foods such as tea, coffee, butter, cheese, jams and sugar, will be: Baking supplies (matzo meal, nuts, eggs, chocolates, vanilla sugar, caster and icing sugar) ; bottled delicatessen ; Passover soups, soup cubes and sauces ; canned and dried fruits and fruit juices. You will be able to use the normal pack of frozen vegetables (other than corn, peas, and beans) ; and frozen fruits, provided that they have not been prepared with sugar. Special milk is also available in many towns.

Allow about 2 lb per head of matzot of all kinds (including tea matzot and crackers)—you can always supplement your supplies if necessary during the week, and any leftovers will keep indefinitely if stored in a cool, dry cupboard.

If you are in any doubt about what foods are permitted at Passover, it is wise to consult your local Rabbi. However, I have found that excellent practical advice can be obtained from a Jewish grocer who is under the supervision of the local Beth Din. A word of warning: do not get "carried away" when giving your order, or you may find yourself loaded with supplies that it will take until the following Passover to use up!

(3) Special Cleaning of the Larder and Kitchen

Plan the cleaning of these rooms in such a way that everything has been done two or three days before the Festival, except those cupboards that are to hold the Passover utensils and supplies, the cooker and the refrigerator.

The cupboards. As each cupboard is turned out in succession, it can be loaded with the everyday pots and pans, and only the minimum china, silver and cooking ware left in use until the eve of the Passover. Those cupboards that are to be used during Passover should be thoroughly washed out, and the shelves and drawers relined with plastic or paper. The larder, or larder cupboard, should be cleaned in the same way, and any chametz cans and packeted foods put away out of sight so that the shelves are left clear for the Passover order.

The appliances:
(a) *The refrigerator.* Plan to use up any perishable foods containing chametz in the week before Pesach. The day you expect the Passover order of perishable foods, thoroughly clean the interior and exterior of the refrigerator. A variety of new plastic containers should be bought and these can then be kept for Passover use alone, and stored with the other Passover pots and pans during the rest of the year.

(b) *The cooker.* If you intend to bake for Passover, you will need to clean the oven three or four days before the Festival. The night beforehand, the interior should be painted with a caustic oven cleaner, so that when it is wiped out next morning, every trace of food residue has been removed. The hot plate must be made red-hot to burn out any possible chametz and should also be thoroughly cleaned with boiling water and Passover detergent.

(c) *Washing-up equipment.* You will need duplicate sets of washing-up equipment initially to wash the Passover pots and pans before use, and then for general use during Passover week.

(d) *Preparation counters.* As the ordinary counters and chopping boards cannot be used, it is a good idea to cover several pieces of blockboard with laminated plastic offcuts to use instead.

(e) *Pots and pans.* While it is possible to kasher (ritually clean) certain everyday equipment so that it can be used during Passover, the process is rather complicated, and it is far simpler to keep a separate set of pans, china and cutlery for use during this one week. The exception is table glassware (not cooking ware), for this is simply soaked in cold water for three days, with the water changed every twenty-four hours. (If you do wish to kasher any special utensils, such as the electric mixer, ask for specific instructions from your local Rabbi.)

The nucleus of a stock of Passover pots and pans can be built up from duplicate wedding presents, and added to little by little during the years—often with gifts from other members of the family whose needs are diminishing as yours increase. During the year, these supplies should be locked away in a high cupboard, or wrapped in plastic bags or newspapers and stored in boxes in a corner of the garage or utility room. The night before Pesach, they should be brought down, thoroughly washed in mild detergent, dried with newly laundered tea-towels and put away in the prepared cupboards and drawers. Remember that, in addition to cooking equipment for meat and poultry, a complete set of kashering equipment will be needed for use during Passover week.

(4) Passover Baking

Although excellent confectionery can be bought for Passover, it is worth making at least one or two kinds of cakes and biscuits at home, for home-baked goods are far cheaper and seem to keep longer than many of the commercial varieties. Plan to do the baking three or four days before Pesach, when your oven has been newly cleaned (see above). You will need to get down the Passover baking equipment and wash that in readiness as well. However, as success in Pesach baking depends to a large extent on experience, it is a good idea to "apprentice" oneself to an older member of the family or a friend who has a good reputation for her Pesach cakes. In any case, it is far easier to do the baking in company, so that it can be arranged on a "conveyor belt" system, a method which is far less tiring than when one has to do every part of the preparation oneself.

Several days beforehand, plan exactly what you are going to bake. As some recipes need all whites and others all yolks, select those recipes that will use up an equal quantity of both. If you do have any egg whites left over, put them in a plastic container and refrigerate them for use later in the week. Left-over egg yolks can be used up in mayonnaise, or put in a plastic container, and refrigerated for use within the next twenty-four hours. You will need new cake tins in which to store the Passover cakes when they are cool.

Making jams and preserves. Home-made jams and preserves make excellent gifts for the immediate family, or to take with you when visiting friends. Lemon curd is especially easy to make, and is useful to have in stock to spread on matzo crackers or in sponge cakes. Most families have their own recipes for "eingemacht" (fruit conserves), and again it is better to help an experienced member of the family than to try and make these without supervision from the start.

Cooking before and during the Festival. This follows the pattern of any Yomtov, with these exceptions: flour and cornflour are not allowed, so the thickening of sauces will have to be done with potato starch, using half the usual quantity. Soups made with pulses and cereals (such as peas, beans, lentils and barley) cannot be used, but many others can be served, such as chicken, tomato, borscht, cabbage borscht, and both meat and milk vegetable soups. One can also buy a large variety of packeted soups with a Passover label, which can be used either by themselves or to augment the home-made varieties. Ordinary pastry cannot be used, but an excellent Passover version (made with crushed crumbs instead of flour—see recipe), can be made instead. Meat and fish can be cooked in the normal way, and there is now a huge variety of cooked meats, salamis and sausages produced for Passover use.

As on any other Festival, cooking is permitted on the first two days of Passover, but it is better to get as much done as possible beforehand.

The last meal containing "chametz". On the morning of the eve of Pesach, breakfast should be completed by 9.30 a.m., after which no chametz should be eaten until the end of Pesach. After breakfast, the few remaining everyday pots, pans and crockery should be stored away, and the Passover utensils, which have already been cleaned and stored in their cupboards, can be brought out into use. No matzo should be eaten or wine drunk until the Seder service that night.

(5) The Preparation of the Seder Table and Its Contents

The Seder meal is unlike any other eaten in a Jewish home, for it is directly symbolic, both in the way the table is prepared and in the order of the Haggadah service that precedes it, of the last meal that the Jews ate before they left on their exodus from Egypt.

When the day comes on which you intend to conduct your own Seder service, this is the way to go about it:

Setting the Seder table. Early in the afternoon of the Eve of Passover, the table is laid with a snowy cloth, and the freshly polished candlesticks are put on their tray. As it is traditional to invite guests (especially those who might otherwise be alone on this night), there are usually many chairs to be set at the table. A wine glass is set for each guest. In the centre of the table is set a special large cup for Elijah the Prophet. (As the glasses will be refilled no less than four times during the meal, it is a good idea to set each glass on a small plate to avoid spilling wine on to the tablecloth.) The cutlery for the meal should not be put on the table, but arranged in place settings on a tray at the side, so that the table can be set just before the meal is served. It is traditional for the men to lean back in comfort during the meal, so cushions should be put on the chairs of the men guests. Near the seat of the host, place a small table containing a basin, jug and hand towel. Just before the Seder service starts, the jug can be filled with water for the washing of hands during the service.

The symbolic foods. To the man of the house falls the duty of arranging the symbolic foods on the table, and full details of the correct order are given in the Haggadah.

114

(There should be a Haggadah for each guest round the table.) However, the different dishes will have to be prepared by the housewife beforehand. One can buy dishes specially designed to hold each of the different foods; otherwise each can be put in a separate glass dish arranged on a flat platter. They are:

(1) *A Roasted Shankbone of a Lamb*
This recalls the lamb that the Jews were told to sacrifice on the night before they left Egypt.

> Very often a cooked chicken's neck is substituted. This is "roasted" by holding for one minute in the flames of a gas cooker, or browning under an electric grill.

(2) *A Roasted Egg*
This is symbolic of the festival offering brought into the Temple at this season.

> The egg is hard-boiled, then "roasted" like the shankbone.

(3) *A Root of Horseradish*
This symbolises the bitter life the Jews endured during their slavery.

> Horseradish can be bought from any greengrocer.

(4) *A Dish of Salt Water*
This is thought to recall the tears they shed during captivity.

(5) *A Sprig of Parsley or Watercress*
This is said by some to symbolise the "springtime" of new hope, when they went towards their promised land.

(6) *Charoset*
This recalls the mortar with which the Jews were forced to make bricks when they built the cities of Pithom and Ramses for their Egyptian taskmasters.

> Charoset is a mixture of minced apples, walnuts, cinnamon and wine, mixed to a paste-like consistency (see recipe). Enough should be made to last for both Sedarim.

In addition, the husband arranges on the table three matzot, covered with a special cloth or "matza decke" which has a separate pocket for each matza, and is embroidered like the "challah decke" used on Friday night. The three matzot are frequently referred to as the

Cohen, Levi and Yisrael. The middle matzo will be broken during the service, and part of it will become the Afikomen which is hidden by the head of the house, and searched for by the children after the meal.

All the crockery and silverware should be ready on a side-table or trolley, together with prepared food and condiments. Below I give two suggested menus for the Seder meal—one meat and the other milk. Some communities traditionally start with a dish of eggs in salt water. How these are prepared depends on family custom, some people slicing the eggs into the salt water and other families serving them whole. In general, however, for each guest allow one hard-boiled egg, $\frac{1}{4}$-pint water and $\frac{1}{2}$ a level teaspoonful of salt.

If there are more than six guests, it is advisable to have one bottle of wine at each end of the table, so that the glasses can be swiftly refilled during the Seder service.

All these preparations should be completed before the candles are lit at the commencement of the Festival.

On the final day of Passover, as soon as the Festival has ended, the Passover pots can be put away, and "chametz" brought out once more. The house then slips into its normal routine for another year.

Passover Foods

Matzo (together with matzo meal of varying textures that is made from it) is the main ingredient of Passover cookery. The first matzo, or unleavened bread, was baked by the Jews on the night they left Egypt. In Egypt, they had learned to bake a bread leavened with yeast—a discovery that originated in the Nile Delta. On this occasion, however, they rolled out their unrisen dough, and baked it on "gridirons" laid over the heated coals of a fire.

The "kremslach" or matzo pancakes, which vary from simple "hot cakes" of meal, egg and water to sweetened fritters stuffed with fruit, recall the meal cakes that were offered as sacrifices in Bible times. The custom of making "eingemacht"—rich preserves of dried fruits or beetroot—is of more recent origin, and symbolises the sweetness of the land to which the Jews turned their eyes when they left Egyptian slavery.

Preserves to Make

Lemon curd ; * eingemacht (fruit conserves) ; beetroot ; * apricot and almond ; lemon and walnut ; stuffed prune and almond ; pineapple and orange marmalade.

Confectionery to Bake

Coconut kisses ; * cinnamon balls ; * coconut pyramids ; * date and walnut kisses ; * Passover ring sponge. *

Seder Menu (milk meal)

Wine ; matzot ; charoset ; eggs in salt water
Halibut in egg and lemon sauce ; * Salmon and salads ; * new potatoes
Brandy and apple flan *
Coffee

Seder Menu (meat meal)

Wine ; matzot ; charoset ; eggs in salt water
Gefulte fish ; * horseradish sauce
Chicken casserole ; * roast potatoes ; * baby carrots and cauliflower
Fresh pineapple slice, topped with orange ; Passover liqueur
Chiffon sponge *
Coffee

* Denotes recipe in Bride's Cookery Course.

Shavuot (Feast of Weeks or Pentecost—6th Sivan)

In earlier days, Shavuot was celebrated as a great agricultural festival, when the start of the wheat harvest was marked by offerings of newly baked bread. Every man brought the first fruits of his crops to the Temple in Jerusalem, while his wife ground flour from the new season's wheat, and baked special cakes and bread in honour of the occasion. Today we commemorate those early days by decorating the house with seasonal flowers and plants, and by taking them as gifts to our friends.

Milk, cheese and honey are the symbolic foods of this Festival, and they are made into some of the most delicious dishes of the Jewish cuisine. From milk (sweet as the fragrance of the harvested fields) is made cream cheese. From cream cheese are made the cheese cakes, the blintzes, the kreplach and the noodle casseroles that so enrich the table on this occasion.

In Bible times, to symbolise the richness of the Torah for both body and soul, honey and milk were used in the same dish—especially in cheese cakes, which were further enriched with Jordan almonds. Today we sweeten our cheese with sugar and flavour it with vanilla and lemon, but we still put honey into our Shavuot cakes and spread it on our bread.

Although most of the traditional dairy dishes have a long culinary history, there are other recipes of more modern origin, which are equally suitable for serving at Shavuot. These include cream-cheese dips, salads, uncooked cheese cakes and sauces made with soured cream. While cooked dairy dishes, such as blintzes and cheese cakes, can be frozen very satisfactorily, uncooked cream cheese should not be frozen, but bought as late as possible before the Festival. The rich double-cream cheeses are excellent to serve on bread, but for cooking purposes, cooking "kaes" and cottage cheese are better, because they are drier and lighter in baked and fried dishes.

*Suggested Dairy Meal for
Shavuot*

Chilled borscht *
Cheese blintzes *
Fresh salmon ; * mayonnaise sauce ; * new potatoes ;
garden peas
Liqueur fruit salad * and cream
Coffee

Suggested Baking for Shavuot

American or traditional cheese cake ; * Jodekager *
(Danish butter biscuits) ; Yomtov chocolate cake with
peppermint icing ; * quick kichlach ; * wine and spice
cake. *

* Denotes recipe in Bride's Cookery Course.

6

BRIDE'S COOKERY COURSE

BRIDE'S COOKERY COURSE

The recipes and cooking instructions that follow are not intended to form a comprehensive book of Jewish cookery.

I have simply set out to devise a cookery course for the new Jewish housewife, which will enable her to meet with confidence all the cookery situations with which she is likely to be faced during the first year or two of her marriage. I have also included all the traditional recipes mentioned in the sections dealing with the preparations for Festivals and Shabbat.

I have written the recipes with the really inexperienced cook in mind. So, in addition to giving exact weights, measures, quantities and oven temperatures, as well as extremely detailed descriptions of the different processes in cookery, I have tried to paint a picture in words of how different mixtures should look, smell, feel and taste at different stages in their preparation.

To become a good cook one must have patience, love for both family and food and, above all, reliable recipes.

The recipes that follow I have developed and perfected during the past twenty years. They can be said to be "family tested" in every sense. The course itself represents the culinary knowledge and experience of myself, my relatives and friends, and the innumerable good cooks whom I have had the good fortune to meet in many parts of the world.

The patience—and the love—I leave to you!

Rules for Success

To cook any dish with certain success, it is well to train yourself from the start to follow these rules :

(1) The day before, read the recipe carefully, so that you can be sure to have the right ingredients and equipment ready, and can estimate how long the dish will take to make.

(2) Before you start, read the recipe again from beginning to end, and go over each process in turn in your mind.

(3) Get out all the ingredients and utensils mentioned in the recipe. Put the ingredients on one small tray and the utensils on another. This will help you to keep your working space in order.

(4) Set the oven (if used).

(5) Weigh or measure each ingredient with care. To do this with the necessary accuracy you will need :

(a) Reliable scales. I prefer balance scales with weights from ½ oz. to 2 lb., to spring scales with an indicator dial.

(b) Measuring spoons. These must bear the stamp of approval of the B.S.I. (British Standards Institution).
All spoon measures in the recipes are level unless otherwise indicated.

(c) A pint glass liquid measure. This is marked in levels at intervals of one or two fluid ounces. This measure should be used to measure fluid (fl.) ounces in the recipes.

(6) Fill a jug and a washing-up bowl with hot water and detergent. (As you finish with utensils, put them to soak in this solution—tools in the jug and larger equipment in the basin. Those that you will need later in the recipe can be rinsed and left to drain.)

(7) Proceed with the cooking, doing each part in the order in which it is given in the recipe. Work at a steady pace but never rush, or your efforts are likely to end in failure, particularly when you are inexperienced.

(8) If there is time before the meal is served, wash all the cooking utensils and leave them to drain after a final rinse in very hot water—they will then dry and be ready for putting away before the main washing-up is started after the meal. If there is no time, leave the utensils soaking in detergent and hot water, and they will then be very easy to clean after the meal. Before it is finally put away, metal equipment should be left to dry completely in the warming drawer of the oven, or in the cooling oven itself after the heat has been turned off.

Note: 2 teaspoonfuls equal 1 dessertspoonful
4 teaspoonfuls equal 1 tablespoonful
2 dessertspoonfuls equal 1 tablespoonful
1 fl. oz. equals 2 tablespoonfuls
20 fl. oz. equal 1 pint, which equals 40 tablespoonfuls

Level spoonfuls are measured by filling the spoon above its rim, and then levelling it by drawing the straight side of a knife across the bowl.

Quantities For Two

No precise figure can be given for the amount of food of different kinds to buy for two people. Certain foods shrink a great deal during cooking, so that only half the weight purchased appears on the table. Other foods (which keep well) are more economical when bought in amounts that will do for two people on two separate occasions. Then, people's appetites for different foods vary a great deal. In some cases, one could well eat far more of a luxury food—such as smoked salmon—than it would be an economic proposition to buy!

For these reasons, the amounts suggested below are only guides to the *average* amount of a particular food that two people might expect to eat at any one meal. The foods are all *raw,* except when otherwise indicated.

	Food	*Quantity*
Fish	Cutlets or steaks, e.g. salmon, halibut hake, plaice	¾–1 lb.
	Fillets	½–¾ lb.
	Smoked salmon (served alone)	3 oz.
	(as part of mixed hors-d'œuvre)	2 oz.
	Pickled or schmalz herring	1–2 fillets
	Trout (1 fish each)	1–1½ lb.
Meat	Lamb chops (shoulder)	2
	Lamb cutlets (first cut)	4
	Liver (for grilling)	8–12 oz.
	(for chopping—prepare minimum ½ lb.)	4 oz.
	Mincemeat (prepare 1 lb.)	½ lb.
	Sausages or saveloys	½ lb.
	Pickled brisket and other cooked meats	4–6 oz.
	Salami (to serve raw)	4 oz.
	Vorsht for frying	½ lb.
	Steak for grilling or frying	¾–1 lb.

Food	Quantity
Boneless beef or veal for braising or stewing	½ lb.
Breast of veal or lamb (including bone)	¾–1 lb.
Wing rib (not recommended unless hung)	1 rib

Note: Do not try to roast or boil a joint weighing less than 2½ lb., as there is too much shrinkage during the cooking to make it an economical meal. Do not braise a *piece* of meat smaller than 1½ lb., though *slices* of steak at least ¾ inch thick will braise to perfection.

Fruit

Apples, pears and bananas (2 average)	½ lb.
Plums, apricots, rhubarb, etc. for stewing (do not cook less than 1 lb. at a time)	½ lb.
Raspberries, strawberries and other dessert fruit to be served uncooked	½ lb.

Vegetables

Artichokes (globe)	2
Asparagus (as an accompaniment)	6 stalks
(as a course by itself)	12 stalks
(quantity may be as low as 6 if stalks are fat and price is high)	
Aubergine (for stuffing, sautéeing) 1 oval	8–10 oz.
Avocado (on the half shell)	1
Broad beans (in their shells)	1–1½ lb.
French or runner beans	½–¾ lb.
Butter or haricot beans (dried)	2 oz.
Beets	1 lb.
Brussel sprouts, cabbage	½ lb.
Spring cabbage (which has a lot of waste)	1 lb.
Cauliflower	1 small head
Carrots	½ lb.
Corn on the cob	2 ears
Celery (heart for salad, outside for soup)	1 medium head
Courgettes	½–¾ lb.
Leeks (as vegetable)	¾–1 lb.
Lettuce	1 medium
Mushrooms (served by themselves)	4–8 oz.
Garden peas (in shell)	1–1½ lb.

Food	Quantity
Potatoes (for boiling or mashing)	1 lb.
(for chipping)	¾ lb.
Spinach	1 lb.
Tomatoes	6 oz.
Watercress	1 bunch

(Frozen vegetables indicate number of servings on packet)

How to Adapt Recipes for the Jewish Kitchen

Many recipes published in general cookery books must be adapted in some way before they can be used in a Jewish kitchen.

This may be for any of the following reasons: They contain non-kosher ingredients; they combine meat and dairy products in the same dish; or they include a dairy ingredient in a recipe one wishes to use in a meat meal.

To make such recipes acceptable, substitute ingredients must be used which, while they satisfy the requirements of the dietary laws, do not radically alter the flavour and texture of the original dish.

Here are some of the more common "forbidden" ingredients and the most satisfactory substitutes.

Butter

To Fry Meat or Poultry
Substitute for each 1 oz. of butter: 1 tablespoonful of rendered chicken fat and 1 dessertspoonful of oil; or 2 tablespoonfuls of oil; or a pre-packed pareve chicken fat substitute.

To Sauté Vegetables for a Meat Casserole or Soup
Substitute an equal amount of margarine.

To Fry or Roast Potatoes
Substitute an equal amount of oil, plus a nut of margarine to give flavour.

In a Pudding After a Meat Meal
Substitute an equal amount of margarine and use water instead of milk to mix.

In Pastry After a Meat Meal
Substitute 4 oz. margarine and 1 oz. white fat for each 5 oz. of butter.

With Vegetables in a Meat Meal
Substitute an equal amount of margarine, and flavour with a squeeze of lemon juice before serving.

129

In a Chicken Soup or Sauce
Substitute an equal quantity of chicken fat (preferably) or margarine.

To Fry Pancakes After a Meat Meal
Substitute white cooking fat.

Milk

In a Batter (*For Pancakes or Yorkshire Pudding*)
Substitute an equal quantity of water, plus 1 tablespoonful of oil for each ¼ lb. of flour. Use two eggs instead of one. Yorkshire pudding made with water is crisper and has less "body" than when made with milk. Pancakes are thinner and lighter, with a less "cakey" texture.

Cream

To Thicken a Chicken Sauce or Soup
Substitute ¼ pt. chicken stock, 1 egg yolk and 1 teaspoonful cornflour for each ¼ pint of double cream. Slake the cornflour with the stock and stir in the yolk. Pour on the hot mixture slowly, stirring well. Return to the pan and reheat until steaming. (If mixture is still too thin, beat into it another egg yolk.)

Note: There is no satisfactory domestic pareve substitute for the cream used in a cold mousse or soufflé.

Chicken Stock

In a Milk Soup or Sauce
Substitute an equal quantity of water flavoured either with a bottled vegetable extract or with a monosodium glutamate product, such as "Accent". Add an extra nut of butter or tablespoonful of cream to enrich the soup before it is served.

Shellfish

In a Fish Cocktail
Substitute an equal weight of a firm white fish (such as halibut or sole) poached and cut into bite-sized pieces.

In a Creamed Dish or Filling For Vol au Vent Cases
Substitute an equal quantity of flaked cooked salmon, halibut or haddock.

In a Batter-Coated Dish
Substitute an equal weight of raw sole, cut into bit-sized strips. Coat with batter and fry as directed in deep fat.

Smoked Meat (Bacon or Ham)

In a Savoury Flan such as Quiche Lorraine
As the meat is used mainly for flavour, use a savoury substitute, such as black olives, sautéed onions, finely diced anchovies or sautéed mushrooms.

In Mixed Grills
Substitute kosher smoked sliced veal or beef.

In a Meat or Chicken Casserole
The flavour of smoked meat in a casserole is strange to the Jewish palate, and it is best not to use a substitute, but to omit it altogether. (For example in "Boeuf Bourgvignonne".)

How to Substitute Meat Cuts

The following kosher cuts from the forequarters of the animal can be satisfactorily substituted for hindquarter cuts mentioned in specific recipes.

Substitute

First cut shoulder steak or *sliced bola* for any braising or stewing cut such as *round steak*

Corner of bola (for braising) for topside or silverside of beef

Pickled brisket for pickled silverside (it is nicer as well)

Boned and rolled wing rib for sirloin

Boned eye of wing rib (sometimes known as "fairy steak") for rump, sirloin or point steak. (The rib steak is in fact "entrecôte")

Shoulder of lamb for leg of lamb

Boned shoulder of lamb for lamb fillet

Boned out shoulder or breast of lamb for boned leg (for kebabs)

Boned and sliced veal and shoulder for escalopes

Boned and cubed shoulder or breast of veal for leg of veal (in casseroles such as sauté de veau Marengo)

Double lamb shoulder chops for chump or loin chops or lamb steaks

Minced bola for minced beefsteak (in grilled hamburgers)

Note: All meat which is to be grilled, spit-roasted or baked in an uncovered dish (using dry rather than moist heat) should be koshered, then hung in the butcher's cold room, or kept in a commercial or domestic freezer for ten days before use. This helps to tenderise it.

7

RECIPES

Passover Cookery

The recipes below in no way constitute a comprehensive list of all the dishes that reflect the spirit of Passover. However, they do comprise a basic repertoire which will suffice for the early years. I have included some specialities of the Seder table, which it is pleasant to make and take as a contribution to the Seder table of parents and friends.

Lemon Curd

3 large lemons
3 eggs, or 4 egg yolks, or 1 whole egg plus 3 yolks (whichever is most convenient)
½ lb. sugar
4 oz. unsalted butter

Lemon curd keeps for six weeks in the refrigerator. It is often made with the egg yolks left over from baking biscuits, such as cinnamon balls and macaroons. Empty ½-lb. honey or preserve jars (which have been made kosher for Passover) are useful for storing lemon curd.

Grate the rind off two lemons and squeeze the juice of all three. Allow to infuse, all morning if possible. Put the sugar in a bowl in a warm oven to heat through, while you melt the butter in a basin standing in a pan of boiling water. Add the sugar and the strained juice. When the sugar mixture is smooth, pour a little over the beaten eggs, then return to the pan and stir with a wooden spoon until the mixture just coats the back of the spoon (it thickens as it cools). Pour into hot, dry jars (most easily warmed by standing in a warm oven—Gas No. ½, 250° F—for ten minutes). Cover with wax discs. Leave till cold, then cover with tinfoil and refrigerate. Makes 1½ lb.

Beetroot Eingemacht

2 lb. cooked beets (or 2½ lb. raw beets cooked in boiling water for half an hour and then skinned when cool)
2 lb. granulated sugar
3 unpeeled lemons
½ oz. ginger
4 fl. oz. water
¼ lb. blanched split almonds

This traditional beetroot conserve must be cooked until it goes brown—a sign that the sugar in the beets has caramelised, giving the jam its inimitable flavour.

Cut the cooked beets into slivers each ¼ inch wide and 1–2 inches long. Put into a heavy pan with the sugar and the water. Stir until the sugar dissolves, then simmer uncovered for one hour. Meanwhile, wash the lemons well, slice and cut into pith-free segments. Add to the beets and cook for a further hour. At this stage the beets will look slightly brown and transparent. Finally, add the nuts and the ginger and cook for a further half hour. (At all times the contents of the pan must be barely bubbling.) The preserve thickens as it cools. Ladle the hot jam into warm jam jars which have been heating for ten minutes in a low oven (Gas. No. ½, 250° F). Cover with greaseproof discs. When quite cold, cover with Cellophane or foil covers and tie down with rubber bands. Makes nearly 4 lb. of jam.

Choconut Kisses

2 egg whites
4 oz. sifted icing sugar
2 oz. desiccated coconut
4 oz. kosher Passover plain chocolate

Beat the whites with a rotary egg whisk until they hold stiff peaks that do not topple sideways when the beaters are withdrawn. Add the icing sugar a tablespoonful at a time, beating until stiff again after each addition. Fold in the coconut and the chocolate chopped into ¼-inch rough cubes.

Put in little heaps on an oiled baking sheet, allowing 2 inches between each kiss. Bake in a slow, moderate oven (Gas No. 3, 325° F) for twenty minutes, or until the kisses feel crisp to the touch and lift off easily from the tray. Store in an airtight tin when cold. Makes about twenty kisses.

Cinnamon Balls

2 egg whites
4 oz. caster sugar
½ lb. ground almonds
1 level tablespoonful cinnamon

Do not bake these biscuits for longer than specified, or they become more like cannon balls than cinnamon balls. Beat the whites till they hold stiff peaks. Fold in all the remaining ingredients. Form into balls with wetted hands. Bake on a greased tray at Gas No. 3 (325° F) for twenty-five minutes, till just firm to the touch. Roll in icing sugar while warm, and again when cold.

Coconut Pyramids

4 egg yolks or 2 whole eggs
½ lb. desiccated coconut
4 oz. caster sugar
Juice and rind of half a lemon

This is a useful recipe to utilise egg yolks left over from a batch of "kisses". However, two whole eggs can be used if it is more convenient.

Set the oven at Gas. No. 5, 375° F. Beat the yolks and the sugar with an egg whisk until they are thick and creamy, then beat in the lemon juice and rind and stir in the coconut.

Have ready a small basin full of cold water and an egg cup. Dip the egg cup into the water, then fill with some of the mixture. Turn the pyramid out onto a greased tray. Repeat the process, rinsing the egg cup in the cold water when necessary, to prevent sticking. Bake the pyramids for eighteen to twenty minutes or until a golden brown. Makes about twenty-four pyramids.

Date and Walnut Kisses

These little biscuits are crisp outside, and soft and fruity within.

2 egg whites
4 oz. sifted icing sugar
¼ lb. shelled walnuts
¼ lb. blanched almonds
¼ lb. dates

Set the oven at Gas No. 3 (325° F). Scissor the dates into small pieces, and roughly chop the walnuts and almonds. Put the whites into a large bowl, add a pinch of salt, then beat with a rotary egg whisk until they hold stiff glossy peaks that do not topple sideways when the beater is withdrawn. Beat in the icing sugar a tablespoonful at a time, beating until stiff after each addition. Finally, fold in the nuts and dates.

Drop from a dessertspoon in little heaps spaced out on a greased baking sheet. Bake for twenty minutes until the kisses feel crisp to the touch and are a pale golden colour. When quite cold, store in an airtight tin. Makes about twenty-four.

Lemon Mousse

This is a refreshing sweet which can be adapted for both meat and milk meals. The secret of success is to make sure that the jelly mixture and the meringue are of a similar stiffness when they are blended together, otherwise the thinner mixture may sink to the bottom of the mousse.

3 oz. lemon juice (approximately two large lemons)
The grated rind of 2 lemons
3 large eggs
1 Passover orange or lemon jelly
3 oz. caster sugar
6 tablespoonfuls orange juice

Put the jelly and orange juice into a pan and stir over a gentle heat until the jelly liquefies (do not let the liquid boil). Put the yolks into a basin and beat until frothy with a rotary whisk. Add the sugar gradually, beating continually, until the mixture is thick and mousselike and the mixture falls in a steady "ribbon" when the beaters are lifted out of the bowl. Add the lemon juice and continue to beat for a further few minutes. Stir in the lemon rind and then the dissolved jelly. Put in a shallow casserole and leave in the refrigerator until the mixture becomes thick and syrupy but has not set. If it has not thickened evenly, whisk it for two minutes until it is of an even consistency.

Put the whites into a bowl with a pinch of salt and whisk until they hold firm but glossy peaks, then beat in two level teaspoonfuls of caster sugar. Take the jelly out of the refrigerator and fold into the meringue. Spoon into a deep glass dish and leave to chill.

For a milk meal, whip ¼ pint of double cream with the tops of two bottles of milk until it has thickened to a meringue consistency. Fold the cream into the thickened jelly and then fold this mixture into the meringue.

This makes a sweet for six to eight people.

Passover Ring Sponge

4 oz. sifted cake meal (or fine matzo meal if not available)
1½ oz. potato flour
Pinch of salt
7 oz. caster sugar
5 eggs
2 fl. oz. oil (4 tablespoons)
1 teaspoonful lemon juice
2 fl. oz. orange juice (4 tablespoons)
1 teaspoonful orange rind

This is an excellent sponge cake to make for your first Passover as a housewife, as it is certain to rise, even if you have never made a Passover sponge before. It can be served plain, or split and filled with canned fruit and cream or with lemon curd blended with twice its volume of whipped cream.

Oil a 9-inch tube or ring tin. Sieve the cake meal, the potato flour, the salt and 5 oz. of the sugar into a mixing bowl. Blend the egg yolks, the oil, the lemon juice and the orange juice. Add the rind, and then stir this mixture into the dry ingredients. Beat well with a wooden spoon to form a smooth, slack batter. Whisk the egg whites until they hold stiff peaks, then whisk in the remaining 2 oz. of sugar a level tablespoonful at a time, beating after each addition until the mixture holds stiff peaks.

Use a metal spoon to fold the meringue mixture into the batter until well blended. Turn the mixture into the tin and bake in a fairly slow oven Gas No. 3 (325° F) for one and a quarter hours.

Turn the cooked cake upside down on a wire rack and leave until it is quite cold. Loosen the edges lightly with the tip of a knife and slide the cake out of the tin. Store in an airtight tin.

This cake will keep fresh for the whole Passover week—if it lives that long !

Brandy and Apple Flan

The Crust
½ **pint sponge cake or prelato crumbs (measure in glass measure, or use 1 large tumblerful)**
2 oz. butter
2 oz. caster sugar
½ **teaspoonful cinnamon**

The Filling
1½ lb. cooking apples, peeled, cored and sliced
2 tablespoonfuls apricot jam
1 oz. butter
4 oz. sugar
Grated rind and juice of half a lemon
1–2 tablespoonfuls brandy or rum (optional)

This is a delicious sweet to make for the family Seder. The sponge flan case can be used in many ways ; filled with a fruited jelly, or with canned fruit alone, or with fresh pineapple blended into sweetened whipped cream.

Cream butter, sugar and cinnamon, then work in the crumbs. Spread over the bottom and sides of a shallow 8-inch glass pie dish. Put in a quick moderate oven (Gas No. 5, 375° F) for ten minutes or until golden brown. Leave to cool.

Melt butter in pan, then add apples in layers, alternately with the sugar, lemon rind and juice, and apricot jam. Put on the lid and cook gently until the apples are tender. Cool, then stir in spirit. Spoon into baked crust and top with unsweetened whipped cream, spiked with toasted almonds.

Serves six.

Further recipes suitable for Passover appear in other sections.

Hors-d'œuvres

**4 hard-boiled eggs (simmered for twelve
minutes, then covered with cold water until
needed)**
½ medium onion
¼ level teaspoonful salt; pinch white pepper
**1 rounded tablespoonful chicken fat
(approximately) to bind**

Chopped Egg and Onion

This is a delicious hors-d'œuvre served on a plate like chopped liver or spread on thick fingers of challah. It should be made the same day it is to be eaten. Some people like to make it with spring onions, but you do need to know your eating companions!

Using a "hackmesser" (straight chopper) or two-handled chopper that fits into a special bowl, coarsely chop the egg and onion in separate piles. Mix them together on the chopping board and continue to chop until the mixture is extremely fine and there is only a suspicion of oniony texture when a little of the mixture is tasted. (Do not be tempted to use the mincer, as this squashes the onion and makes it watery.)

Turn the mixture into a bowl and use the rendered chicken fat to bind it into a pasty mixture that just holds together. Stir in the salt and pepper, and mix well again. Spoon into a shallow platter and flatten the surface with a knife, then mark it into a geometrical design. Cover with foil and chill for an hour before serving.

Serves two to three as an appetiser, but will serve six, spread on biscuits.

2 salt herrings
**1 hard-boiled egg (simmered for twelve
minutes in water to cover)**
Half a small, tart dessert apple
Half a medium onion (finely grated)
2 level teaspoonfuls sugar
1 level tablespoonful fine meal
2 tablespoonfuls vinegar and speck of pepper

Chopped Herrings

The seasoning of chopped herring is very much a matter of taste. You may, for instance, use fresh lemon juice instead of vinegar, and crumbled sweet biscuits in place of fine meal. If you start with the balance of flavours I suggest below you can then adjust it as you wish.

The day before, cut the heads off the herrings, slit the belly and remove the entrails. Place in a glass casserole and put under the cold water tap, with the water running in a gentle trickle. After an hour, turn off the tap and leave the herrings covered in cold water overnight. Next day, lift them out of the water and drain well. Put on a board and slit the skin down the centre back, when it can be peeled off easily from both sides. Flatten the back of each herring with the palm of the hand, turn it over and lift out the centre bone. Remove any other bones which may be sticking out.

Cut the fish up roughly, and put on a chopping board kept specially for the purpose. Add the egg, the apple and the grated onion, and chop until all the ingredients are very fine. Now sprinkle on the meal, the vinegar and the sugar, mixing well. The meal should be sufficient to soak up excess juice. If not, add a little more. Taste, and add a little more vinegar or sugar if necessary. Spoon the herring into a shallow dish, smooth level, cover with foil and chill. Just before serving, the herring can be garnished with the sieved hard-boiled yolk of another egg.

Chopped herring can be served on a plate, garnished with a lettuce leaf and a slice of tomato and gherkin, or on crisp biscuits, but in this case, do not spread it until ten minutes beforehand, or the biscuits will go soggy.

Serves four people as an appetiser, but will make enough, spread on biscuits, for eight.

Liptauer Cheese

4 oz. cream cheese
1 oz. butter
1 inch anchovy paste from a tube or
  1 teaspoonful from a jar
1 level dessertspoonful chopped capers
1 teaspoonful made mustard
1 level dessertspoonful paprika pepper
Pinch each of pepper and celery salt
1 level dessertspoonful chopped chives

This is a delicious cheese spread or dip, which it is most appropriate to serve to visitors at Shavuot. It will keep for a week under refrigeration.

Have the butter at room temperature for an hour beforehand. Cream with a wooden spoon until soft, then beat in the cheese and all the remaining ingredients. Leave for several hours in a covered dish for the flavours to develop.

Spread on savoury biscuits, or use as a filling for 1-inch lengths of celery, or let down to a creamy consistency with soured cream and use as a dip, using crisps or savoury biscuits as scoops.

Melon Hors-d'œuvre

A really choice, ripe melon needs little embellishment. Whatever the variety it should be chilled for half an hour

after it has been prepared. Small canteloupe-type melons like the Israeli Ogen and the French Charentais (which are both in season for Rosh Hashanah) should be cut in halves or thirds according to their size, and the pips removed. Caster sugar can be passed at the table but this should not be necessary if the fruit is choice. *Honeydew melons* are prepared as follows:

Cut the melon in half, and scoop out the seeds. Cut each half into two, three or four slices according to the size. Take each slice in turn, and with a sharp knife cut between the flesh and the skin. Leave the flesh on the skin, but cut it into 1-inch slices, each large enough for a mouthful. The slices can then be pushed to alternate sides to make the melon look more attractive. Arrange them on a serving plate, sprinkle lightly with caster sugar and then generously with lemon juice. Put uncovered in the refrigerator for half to one hour, by which time they will be covered in a delicious lemon syrup.

For a Yomtov meal, thread alternate slices of pineapple, grape and glace cherry onto a cocktail stick and spear in the centre of the melon slice. If only half the melon is sliced, cover the remainder with foil and leave at the bottom of the refrigerator. Use within twenty-four hours.

Pickled Herrings

3 salt herrings
½ pint mild white vinegar or 1 part of (20%) acetic acid diluted with 2 parts of cold water to make ½ pint liquid
1 large onion, sliced thinly
Half a large, unpeeled lemon, sliced
2 level teaspoonfuls pickling spice
10 peppercorns
2 bayleaves
1 level tablespoonful brown sugar

Behead the herrings, slit the belly and remove the entrails. Put the fish in a glass casserole (so that the smell will not linger) and put under the cold water tap. Leave the water running in a gentle trickle. After an hour, turn off the tap, and leave the herrings overnight, covered in cold water. Next day, lift them out of the water and drain well. Put on a piece of paper; scrape with a blunt knife to remove loose scales. Wash again under the cold water tap and put on a board. Open the front, then turn over and press the back with the flat of the hand. Turn over again and you will find that the backbone can be lifted out easily. Remove any other loose bones. Sprinkle each herring very lightly with white pepper, add two or three thin rings of onion, then roll up from the tail to the head. If the herrings are very large, you may find it easier to split them lengthwise before rolling.

Skewer each herring closed with a wooden cocktail stick. Put in a glass jar in alternate layers with the sliced lemon, the onion and the spices. Put the water, vinegar and the sugar into a pan and bring to the boil. Immediately the liquid bubbles, turn off the light and leave until it is luke-warm. Pour over the herrings. Cover and refrigerate for two days before using. The herrings will keep under refrigeration for several weeks, but they do tend to become more acid as the weeks go by.

Enough for two people on three different occasions.

Serve in ½-inch slices, either speared on a cocktail stick with a drink, or as an hors-d'œuvre garnished with the pickled onion slices, tomato and cucumber.

Chopped Liver

½ lb. liver
2 hard-boiled eggs (simmered for twelve minutes, then plunged in cold water till required)
1 medium onion
½ level teaspoonful salt
10 grinds black pepper
Rendered chicken fat to bind (about 1 rounded tablespoonful)

Calf and ox liver may both be used to make chopped liver, but the flavour is sweeter and the texture softer when calf liver is used. This, however, is only available occasionally. It is also much more expensive than ox liver.

In either case the liver must be koshered beforehand (see "How to Kosher Meat and Poultry", p. 149).

Put the koshered liver into a saucepan with half the onion. Cover with cold water. Bring slowly to the boil, cover and simmer for ten minutes over very gentle heat. Drain the liver thoroughly and discard the half onion. Remove the outer skin. Put through the medium blade of the mincer the cooked liver, the half raw onion and the whole of one egg and the white of the other. Put in a basin with the salt and pepper and add the chicken fat to bind it together. If the mixture looks crumbly, add a little more soft fat. Turn into a shallow dish and smooth the surface flat. Refrigerate covered with foil (chopped liver will keep in the coldest part of the refrigerator for two days). Just before serving, push the remaining hard-boiled egg yolk through a metal sieve onto the surface of the liver. Serve with sliced challah or matzo crackers.

This makes enough for three generous portions as an appetiser, or will serve six when spread on biscuits.

1 whole schmalz herring or two fillets
Spring onions or Spanish onions
Tomatoes, and fresh cucumber
Lemon juice or vinegar
Black pepper

Schmaltz Herring Hors-d'œuvre

Schmaltz or matjes herrings can now be bought ready-filleted from many delicatessen shops. Otherwise, the whole fish have to be skinned and filleted at home. In either case the fish will only need to be soaked for an hour or two, as they are smoked rather than salted during the curing process.

Soak the fillets for one hour. Whole fish should be beheaded and slit down the belly and the entrails removed, then covered in cold water and soaked for two hours. Drain thoroughly, press down on the back to flatten, then remove the centre bone. To skin, slit the skin down the centre back, and then peel it off on either side.

To Serve

Half an hour before dinner, cut the fillets of fish into 1-inch slices and arrange in a narrow shallow dish, surrounded by alternate slices of tomato and fresh cucumber. Over the fish squeeze just enough lemon juice or vinegar to moisten it and point up the flavour. Sprinkle with several grinds of black pepper, and then some finely sliced spring onion or raw Spanish onion. Serve with black bread or challah. Enough for two.

A Guide To Kosher Meat Cuts And How To Cook Them

The best kosher butchers now cut and prepare their meat to suit all modern methods of cooking. They kosher and freeze steaks for grilling and frying; they kosher and hang joints for spit roasting or oven roasting; they use electric saws to slice meat neatly for braises and casseroles. Of course, the number of different cuts available in a kosher butcher shop is limited because they do not include any meat from the hindquarters of the beast. However, a huge variety of dishes can be made with the parts that are permitted, provided each part is used in the most suitable way.

Note: Freezing meat helps to tenderise it, thus making it suitable to fry or grill. To conform to the laws of kashrut, it must first be koshered, and it can then be stored in the freezer for any length of time.

Hanging meat helps to tenderise joints used for roasting, such as rib or bola (see note below on roasting bola). The meat must first be koshered and then loosely wrapped (to prevent drying), before hanging at a temperature of between 32° F and 34° F for seven to ten days. As this is colder than the temperature of the normal domestic refrigerator, it should be hung by the butcher before the meat is delivered to your home.

Fresh beef is a bright red when first cut, but darkens on standing in the air. *Tender beef* is usually flecked with fat, rather like marble, and is surrounded by a creamy layer of it.

Fatless meat cannot be tender. The inside of the bones should be rosy, and the meat firm and moist to the touch, and very smooth.

Beef

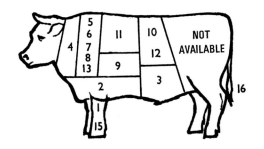

1. *Shin beef.* Soup and beef tea; makes a flavoursome, if rather fibrous, pressure cooker stew.

2. *Brisket:* (a) *Thin end.* For tsimmes—used sliced, with a marrow bone.

   (b) *Point.* Covered roasting—in fat without

145

liquid, 40 minutes to the lb. Only economical in a 4-lb. joint or over. Meaty but fatty (middle brisket has thinner layer of fat). *Note:* Brisket is really too thick to roll. Excellent for pickling.

3. *Flank.* Needs rolling. Cheap. Sweet when pot roasted, but must be pressed and served cold, or it falls to bits. Also for pickling.

4. *Neck steak.* Mincing or stewing—has plenty of ''body''.

5. *Chuck or back steak.* Stew, mince or cook with wine.

6. *Shoulder steak.* First cut for braising, cut $\frac{1}{2}$-inch thick, or for casseroles—excellent for goulash or boeuf bourguignonne, cut in 1-inch cubes. If hung for ten days, it can be fried.

7. *Blade steak.* Braise in slices, or pot roast in one piece. The thin gristle running through can be nicked out before serving.

8. *Alki or round bola (part of shoulder steak).* Braise, cooked with plenty of its own fat (dice fat then use to brown meat). Good, hot or cold.

9. *Top rib.* Similar to flank. For borscht, cabbage soup, cholent.

10. *Wing rib.* Roasting: can be boned out for spit roasting, or shortened rib on bone can be spitted—keeping bone in adds to flavour.

11. *Lid of rib (top of back rib).* Rolled, then roasted or spitted. Excellent cold for sandwiches.

12. *Rib steaks.* Boned out and cut $\frac{1}{2}$ to $\frac{3}{4}$ inch thick for grilling or frying.

13. *Bola:* (a) *Corner.* Braising, with plenty of its own fat. Hung bola can be open-roasted very slowly, loosely foil-covered for half the time, allowing 40 minutes to the lb.

    (b) *Slice.* Braising (Swiss steak, or cooked in tomatoes). Bola, frozen, then cut paper thin can be used for ''Steak Diane''.

14. *Liver.* Chopping. Young beasts' liver need only be grilled; older animals' liver should be grilled to kosher, then simmered in salted water for half an hour. (Not illustrated)

15. *Knuckle and shin beef.* For soup.

16. *Oxtail.* For soup (not available in some towns).

Mincemeat should always be used as soon after mincing as possible, as the number of cut surfaces makes it deteriorate more quickly than other meat. All meat should be completely cooked before storage; partially cooking meat raises the internal temperature just enough to encourage the growth of bacteria, without being sufficiently high to kill them.

Veal

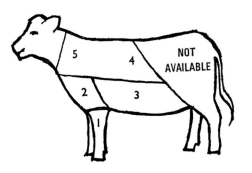

Good veal is between six and eight weeks old, the flesh milky rather than pink in colour. An older animal which is too young to be classified as beef is called a "Sterk".

1. *Shank of veal.* In thick soups such as barley and hobene gropen; for calve's foot jelly or meat casseroles, such as "osso bucco". It must be cut with an electric saw.

2. *Shoulder.* The thick part of the shoulder can be plain roasted, the blade end boned out, stuffed and braised. Use plenty of fat, flavour with bayleaf and onion, cook in a covered casserole.

3. *Breast.* Have it boned and pocketed or boned and rolled, then stuffed. Braise. Add the juice of an orange, glass of wine in last hour.

4. *First cut chops.* Braise. Also for kebabs, and veal scallops in wine.

5. *Shoulder chops.* Boned out, koshered, frozen and sliced for schnitzel.

6. *Calf liver.* Grill to kosher, then slice and smother with onions in frying pan. Or use for chopped liver.

Lamb

Good lamb joints have plenty of light pinkish meat, creamy, mellow fat, and very little bone.

1. *Neck and scrag.* For Scotch broth.

2. *First cut chops* (*cutlet*). For grilling. There are twelve in each beast.

3. *Middle neck.* For casseroling.

11

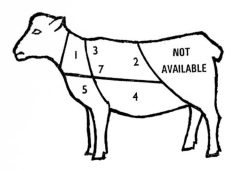

4. *Breast.* Casseroled with spring vegetables. Can also be stuffed.

5. *Shoulder.* Roast. Can also be boned and rolled.

6. *Kidneys.* To sauté and stew where available. (Not illustrated)

7. *Shoulder chops cut with cutlet.* Fry, then casserole until tender. Known as "man's chop" because of size.

How To Kosher Meat And Poultry

It is now possible to buy pre-packed meat and poultry which has been koshered under rabbinical supervision and can therefore be cooked without any further ritual preparation. (Butcher's mince is always prepared from prekoshered meat.)

However, when the food has to be koshered *at home,* the following procedures should be followed for all kinds of meat, bones, poultry and giblets, with the exception of liver and grilling steaks (see alternate instructions below).

(1) Meat and Poultry (Including Bones and Giblets)

(All poultry must be drawn and the feet skinned before it is koshered).

(a) As soon as possible after the food has been delivered, put it into a deep plastic or enamel bucket and cover it completely with cold water.

(b) Leave it to soak for half an hour.

(c) Take it out and place it on a wire or plastic draining grid, tilted so that the liquid can easily drain away. Leave it to drain for five minutes.

(d) Thoroughly sprinkle every surface with koshering salt. (This can be obtained from a kosher butcher or grocer.)

(e) Leave for one hour.

(f) Rinse the food three times in cold water, to remove all traces of salt and blood.

Meat and bones should then be well dried with a paper towel and cooked at once, or stored until required in the refrigerator or freezer (see section on "How to Store Food").

Poultry and giblets must be scalded as follows:

(a) Stand the fowl in a bowl and pour boiling water over it from a kettle.

(b) When cool enough to handle, scrape the skin of the bird with a blunt knife, to remove any pin feathers or coarse bits of skin. Look inside the body cavity to make sure it is absolutely clean, and that no traces of the entrails remain. Trim off any loose skin from the giblets. Dry thoroughly, cook at once, or store in the refrigerator or freezer.

In an emergency, to ensure that food can be cooked before the commencement of Shabbat, the koshering time may be reduced by half. In this case, the food is soaked for fifteen minutes only, and then left in salt for half an hour.

(2) Liver

As liver contains too much blood to be effectively koshered by soaking and salting, the following method is used instead:

(a) A thick piece of liver should be cut open, thinner slices should be cut across the surface to facilitate the removal of the blood.

(b) Wash the liver thoroughly in cold water, then sprinkle it on both sides with cooking salt (koshering salt is too coarse for the purpose).

(c) Place the liver on a sheet of foil and lay it in the grill pan. Grill gently until it changes colour, turn and grill on the second side in the same way.

Alternatively, the salted liver can be placed in a wire basket or on a wire grid *over* a gas flame and cooked in the same way, until it has changed colour on both sides.

(d) Calf liver can now be served without further preparation, or it can be put in a frying pan and "smothered" with fried onions. Ox liver must be tenderised by simmering in salt water for half an hour. It can then be used for chopped liver. (The foil on which the liver was grilled should be discarded after use. If a wire basket or grid is used, it should be held over the flame to burn off any residue, then washed, wiped and stored.)

(3) Steaks

Steaks which are to be grilled do not need to be soaked and salted. The grilling process draws out the blood from the meat, and this is considered to satisfy the requirements of Kashrut.

Note: All utensils used to kosher food should be kept exclusively for that purpose. After use, they should be washed and wiped with a special cloth, then stored separately from other kitchen equipment.

To Braise Meat

A joint suitable in size for two is too small to dry roast, as it shrinks and dries up when exposed to fierce heat. It is far more satisfactory to braise a 3-lb. piece of meat rather as one does a fowl. Half can be eaten hot, and the remainder served cold with chips, or minced for a meat pie or blintzes.

Braised Bola Printanière

3 lb. corner of bola, with 1 level teaspoonful salt, 1 level teaspoonful dry mustard, and 2 level teaspoonfuls flour rubbed into it
1 tablespoonful of cooking fat or oil
2 small onions, 2 stalks of celery, 2 carrots, half a small green pepper, all coarsely sliced
Half a clove of garlic

Set the oven to Gas No. 3 (335° F).

In a heavy-based casserole, melt the fat and brown the meat quickly on all sides. Lift it out onto a plate. Into the same fat put the onion, cooking until soft, then add all the remaining vegetables and stir them well to absorb any remaining fat. Sprinkle with a little additional salt and ten grinds of black pepper. Add a bayleaf, a sprig of parsley and half a small cup of boiling water. Stir the contents of the casserole thoroughly, then replace the browned meat on the savoury vegetable bed. Put on the lid and put in the oven. When the liquid starts to bubble (after about fifteen minutes), turn the oven down to Gas No. 1 (300° F) and cook for two and a half to three hours, depending on the weight of the meat. Allow forty-five minutes per pound, and forty-five minutes for the piece.

Ten minutes before serving, take off the lid and allow the surface of the meat to become crisp.

To serve, put the meat on a hot dish. Push all the vegetables and cooking liquid through a sieve into a small pan. Skim off the excess fat, heat to boiling, season with salt and pepper and serve with the meat.

For two people there should be sufficient meat to serve once hot, once cold and once minced, in a pie or other dish.

Braised Brisket

3 lb. corner of brisket, 1 tablespoonful meat fat
6 pickling onions
2 large potatoes, 2 medium carrots
1 bayleaf, 6 peppercorns, 2 level teaspoonfuls
   salt, 10 grinds black pepper
Half a small cupful boiling water

As the fat that melts off brisket is so tasty, it makes an ideal medium in which to cook potatoes and carrots. Left-over brisket should be forced into a basin, covered with a saucer and a 2-lb. weight and then refrigerated. Next day it will cut to perfection.

Brown the meat quickly in the hot fat. Sprinkle with the seasonings. Put in a casserole surrounded with the onions and the boiling water. Cover and cook in a slow oven (Gas No. 1, 300° F) for three hours. One hour before the meat is ready, surround it with thick slices of potato and carrot. Serve the brisket cut in thick slices, together with the potatoes and carrots in the delicious meat juices.

Note: If you use an enamelled roaster or glass oven casserole, instead of one made of enamelled steel or oven-proof earthenware, you may need to use a slightly hotter oven—the liquid should barely bubble in the casserole all the time.

Serves four to six, with some left for sandwiches.

Mincemeat

1 lb. twice-minced shoulder steak
1 dessertspoonful chicken fat or soft
   margarine
2 level teaspoonfuls salt
10 grinds black pepper
1 egg
Half an onion, finely grated
1 thick slice of white bread (the crust
   removed) soaked till soft in cold water

Mincemeat is extremely versatile. Using a basic mixture (see recipe left) one can stew it in tomato and herb sauce; stew it in a sweet and sour sauce; roast it; make meat balls for soup; make a mincemeat pie and many other dishes. Always ask for *twice-minced shoulder steak*. This is dearer than plain "mince", but far meatier and with less gristle content.

Beat the egg until frothy, then stir in the onion, the seasonings and the soaked bread, which should first be squeezed as dry as possible and broken up with a fork. Leave for ten minutes, then add the mincemeat and blend thoroughly with a fork, until no traces of the bread are visible.

1 lb. recipe mincemeat mixture
1 large onion, sliced or chopped as preferred
2 tablespoonfuls oil
¼ pint meat bouillon or thin left-over gravy
1 small bayleaf
1 tablespoonful flour mixed with a pinch of
**   salt and pepper**

Meat Ball Casserole

Wet the hands under the cold water tap. Take large spoonfuls of the raw meat mixture and form into balls the size of small apples, then flatten slightly into a patty. There should be six.

Put the seasoned flour onto a piece of paper, and dip each patty into it. Shake off any excess flour. Heat the oil in a heavy frying pan for four minutes, put in the meat balls, and fry steadily until they are a rich brown on both sides. Remove the meat, and in the same fat fry the onions until they are soft and golden, but not crispy. Add the bouillon or gravy to the pan with a further sprinkle of salt and pepper and the bayleaf. Stir the pan well to release any meat juices which may have stuck to the bottom.

Arrange the patties in a shallow uncovered casserole, in which they can fit side by side. Pour the gravy round them, and cook slowly at Gas No. 1 (300° F) for forty-five minutes. Alternatively, the meat can be put back into the frying pan surrounded by the onions and gravy, and left to cook very gently for the same time, turning the meat once or twice.

This will serve two people, with enough left over for lunch for one.

1 lb. twice-minced shoulder steak
1 level dessertspoonful chicken fat or
**   margarine**
1 egg
2 heaped tablespoonfuls fresh breadcrumbs
1 level teaspoonful dry mustard
1 level tablespoonful medium matzo meal
¼ medium onion (grated)
1 level tablespoonful tomato ketchup
1 level dessertspoonful H.P. or similar savoury
**   sauce**
1 level teaspoonful salt
Speck of black pepper

Savoury Meat Loaf

This is excellent hot or cold, when it makes delicious sandwiches.

Beat the egg with all the seasonings, then add the grated onion, the matzo meal and the breadcrumbs and leave to soak together for half an hour. (If the bread is too fresh to crumb, cut a 2-inch slice, remove the crust and cut it into tiny cubes—it will soften in the liquids.) After half an hour, add the meat and the fat, and blend thoroughly with a fork. Shape the meat into a loaf and place it in a shallow square casserole or roasting tin which is about 2 inches wider all the way round.

In a small frying pan, melt a level tablespoonful of chicken fat or oil, and gently fry a tablespoonful of coarsely chopped onion. When the onion is golden, add ¼ pint of meat or chicken stock or thin gravy, stir well, then pour round the loaf. Bake at Gas No. 6 (400° F) for fifteen minutes, then turn down to Gas No. 4 (350° F) for a further forty-five minutes. Baste the loaf twice while it is cooking, using the juices in the pan. Ten minutes before the loaf is ready, mix 2 level teaspoonfuls of cornflour with half a cup of water or stock, and pour round the loaf, blending with the pan juices. Serve the loaf in thick slices with the gravy.

Left-over loaf should be foil-wrapped and refrigerated. Serves two to three plus left-overs for sandwiches, or to serve with chips.

How to Stuff Cabbage

Ashkenazi and Sephardi Jews alike eat stuffed cabbage in celebration of Succot, but they prepare it in different ways. The gevikelte kraut of the West has an ordinary mincemeat stuffing, and a sweet and sour meat sauce. The holishkes of the Middle East are stuffed with meat and rice, and cooked in a sweet and sour tomato sauce. Both are equally delicious. It is not worth making holishkes just for two, but as they keep extremely well, left-overs from the following recipes can be served on succeeding days. They are even delicious cold as an hors-d'œuvre.

If possible, make the bundles the day before they are to be served. Soaking in the sauce overnight improves the flavour.

Gevikelte Kraut (Cabbage Bundles)

Set the oven at Gas No. 4 (350° F).

The Stuffing
1 head of winter cabbage
1 lb. twice-minced raw shoulder steak
2 level tablespoonfuls medium matzo meal
Half a grated onion
½ level teaspoonful salt, speck of pepper
1 egg

Remove the stalk from the cabbage by making a triangular incision, then plunge the head into a pan of boiling water. Bring back to the boil, then simmer gently for five minutes. Tip into a colander and put under the cold tap. Drain. Turn the cabbage, so that the stalk end is towards you.

Cut each leaf in turn free from the cabbage—you should get about twelve to fourteen perfect leaves from an average cabbage. If you are short of this number, you can always "patch" several together. Remove any tough stalk from the base of each leaf.

Have all the stuffing ingredients blended together in a bowl, ready. Put a tablespoonful at the base of each leaf,

155

turn in the sides, and roll up into a "parcel". Take the roll and squeeze it gently in the palm of the hand to stop it unrolling. Lay the rolls in a wide shallow glass casserole, an enamel roaster or an enamelled iron dish.

The Sauce
2 rounded tablespoonfuls golden syrup
1 tablespoonful vinegar
1 bayleaf, 6 peppercorns, 1 level teaspoonful salt
Water or beef bouillon

Sprinkle the seasonings over the bundles, then add enough water or (preferably) beef bouillon barely to cover them. Cover the casserole and put in the oven. Leave until the sauce simmers (about fifteen minutes), then turn the oven down to Gas No. 1 (300° F), and continue to cook for at least two hours, though longer will improve the flavour. Ten minutes before you take out the casserole, take off the lid to brown the tops of the bundles. Taste the sauce, and add more syrup or vinegar if necessary. Makes twelve to fourteen bundles. Serves four to six as a main course.

Holishkes

Set the oven at Gas No. 4 (350° F).

Chop the onion finely, then fry gently in the chicken fat until golden. Add the rice to the pan, stir well and cook for two or three minutes. Stir in the stock, cover and cook for a further five minutes, or until the stock has been absorbed by the rice. Stir this mixture into the raw meat, add the seasonings and mix thoroughly.

The Filling
1 firm head of winter cabbage
1 onion
2 level tablespoonfuls rendered chicken fat or margarine
4 level tablespoonfuls long-grain (Patna) rice
¼ pint chicken bouillon (use cubes)
1 lb. twice-minced raw shoulder steak
½ level teaspoonful salt, ¼ level teaspoonful white pepper

Remove the stalk of the cabbage by making a triangular incision, then plunge the head into a pan of boiling water. Allow to simmer for five minutes, then tip into a colander and put under the cold tap. When cool enough to handle, remove the leaves by cutting each one in turn free at the stem end. Cut out any coarse stalk from each leaf. Put a tablespoonful of filling at the base of each leaf, fold in the sides and roll up into a bundle. Squeeze between the palms of the hand to seal. Lay the holishkes side by side in a casserole of glass, enamelled iron or enamel—it should be wide enough to accommodate them in one layer.

Sweet and Sour Sauce
4 level tablespoonfuls soft brown sugar
Juice of 1 large lemon
1 small can of tomato purée, two canfuls of cold water

Mix all the sauce ingredients together and pour over the holishkes, which should be barely coated with liquid.

Cover and put in the oven for about fifteen minutes, or until the sauce starts to simmer. Turn the oven down to Gas No. 1 (300° F) and continue to cook for at least two hours, though longer will improve the flavour. Ten minutes before you take out the casserole, remove the lid to brown the tops of the holishkes. Taste the sauce and add more lemon juice and brown sugar if required.

Makes twelve to fifteen holishkes. Serves four to six for a main course.

To Stew Meat

Meat cooked in a savoury sauce can be one of the most delectable of dishes, if certain rules are followed:

(1) Always brown the meat to develop its flavour and to seal it, thus preventing the total escape of the meat juices into the cooking liquid.

(2) Use only enough liquid to cover the meat, so that the meaty flavour does not become diluted.

(3) Make sure that the liquid never boils, but "shivers" all the time, so that the cooked meat is soft without being stringy.

Savoury Goulash

1 lb. bola, cut into $\frac{1}{2}$-inch cubes
1 oz. meat fat or 1 tablespoonful oil
Plenty of black pepper
1 large onion, sliced wafer thin
1 level dessertspoonful brown sugar
2 level teaspoonfuls salt
1 bayleaf
$\frac{3}{4}$ pint water or meat stock made with a bouillon cube
1 level tablespoonful of cornflour dissolved in 4 tablespoonfuls of cold water

This basic recipe can be varied in any of the following ways:

(1) Tinned tomatoes can be substituted for all the liquid.

(2) Red wine can be substituted for half the liquid.

(3) The bay leaves can be omitted and 1 level dessert-spoonful of paprika pepper sprinkled on the meat as it is browning in the fat.

Heat the fat or the oil in a heavy frying pan or oven casserole, sprinkle with the black pepper, then put in the meat and brown briskly on all sides (make sure the meat is well dried beforehand on a kitchen paper towel, or it will not brown). Add the onions, sprinkle with the brown sugar and continue to cook until the mixture is a really rich brown. Pour in the water or stock, the bay leaf and the salt. Cover and simmer for one and a half hours on the top of the stove or two hours in a slow oven (Gas No. 1, 300° F). Adjust the temperature so that the liquid is barely bubbling all the time. Add the dissolved cornflour and continue to cook for a further three minutes. Taste and add more seasonings if necessary. This serves two to three.

To Make a Meat Pie with a Single Crust

Cook the mixture as above but allow it to cool, then spoon into a pie dish 2 inches deep with a ½-inch rim all the way round. Roll out a packet of frozen puff pastry until it is the thickness of a penny, and ½ an inch wider all the way round than the top of the pie dish. Trim off this extra ½-inch, and lay it on the dampened rim of the dish. Dampen the strip of pastry in turn, then carefully transfer the remaining pastry to the dish, pressing it down well onto the pastry rim that is already in position. Use a fork to crimp the edges of the pie. If you have a little beaten egg, use it to paint the top of the pie. Otherwise, leave it plain. Bake in a hot oven (Gas No. 8, 450° F) for twenty minutes.

To Make a Meat Pie with a Double Crust

Divide a packet of puff pastry in half, and roll one half to fit the bottom of a 7- or 8-inch pie dish. Spoon in the cooled meat mixture. If there is too much gravy, omit it and serve separately. Dampen the edges of the pie, then cover with a second crust rolled from the remainder of the pastry. Crimp the edges firmly with a fork, brush with egg or leave plain, and bake for ten minutes at Gas No. 8 (450° F), then for a further fifteen minutes at Gas No. 7 (425° F).

Both pies will serve four people.

To Make a Dumpling Crust

Sieve 3 oz. of self-raising flour with a pinch of salt and 1 level teaspoonful of baking powder and rub in 1½ oz. margarine until the mixture resembles coarse crumbs. Stir in a teaspoonful of chopped parsley and about 2 tablespoonfuls of cold water—enough to make a stiff dough. Gently roll out the dumpling on a floured board to fit the top of the casserole in which the meat mixture is bubbling. Three-quarters of an hour before the meat should be done, top the casserole with the dumpling crust, cover with the casserole lid and continue to cook. When the meat is ready, the crust will have become puffy and brown.

Serves four.

To Cook Lamb Chops

Chops are better grilled than fried, as they are then less greasy. They do not need to be frozen like beef steak, but should be kept in the chiller tray of the refrigerator for three days (after they have been koshered) before they are cooked.

Ask the butcher for first cut lamb chops—they have the most meat and the least bone. They should be cut ¾ inch thick, if they are to be juicy when cooked. Trim off all but a very thin edging of fat from each chop, then give them a sharp pounding with the end of a rolling pin or a special cutlet bat.

An hour before you intend to grill them, put enough oil to cover the bottom into a shallow dish. Into it cut up a clove of garlic and a sprig of fresh rosemary or a pinch of the powdered herb. Now put the chops into the oil and turn to coat them. Turn them once or twice in the following hour so they are well and truly steeped in the flavoured oil.

Fifteen minutes before you plan to serve them, heat the grill for three minutes. Arrange your chops on the grid of the grill pan, pouring over any excess oil. Put the grill pan 4 inches below the heat and grill for five minutes on each side, or until the chops are a really rich brown. Serve at once.

To Cook a Steak

While frying and grilling steaks cost more per pound than less tender cuts, they are very quick to prepare, and there are no left-overs to use up. This makes them a good proposition when cooking for two, particularly if you have been out at work all day. Kosher steaks can be grilled under a really efficient grill, but I think they are more satisfactory, particularly for new cooks, when they are sautéed on top of the stove.

Steak Sauté

Ask the butcher for two ¾-inch thick steaks cut from the eye of the rib (what the French call "entrecôte"). Allow 1 lb. of meat for two good portions. The meat should have been koshered by the butcher and frozen for ten days before it is sold. Put the defrosted steak on a chopping board and nick it with a sharp knife wherever you see a layer of gristle between the fat and the meat. This stops it from curling in the pan and cooking unevenly. Dry the steak thoroughly, using a paper towel.

159

Choose a frying pan with a good, solid, machine-ground base. Fry the steak in oil—about 2 tablespoonfuls to cover the bottom of the pan to the depth of $\frac{1}{16}$ of an inch. Add a teaspoonful of rendered chicken fat if available. (Put empty pan on a medium light for a minute or two to heat through—this stops any sticking—and then put in the oil.) Give it four minutes to become hot enough. To test, gingerly lower your steak into the fat. As the first corner touches the oil it should sizzle encouragingly. If it just makes a sad "plop", wait a bit longer. The fat should cook the first side of the steak to a rich brown in four minutes.

Remember, the cooking of a steak does not tenderise it; it merely browns the outside appetisingly and cooks the inside to the colour you like. Overcook a steak, and it gets progressively tougher.

Turn the steak when it is brown, using a slotted spoon or spatula never a knife, which might pierce it and cause the escape of the juices. After another four or five minutes, the steak should be "à point"—that is pale pink inside, and a rich brown outside. To test, press it with your finger. It should resist slightly instead of being soft like a fresh steak. But perhaps more surely, nick it with a knife and have a look. Allow a total of ten minutes, depending on the thickness of the steak. And remember it will cook a little more in the few minutes it is in the oven, while you are making the sauce.

Transfer the cooked steak to a heated platter and turn your attention to the pan. Pour off all the cooking fat except a teaspoonful or two. Turn the heat down and add a wineglassful of red or white wine (dry) or white vermouth, or the same amount of gravy left over from a roast or a braise, or even stock made from a bouillon cube. Swirl this liquid round in the pan to loosen the delicious sediment sticking to the bottom. Allow it to simmer for a minute to concentrate the flavour. Add a few drops of Worcestershire sauce, a few grinds of black pepper, a pinch of salt. Pour over the steak and sprinkle with chopped parsley. Enough for two.

To Render Chicken Fat

Chicken fat, fat-impregnated skin
1 onion (roughly chopped)

Before a fowl is boiled or casseroled, the excess fat and the fat-impregnated skin at the back should be removed, so that it can be rendered down for use in dishes like chopped liver and knaidlach.

Cut the fat and the fatty skin into 1-inch squares and put into a heavy pan. Cover with cold water, and bring to the boil. Reduce the heat until the contents of the pan are barely bubbling, then cover with a lid and allow to simmer in this way for twenty minutes, or until the fat has melted. Uncover and continue to simmer gently, until all the water has evaporated and only liquid fat remains—when the bubbling will have stopped and the surface of the liquid will be still. Now add a coarsely-chopped onion and continue to cook gently until the onion is golden brown. (Be sure to keep the light low, or the fat will start to smell and burn.) Cool the fat in the pan for ten minutes, then strain it off into an earthenware dish and allow it to cool. The cracklings (or grebene) of skin are delicious on matzo or bread. Store the cooled and covered chicken fat in the refrigerator.

An Alternative Method Using the Oven

If the oven is already heated to cook another dish, the fat may be rendered at the same time. Cut it up in exactly the same way, but add the onion at the beginning. Put into a small earthenware dish and leave in a low oven until the fat has melted—this may take an hour or two. Strain and store in the same way.

To Casserole a Fowl

A fine plump fowl has, perhaps, more flavour than any other kind of bird. However, as its flesh tends to be dry, it must be cooked in gentle moist heat. The best way is to braise it slowly on a bed of lightly fried vegetables, in a covered casserole just large enough to contain it.

The bird can be whole or jointed, stuffed (with helzel or breadcrumb mixture) or left plain. The vegetables used can be varied with the season, but the basic method is always the same.

Turn the oven on to Gas No. 4, 350° F. Mix together the salt, pepper, flour and paprika, then rub into the skin of the bird. In a heavy casserole, heat the oil and fry the onion until it is soft and golden, then add all the remaining vegetables and stir over gentle heat, until they have absorbed most of the fat. Put the bird in and turn it in the hot fat

1 fowl, 4–5 lb. in weight, koshered and scalded, then stuffed or left plain
1 tablespoonful oil
1 large onion, thinly sliced
1 carrot, cut in thin slices
2 soft tomatoes, or 2 teaspoonfuls tomato purée
1 bayleaf
2 level teaspoonfuls paprika
2 level teaspoonfuls flour
1 level teaspoonful salt
10 grinds black pepper
1 crushed clove of garlic
Half a cup chicken soup or chicken stock made with a cube
Any or all of the following may be added if they are available:
Half a green pepper, deseeded and cut into strips
3 stalks of celery, cut into dice
2 oz. mushrooms, cut into slices

until it has turned pale gold. Pour the stock or soup down the side of the casserole. Cover and transfer to the oven. After fifteen minutes, turn the oven down to Gas No. 3, 335° F and cook for three hours, or until the bird is a rich golden brown and the leg can be moved easily in its socket.

During cooking, the liquid should be bubbling very gently. If it is too violent, turn the oven down to Gas No. 2 (315° F). Baste twice with the pan juices. If dinner is delayed, the oven can be turned down to a "keep hot" or minimum setting, and the bird will come to no harm.

To serve, lift the bird onto a warm platter. Skim off as much fat as you can. The gravy can be served as it is, or it can be pushed through a sieve into a pan containing 2 level teaspoonfuls of cornflour, slaked with 2 tablespoonfuls of cold water. Bring the gravy mixture to the boil, then simmer for three minutes. Taste, re-season if necessary, and serve.

Serves four to six.

To Casserole Joints of Fowl

This is useful if you want to cook only half a bird, or do not wish to carve a hot bird at the table.

Ask the butcher to joint a koshered and scalded bird into six or eight sections, or into four, if only half a bird is used. Sprinkle with salt, pepper and paprika, as with the whole bird, but instead of flouring it, dip each joint in medium matzo meal. Do not fry the joints, but lay them side by side on top of the fried vegetables. Add the chicken soup or stock and cook in exactly the same way. For variety, white wine can be substituted for the chicken stock.

To Brown a Boiled Bird

Set the oven at Gas No. 5 (375° F). If you wish to cook the bird in the soup, but prefer to have it hot and brown rather than cold and boiled, proceed as follows:

Cut the legs off the raw fowl before boiling—this makes the bird easier to handle. Cook the bird and legs in the soup until barely tender—about two hours, or when the flesh of the leg feels soft when prodded with a fork. Lift the bird from the soup and leave covered until needed.

Next day, place the bird and legs in a casserole. Skim the fat off the soup, put it in a frying pan and cook a large sliced onion in it until soft and golden. Sprinkle the bird with a light dusting of paprika and flour, then pour over it the fried onions and the fat in which they were cooked. Cover and cook for forty minutes, or until the bird looks brown and juicy. Uncover and add half a cup of the chicken soup. Cover and reheat for a further ten minutes. Serve the bird in joints with the pan juices.

To Roast a Chicken

1 roasting chicken, about 3½–4½ lb. net weight
½ pint chicken stock or soup
2 oz. margarine
Stuffing

This method keeps a kosher bird moist and juicy better than the conventional English method of roasting without any liquid. The skin is brown and crisp. A small bird for two is best spit-roasted, according to the maker's instructions.

Set the oven at Gas No. 7 (425° F). Sprinkle the inside of the scalded and koshered bird with salt and pepper. Stuff (see recipe below) or insert a nut of margarine and a large sprig of parsley into the body cavity. Spread the bird all over with the soft margarine, and cover the breast lightly with greasepaper or greased foil. Tie the legs together with string, so that the bird is a compact shape. Put in a roasting tin, into which it will fit comfortably without being lost. Stew half a sliced onion and carrot round it and pour in the stock.

Put the bird in the oven for ten minutes, then *open the door quickly*, baste well, then turn the heat down to Gas No. 4 (350° F) and continue to cook for a further hour. Open the oven, again take off the paper or foil and baste the bird well. Add a little extra water if the stock has dried up and no longer covers the base of the tin. Continue to cook for a further half hour, until the leg can be moved easily in its socket and the flesh feels very soft when prodded. If possible, leave the bird in a warming oven for ten minutes before it is carved.

To serve, put the bird on a serving dish, and pour off the juices into a measuring cup. Make up to half a pint with chicken stock or left-over gravy. Return the juices to the baking tin and scrape it well, to release any delicious sediment stuck to the base. Boil the juices down rapidly until they are rich and syrupy. Season with salt and pepper and serve with the roasted bird. Serves four to six.

Savoury Bread Stuffing

2 cups stale challah crumbs (put in liquidiser or
    pull out of crust with a fork)
3 oz. margarine
1 dessertspoonful oil
1 small onion, finely chopped
Pinch each of salt, paprika, black pepper and
    dried oregano
2 tablespoonfuls finely chopped parsley

Put the crumbs and the seasonings into a bowl. Heat the margarine with the oil in a small frying pan, and add the finely chopped onion. Cook gently until the onion is soft and golden, then pour the contents of the pan on to the seasoned crumbs. Toss lightly until all the crumbs are coated with fat. Stuff lightly into the salted cavity of the bird.

Helzel Stuffing

3 oz. plain or self-raising flour, plus
1 oz. semolina or fine matzo meal
3 tablespoonfuls raw chicken fat, finely
    chopped
Half a medium onion, coarsely grated
½ level teaspoonful salt, speck of white pepper

Use this to stuff a casseroled bird; it will not cook sufficiently in one that is roasted.

Mix all the ingredients together with a fork. (If raw fat is not available, use 3 rounded tablespoonfuls of rendered fat. Use this to cook the onion gently for two minutes, then pour on to the dry ingredients and blend well.) The mixture should look slightly moist. If it is too dry, add a little more fat; if too moist in appearance, add a little more semolina or meal. Stuff lightly into the body cavity of the bird.

Carrot Tsimmes

1½ lb. carrots
1 lb. potatoes
1½ lb. slice of brisket
3 rounded tablespoonfuls golden syrup, 2 level
    teaspoonfuls salt
Speck of white pepper
1 level tablespoonful cornflour mixed to a thin
    paste with cold water

It is impossible to make a quick tsimmes—in fact, the more slowly it is cooked the better. Tsimmes simmered for hours has a delicious caramelised flavour that is unique. It reheats to perfection. One cannot make tsimmes for fewer than four, as the flavours cannot develop in too small a dish.

Trim all but a thin edging of fat off the meat, then cut the meat into 1½-inch chunks. Peel the carrots and cut into ½-inch cubes. Put the carrots and meat into a pan, cover with hot water and add 2 tablespoonfuls of syrup and 1 teaspoonful of salt. Bring to the boil, and then simmer for two hours, either on top of the stove, or in the oven in a casserole. Take out and skim off most of the fat or, better still, chill until next day, when the fat can then be lifted off. Drain the meat and carrots from the juice and put into an earthenware, stoneware or cast iron casserole (glass does not brown so well).

Mix the cornflour and cold water, and stir into the carrot

juice in the pan. Bring to the boil, then pour over the carrots and meat. Peel the potatoes, cut into 1-inch chunks and arrange on top of the other ingredients. Add extra boiling water if necessary, to make sure the vegetables are submerged. Sprinkle with the remaining teaspoonful of salt and tablespoonful of syrup. Put in a moderate oven (Gas No. 4, 350° F) for fifteen minutes, or until the casserole is bubbling. Turn the oven down to Gas No. 2 (315° F) for a further three hours.

Uncover and taste; if the juice is not sweet enough add a little more syrup. Leave the lid off for the casserole to brown for a further half hour.

Tsimmes With Dumpling

Rub 2 oz. of margarine into 4 oz. of self-raising flour, just as though you were making pastry. (If you have any rendered meat fat or dripping, you can use that instead of the margarine.) Mix to a soft dough with about 3 table-spoonfuls of cold water.

Arrange this dumpling in the centre of the casserole, and put the cooked carrots and meat and the raw potatoes around it. Continue as in the recipe above.

Tsimmes Simmered Overnight

Use identical ingredients, but omit the cornflour thickening. Arrange the cubed carrots, potatoes and meat in the casserole. Sprinkle with the syrup and salt and barely cover with water. Cover and put in a preheated oven at Gas No. ¼ (200° F) in the coolest part of the oven, usually the bottom. Cover tightly and leave from Erev Shabbat until Saturday lunch. Half an hour before lunch, remove the lid to allow the tsimmes to thicken.

Cholent

1 lb. butter beans (soaked the night before in cold water to cover)
3 lb. piece of boneless brisket
Salt, pepper, paprika, ginger
2 level tablespoonfuls rendered chicken fat
3 onions (sliced), 1 crushed clove of garlic
6 whole peeled potatoes or 1 cupful of washed raw barley

Cholent is the one dish specifically designed to be cooked overnight. It really is not successful if cooked more quickly. That is why you cannot make a cholent for two; it would dry up before it was cooked. However, if you are entertaining on Shabbat or Yomtov, you can use the recipe given below, for it will serve six to eight people (depending on their appetites).

Set the oven at Gas No. 6 (400° F). Rub the meat well with the seasonings. Brown it in the hot chicken fat in a

165

heavy pan. Take out and into the same pan put the sliced onions, cooking gently until soft and golden. Put the meat, the fried onions and any left-over fat into a deep hotpot casserole (brown earthenware seems to cook cholent the best).

On top arrange the well-drained butter beans and whole potatoes, or the washed barley. Add the crushed clove of garlic and the bayleaf. Sprinkle lightly with flour. Add enough boiling water barely to cover the contents of the pot. Cover and put into the oven. When the liquid in the pot starts to bubble (after about thirty minutes) turn the oven right down to Gas No. $\frac{1}{4}$ (200° F). Do not touch the dish until you serve it for lunch the next day.

Borscht

1 small onion
1 small carrot
**2 bunches of young beets or 1½ lb. raw, old
  beets**
**1 quart of meat or chicken stock, or stock made
  from Israeli bouillon cubes**
Juice of large lemon
2 level tablespoonfuls sugar
**2 level teaspoonfuls salt, speck of white
  pepper**
2 whole eggs

Strained beet juice will keep for several days in the refrigerator. The eggs can be added the day the borscht is needed, and any left-over soup will then keep for a further two days.

Scrape the skin off new beets with a blunt-bladed knife, or peel old ones with a potato peeler (be sure to keep the beets on a piece of kitchen paper to avoid staining the counter or chopping board). Peel the onion and carrot. Put the sugar, the salt, the pepper and the stock into a soup pan and add the coarsely grated vegetables. Bring slowly to the boil, cover and simmer for three-quarters of an hour.

Pour the contents of the pan through a coarse sieve into a bowl. Discard the vegetables. Return the liquid to the pan (or refrigerate until required). To thicken the soup : Beat the eggs in a basin until the yolks and whites are thoroughly blended. Bring the soup to the boil and add the lemon juice. Gradually pour a cupful of the hot beet juice onto the beaten eggs, whisking all the time, then return this mixture to the soup pan. Whisk vigorously and reheat until the soup is steaming, but do not let it boil, or it will curdle. Taste and, if the flavour is not equally sweet and sour, add extra sugar or lemon juice. Serve with a boiled potato.

Milchik Borscht

Use water instead of stock, and chill the soup after it has been thickened. To serve, stir $\frac{1}{4}$ pint of sweet or sour cream into the soup and serve chilled in soup cups or wine glasses.

Makes four generous servings.

Soups and Garnishes

Soup Stocks

Stock is a flavoured liquid, from which soups and sauces are made. It is made by simmering the coarser parts of root vegetables with herbs and koshered bones, enriched, if desired, with a piece of shin-beef. To extract the flavour from these ingredients, stock must be simmered very slowly for many hours. However, with a pressure cooker, one can make excellent stock in only an hour. If stock is made the day before the soup, it is easy to lift off any fat that has congealed overnight. Stock is an excellent way of using up odds and ends of vegetables with a good flavour, but too coarse to use in the soup itself.

Koshered bones
The green part of a fat leek
The leaves from a head of celery
Half a white turnip
Half an onion
2 squashy tomatoes
A bayleaf, 10 peppercorns, large sprig of parsley
2 level teaspoonfuls salt

Here Are the Different Ways to Make Stock for Soup

(1) *Bone Stock*

Put the bones and the coarsely cut vegetables into a pressure cooker, and cover with cold water. Add the seasonings. Pressurise at 15 lb. for one hour. Strain out all the vegetables. If the stock is not to be used at once, it can either be refrigerated until next day, or boiled down to concentrate it, then poured into a plastic container and frozen. *Note:* It is not necessary to cut fresh vegetables for stock, but any left-over ends of carrot, half-onions, squashy tomatoes, etc., can be used. In fact, the coarser the vegetables, the more flavour they will add.

(2) *Beef and Bone Stock*

Proceed as above, but add ½ to 1 lb. of shin-beef to the vegetables. The cooked meat can either be served in the soup, or used to make kreplach or other minced meat pastries.

(3) *Cooked Bone Stock*

The bone left from a roast rib makes excellent stock. Proceed as above. Use the stock for barley soup.

1 large onion
2 large carrots, sliced
1 stalk celery
2 squashy tomatoes or 1 teaspoonful tomato
  purée
2 level teaspoonfuls salt
$\frac{1}{4}$ teaspoonful white pepper

(4) *Cooked Chicken Bone Stock*

Break up the carcase of a braised or roast fowl and put it into the pressure cooker, together with the following :

Proceed as for bone stock. *Note:* If you are not using a pressure cooker, simmer the stock in a covered pan for three hours.

Bouillon Cube Stock

For the small family, it is probably a more economical proposition to use commercial bouillon cubes, which are diluted with water according to the manufacturer's instructions. Excellent beef and chicken cubes are available in a kosher pack.

Note: If a soup requires a long cooking time—for instance, barley soup and split pea soup, the bones and meat (if used) can be cooked simultaneously with the soup ingredients. In that case, the bones should be put into the pan, covered with the amount of water specified in the recipe, and the mixture brought to the boil. The scum from the bones should then be carefully removed with a wet spoon before the soup cereals and vegetables are added.

---

2 large potatoes, $\frac{1}{2}$ large onion, both finely
  sliced
1 carrot, grated, the white part of a fat leek,
  finely sliced
1 oz. butter, 1$\frac{1}{2}$ pts. of water
Blade of mace (optional), 2 level teaspoonfuls
  salt, speck of white pepper
$\frac{1}{2}$ pint milk, $\frac{1}{8}$ pt. cream
Nut of butter, 2 level tablespoonfuls cut
  chives, or 1 level dessertspoonful chopped
  parsley

Passover Cream of Vegetable Soup

The potatoes provide the thickening for this delicious soup. If kosher cream is not available, use top milk.

Melt the ounce of butter in a heavy pan. Add the onion, the carrot and the leek. Put on the lid and leave to stew in the butter for ten minutes. Uncover and add the potatoes, mixing the vegetables well together. Then add the water and the seasonings and simmer until the vegetables are absolutely tender—about thirty minutes. Push the contents of the pan (including the liquid) through a sieve or vegetable mill into a basin. In the soup pan, heat the milk and the nut of butter, and when steaming add the sieved vegetable mixture. Taste and add more salt and pepper if necessary. Just before serving, stir in the cream and the chives.

Makes four generous servings.

Barley Soup

2½ pints stock
3 level tablespoonfuls pearl barley
1 carrot, ½ onion, ½ white turnip, white part of a
   leek
Chopped parsley, 1 sprig parsley
1 level teaspoonful salt, speck of pepper

Barley soup is especially delicious when the stock used has been made from a roast rib bone. If ordinary bone stock is used, a little (½ lb.) shin-beef will greatly improve the flavour.

Put the barley into a bowl and cover with boiling water. Then turn into a sieve and rinse well under the cold tap. Cut the carrot, turnip, onion, and leek into small dice. Put the stock (and meat if used) into the soup pan and add the salt and pepper, the barley, the parsley and all the vegetables. Bring to the boil, skim with a wet metal spoon, then cover, reducing the heat until the mixture is barely bubbling. Simmer for three hours, by which time the barley will have thickened the soup. Taste and re-season. There should be plenty of pepper in it. Add a dessertspoonful of chopped parsley just before serving.

Serves four.

Chicken Soup

The feet, the last joint of the wings and the
   giblets of a young fowl (4 lb. dressed weight)
   or roasting chicken; plus a chicken bouillon
   cube
                or
The whole bird or half-bird with the feet,
   wings and giblets alone
3 pints of water
1 whole onion
2 carrots, peeled and cut in four
The leaves and top 2 inches of 2 stalks of
   celery
A sprig of parsley
A squashy tomato
2 level teaspoonfuls salt, pinch of white
   pepper
Any soft eggs from the fowl

Chicken soup is traditionally made by simmering a fowl (or part of one) in water flavoured with a variety of vegetables. However, if the fowl is to be casseroled rather than boiled, or a younger bird roasted or fried, then the soup can be made with the feet and giblets alone, and the flavour strengthened by the addition of a chicken bouillon cube. Chicken soup should always be made the day before it is served, as the flavour is incomparably better on the second day.

Put the water, the salt and the pepper into a large, heavy soup pan, add the feet, wings and giblets, and the bird or the bouillon cube. Cover and bring to the boil. Uncover and remove any froth with a large, wet, metal spoon. Add all the remaining ingredients. Bring back to the boil, then reduce the heat so that the liquid is barely bubbling. Cover and continue to simmer for a further three hours, or until the fowl (if used) feels very tender when the leg is prodded with a fork.

Strain the soup into one bowl and put the giblets and the carrot into another. The fowl, if used, should be put in a separate container. Refrigerate. Next day, remove any congealed fat, and return the soup to the pan. (If there is a thick layer of fat, it can be heated in a pan to drive off any liquid and then, when it has stopped bubbling, cooled and stored like rendered raw fat.) Add the cooked giblets and the carrot (cut into small dice), and reheat slowly before serving. The soup may be garnished with cooked lokshen (vermicelli), mandelen or knaidlach (matzo balls).

This quantity will serve two people generously for two meals. Using the same basic ingredients, chicken soup can be made weaker or stronger by varying the amount of water used.

Second-day chicken stock can be made by simmering the stripped carcase of a casseroled bird for two hours with vegetables using the same mixture as for fresh chicken soup. This stock makes an excellent basis for borscht, and tomato and vegetable soups, and can be strengthened if necessary with chicken or beef bouillon cubes.

Hobene Gropen Soup

1 quart stock
3 level tablespoonfuls hobene gropen
½ lb. shin-beef (optional but nice)
1 level teaspoonful salt, few shakes of white pepper
1 medium potato, 1 medium carrot, 1 medium onion, 2 stalks celery
Large sprig of parsley, 1 dessertspoonful of chopped parsley

A thick, "creamy" soup that is most satisfying on a cold winter's day. Buy the hobene gropen from a Jewish or Polish grocers.

Put the hobene gropen into a small basin and cover with boiling water. Leave to settle while you add the meat to the soup stock, together with the salt. Bring to the boil and skim off any froth with a wet metal spoon. Add the strained hobene gropen, reduce the heat so that the soup is barely bubbling, then cover and simmer in this way for one hour. Meanwhile, cut the potato into ½-inch cubes, and dice the onion, carrot and celery into ¼-inch cubes. Add these vegetables to the soup, together with the parsley sprig. Cover again and simmer for a further two hours, when the soup should be creamy and the meat tender. Remove the sprig of parsley, taste, and add more salt and pepper if required. Sprinkle in the chopped parsley and serve piping hot.

To serve on the second day, add half a cup of water and reheat gently. Serves two people twice.

Half a breakfast cup ($\frac{1}{4}$ lb.) green split peas
4 level tablespoonfuls red lentils
1 level tablespoonful pearl barley
2 level tablespoonfuls haricot beans
1 soup bone, 1 quart water or 1 quart bone stock
$\frac{1}{2}$ lb. soup meat (optional), 1 level teaspoonful salt, ten grinds black pepper
1 large carrot, diced into $\frac{1}{4}$-inch cubes
1 small carrot coarsely grated
1 stalk of celery, diced into $\frac{1}{2}$-inch cubes
The white part of a leek, well washed and thinly sliced
Large sprig of parsley

Lentil, Pea, Barley and Bean Soup

The proportions of the soup cereals can be varied if preferred, and the soup will then have a slightly different flavour and texture each time it is made. For instance, butter beans can be used instead of haricot beans, or the barley may be omitted. But the split pea and lentil proportion should remain the same.

The day before, put the split peas, lentils, barley and beans into a large bowl, cover with twice their depth of cold water and leave to soak and swell overnight. Next day, put the meat and the stock (or the water and bone) with the salt into a large soup pan and bring to the boil. Skim with a wet metal spoon; tip the soup cereals into a fine sieve to remove any excess soaking-water, then put under the cold tap and rinse thoroughly until the water that drains from them is quite clear. Add to the soup pan with all the vegetables except the grated carrot.

Bring back to the boil, then reduce the heat until the mixture is barely bubbling. Cover and simmer for two hours. Uncover and add the grated carrot. Continue to cook for a further hour, stirring the pan occasionally to make sure the soup does not stick to the bottom as it thickens. When the soup is ready, the lentils and split peas will have melted into a purée. Taste and add more seasonings if required. Remove the sprig of parsley.

Left-over soup can have a tablespoonful of tomato purée added, together with $\frac{1}{2}$-cupful of water to thin it down before reheating. Serves four people.

1 quart stock (made from chicken or beef bouillon cubes, bone stock, left-over chicken soup or a stock made from a casseroled chicken carcase—see recipe for stocks)
1 large (15 oz.) can of peeled plum tomatoes
Juice of a large lemon
2 level tablespoonfuls of sugar
4 level tablespoonfuls canned or tubed tomato purée
2 level tablespoonfuls of short-grain (Carolina) rice

Tomato Rice Soup

This is a delicious soup, whose flavour depends to a great extent on the strength of the stock used to make it. Although it is not normally worthwhile making only enough soup for a single day, this recipe is so easy that it can be usefully made from left-over chicken soup. In that case use 1 pint of left-over soup, a small can of tomatoes and exactly half the remaining ingredients.

Put the soup or stock into a soup pan and add all the remaining ingredients, pushing the tomatoes and their juice through a coarse sieve into the pan if you prefer a smooth soup. Bring the soup gently to the boil, then add the rice. Reduce the heat so that the soup barely bubbles, cover and cook very gently for half an hour, or until the rice is tender (bite a grain) and has slightly thickened the soup. Taste. The soup should be slightly sweet and sour. Add a little more sugar or lemon juice if required.

Serves four people.

Gefulte Helzel (Stuffed Neck)

1 fowl's neck, untorn
2 oz. of plain flour, minus 1 rounded tablespoonful (replace this with a rounded tablespoonful of semolina or fine meal—it gives the helzel a better texture)
3 level tablespoonfuls raw chicken fat, finely chopped
1 level tablespoonful raw onion, coarsely grated
Good pinch of salt and white pepper

When you intend to stuff a helzel you will need to tell the butcher, so that he will send you a fowl with the neck intact. The neck of a chicken is too small to be practicable.

Mix all the stuffing ingredients together with a fork. The mixture should look slightly moist. If it is too dry, add a little more fat; if too loose, a little more semolina or meal. With a coarse sewing needle and strong thread, sew up one end of the neck, and fill it with the stuffing mixture. It should be only loosely packed, as it swells during cooking. Carefully sew up the other end. Rinse the stuffed neck with cold water, then pour boiling water over it, to make the skin smooth.

To Cook the Helzel

If the bird is to be boiled, cook the helzel with it in the soup pan, then brown it with the bird for half an hour in the oven. If the bird is not to be browned after boiling, the helzel can be browned in the oven by itself for half an hour, or in the roasting pan with a joint of meat.

If the bird is to be casseroled, and only its giblets used for the soup, then the helzel can be put in the casserole with it and cooked at the same time, and then does not need to be boiled in the soup.

A stuffed helzel will serve four, but can easily be eaten by two.

Knaidlach

1 slightly rounded tablespoonful of soft rendered chicken fat (do not melt it)
1 large egg
2 tablespoonfuls chicken soup or cold water
½ level teaspoonful salt; pinch of white pepper and ginger
2 level tablespoonfuls ground almonds
2 oz. medium matzo meal (about 6 level tablespoonfuls)

These are sometimes called "halkes" or matzo balls. The secret of success is to use sufficient fat to make them tender yet firm. Providing the specified amount of fat is used, the amount of matzo meal may be increased if you prefer a firmer (though equally tender) texture. Ground almonds greatly enhance both the flavour and texture, but if you have none in the house, an equally quantity of medium matzo meal can be used instead.

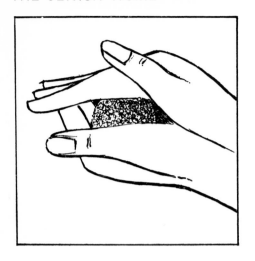

Beat the egg with a rotary whisk until fluffy, then stir in the tepid soup or water, the seasonings, matzo meal and ground almonds. It is a good idea to keep one level tablespoonful of meal in reserve and add it only if necessary, when the ingredients have been well mixed and you can see the texture. The mixture should then look moist and be stiff but still stirrable, yet not stiff enough to form into balls. Refrigerate or chill in a cold larder for at least one hour. (The mixture may be left overnight if convenient.)

Wet your hands under the cold water tap, take a walnut-sized piece of the now stiffened mixture, and roll it into a ball between your palms.

Have ready a large pan half full of boiling water. Add a teaspoonful of salt, then drop in the balls. When the water is barely bubbling, put on the lid, and simmer gently for forty minutes, without looking at the contents of the pan during that time. Uncover, lift out the knaidlach with a slotted spoon, and lower them gently into simmering chicken soup. Serve with the soup. Left-over balls can be allowed to remain in the soup overnight.

Makes eight knaidlach, enough for four people.

Kreplach

One just cannot make kreplach for two—one has to make them for an entire family ! If you feel like trying your hand, expect to have plenty to give away ! Allow yourself plenty of time to roll and cut the dough. The secret of tender kreplach is a dough that is kneaded until it resembles nothing so much as chamois leather.

Stew the beef until it is tender (about two hours) in chicken soup or any stock you are preparing for another meat soup. Allow it to cool, then mince and mix with the beaten egg, the grated onion, the salt and the pepper. Leave while you prepare the dough.

Put the flour and the salt onto a pastry board, make a well in the centre, and drop in the whole eggs, gradually drawing in the surrounding flour until a firm dough is formed. Knead the dough on the board using the heel of

The Filling
½ lb. shin-beef
1 egg
Half a grated onion
Salt and pepper to taste

The Dough
6 oz. plain flour
1 level teaspoonful salt
2 eggs

174

your right hand, until it goes smooth and shiny and becomes chamois-leather like in texture. Take half the dough at a time, and roll it out on the well-floured board until it is as thin as a knife blade. Keep on turning the dough as you roll, so that it does not stick to the board.

Cut the dough into 2-inch squares. On each square put a teaspoonful of the meat filling, then fold over into a triangle and pinch the edges together with your fingers. Have a large soup pan almost full of boiling salted water. Drop the kreplach in and reduce the heat until the water is simmering, cover, and simmer for half an hour.

Remember that the kreplach will swell as they cook, so if the pan seems at all crowded, cook the kreplach in two batches. Take the pan off the light and allow the water to cool for five minutes, then drain the kreplach through a colander. When they are thoroughly drained, put on a plate, cover and refrigerate.

To serve, heat for ten minutes in simmering chicken soup.

Mandlen (Soup Nuts)

3 oz. (approximately) plain flour
½ level teaspoonful salt; 1 dessertspoonful oil
1 large egg

These are delicious served with chicken or tomato soup. Put a dish on the table and let each person add their own to their bowl of soup. Mandlen may be baked or fried, whichever you prefer.

Sieve the flour and salt into a bowl. Make a well in the centre of the flour, and drop in the egg and the oil. Gradually work in the surrounding flour to make a soft dough that you can roll between your fingers into a "sausage". If too stiff, add a drop more oil; if too soft, add a teaspoonful more flour. Work the dough into a ball with your hands, then divide it into three. On a floured board, roll each piece into a pencil-thick length, and cut it into pieces half an inch long.

To bake, arrange the mandlen on a greased, flat baking sheet, leaving room for them to puff up. Bake in a moderate oven (Gas No. 5, 375° F) for twenty minutes, or until golden brown. After ten minutes, open the oven and shake the tray, so that the mandlen will brown evenly. When quite cold, store them in an airtight tin until needed.

To fry, leave the uncooked mandlen for half an hour on the pastry board, for the surface to dry out a little. In a frying

175

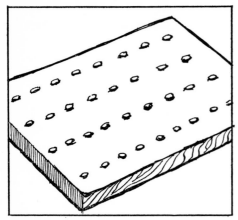

pan put oil to a depth of three-quarters of an inch. After oil has been heating gently for five minutes, drop in one mandel as a "tester". If gentle bubbles appear round it, the oil is hot enough. Put more mandlen into the oil, but do not overcrowd the pan, or the oil will become too cool. Allow them to cook at a steady bubble, turning them so that they brown on all sides. When golden brown, lift out with a slotted spoon, and drain on crumpled tissue paper. When quite cold, store in an airtight tin.

To reheat either baked or fried mandlen, put them in a small heat-proof casserole, and leave for ten minutes in a moderate oven (Gas No. 4 ,350° F).

Makes enough to serve four to six people.

1 large egg
2 oz. self-raising flour
½ level teaspoonful salt
Two grinds of black pepper
2 teaspoonfuls cold water

Quick Mandlen

These are excellent to make at the last moment before a Yomtov lunch, or as a garnish for left-over chicken soup. They are very crisp and puffy, but soften very quickly in soup.

Beat the egg, the water and the seasoning with a rotary egg beater, until the mixture is thick and frothy. Sieve the flour into the egg, and beat with a fork until a batter-like consistency is obtained (about two minutes). In a 9-inch frying pan, place enough oil to come to a depth of half an inch. After five minutes of heating, drop a little of the mixture from a teaspoon. If bubbles appear round it, the oil is ready. Drop teaspoonfuls of the mixture into the oil, leaving room for them to swell. Reduce the heat until the oil is bubbling gently round each soup nut. When bubbles appear on the surface, turn the mandlen over and continue to cook until both sides are a rich brown. Drain on crumpled tissue paper. Put in a heatproof dish and leave in the oven until required. They are not suitable to store.

Makes about fifteen mandlen. Enough for four people, or two if they are very hungry.

Fish

Perfect Fried Fish

Fried fish which is still palatable two days later depends on three main factors: the frying pan, the coating and the temperature of the oil.

The Pan

The ideal fish frying pan can be made either of heavy-cast aluminium or of iron, but in both cases, it must have a thick base that sits evenly on the cooker. The sides should be at least 2 inches high, to prevent the bubbling oil from spattering over the cooker. It should be at least 10 inches in diameter.

After each frying session, the cool oil is poured through a sieve lined with paper tissue into a screw-top glass or plastic jar, and the pan wiped out with tissue paper or newspaper. The base of an aluminium pan needs cleaning with a damp, detergent-filled pad, but that of an iron pan can be wiped clean with newspaper and a damp cloth. A little new oil is added to the old oil each time fish is fried.

If the oil smells acrid after it has been used, it has been overheated and has started to decompose, and should then be thrown away. So should any oil which has become dark and smelly. However, a little of this old oil added to a new panful of fresh oil will help the fish to brown more quickly. I like to fry fish in corn oil, as I think it gives it a crisper, more digestible coating.

The Coating

One can use stale bread, which has been dried in the oven without browning until it becomes crisp enough to mince or liquidise into crumbs. However, I prefer to use prepared crushed cornflake crumbs. They form an even coating which fries to a rich brown, and keeps the fish crisp when it is cold.

The Oil Temperature

It will take about four minutes for a 1-inch deep layer of oil to reach the right temperature for fish frying—375° F—

that is, when a cube of bread browns on one side in thirty seconds. A thermostatically controlled hot plate should be set at this temperature. An oil thermometer takes the guess-work out of frying.

Fried Fish Fillets or Steaks

6–8 fillets or steaks of fish
1 egg
2 tablespoonfuls flour
Coating crumbs

Steaks of sole, hake, haddock, cod, halibut or large plaice should be cut $\frac{3}{4}$ inch to 1 inch thick. Fillets should be 1 inch thick. Fillets of plaice, sole or baby halibut should be cut from fish not less than $1\frac{1}{2}$ lb. in weight.

Wash the fish under cold running water, arrange round the sides of a colander, sprinkle lightly with cooking salt and leave to drain.

Beat the egg with a fork to blend the yolk and the white, then put into a shallow oval dish. Beside this dish put a piece of greaseproof paper, with a cupful of coating crumbs. Next to it put another piece of greaseproof paper with the flour.

Heat the empty pan for three minutes over medium heat, then put the oil into it to a depth of 1 inch, and heat steadily for four minutes. Then test to see that the cube of bread browns in thirty seconds, or the thermometer registers 375° F. Dip the fish in and out of the flour, patting off any surplus. Next dip it in and out of the egg, and finally lay it in the crumbs and pat them on in an even layer. Lift up the fish on a slotted spoon and lower it into the hot oil. Do not overcrowd the pan, or too much cold fish put in too soon will lower the temperature too drastically, and the fish will be soggy. Cook the fish over medium heat with the oil bubbling steadily, until the first side is a rich brown. This will take about four minutes for a fillet, five to seven minutes for a thick steak. Turn it care-fully, using a slotted spoon and a fork, and cook until the second side is brown.

Have ready a shallow casserole filled with crumpled tissue paper. Lift out the fish to drain. If the fillets are not stiff and crisp when they are lifted out, turn up the heat and return them to the pan for a further minute's cooking in hotter oil. Perfect fried fish should look dry and crisp. As soon as it has drained completely, lift it on to a platter and store in the larder until required.

To Fry Fresh Herrings

Have them either filleted, or gutted without being split. (Fish on the bone is more fiddly to eat, but the flavour is more pronounced.) Scrape well with a knife to remove the scales, wash, salt and leave to drain in a colander. Dip in flour and egg, but finish with a coating of medium oatmeal or sieved porridge oats. Fry as above. Serve warm or cold. Allow two medium herrings per person.

To Fry Fish in Butter

Use steaks cut ¾ to 1 inch thick, and fillets cut from 1½ lb. fish. This is a practical mid-week method of cooking fish for two. There is no need to coat the fish in anything other than flour, and the smell of oil is kept out of the kitchen. However, the fish must be eaten hot off the pan, as the butter which is so delicious when the fish is hot, congeals and makes the fish greasy when it is cold. Any filleted or steaked fish that is fried in oil can also be fried in butter; but this is a particularly suitable method for frying a small whole fish, like trout.

Truite Meunière

2 freshwater trout, each ½ lb. in weight
1½ oz. butter, 1 dessertspoonful oil
Plain flour
Juice of half a lemon
Chopped parsley

Ask the fishmonger to leave on the head of the trout and to clean it through the gills. Wash the fish under cold running water, and leave it to drain in a colander, sprinkled with salt. Put about 2 tablespoonfuls of flour onto a sheet of greaseproof paper. Dip each trout into the flour then, using your hands, pat it all over so that only a thin coating of flour remains.

Heat a heavy frying pan without fat for three minutes, then put in the butter and oil. The minute the butter starts to foam (but has not changed colour at all), put in the fish. Cook steadily for five minutes, by which time the underside will be brown. Carefully turn over the fish and continue to cook for a further five minutes. Lift out onto a warm serving dish. Into the butter in the pan put the lemon juice, a pinch of salt and a sprinkle of black pepper. Swirl the sauce round the pan, then pour the juices over the fish; sprinkle with parsley and serve with thick wedges of lemon.

To Grill Fish

Unlike meat, fish does not need a fierce heat, as it is unnecessary to "sear" the outside to contain the juices. Indeed, too high a heat will make the fish dry. Instead, it needs plenty of butter to keep it moist and flavoursome.

To Grill Fish for Two

Use steaks cut ¾ to 1 inch thick, and fillets cut from 1½ lb. fish. Put 1½ oz. of butter in the grill pan or in a flat, cast iron dish just large enough to contain the fish. Put it under a gentle grill to melt without browning—the melted butter should make a thin layer on the bottom of the dish. If not, add a little more butter. The minute it has melted, put the washed and salted fish into the hot butter then turn it over onto the other side. In this way both sides of the fish will be coated with the butter. Sprinkle each piece of fish with salt and pepper and dust very lightly with flour.

Grill gently but steadily without turning, allowing ten minutes for a piece ¾ inch thick, and twelve minutes for one that is 1 inch thick. Two or three minutes before the fish is done, sprinkle with a further dusting of flour, or a light sprinkle of dry bread-crumbs or cornflake crumbs. Baste with the butter twice while the fish is cooking. When the fish is done, the fillets will be a rich golden brown. Steaks will be the same colour, and the centre bone will move easily when pulled.

Serve the fish with the pan juices poured over them, and thick wedges of lemon.

Gefulte Fish

1 lb. hake, ½ lb. haddock or cod (whichever is most choice that week)
Half a large onion
1 dessertspoonful oil
Half a large raw potato
2 level teaspoonfuls sugar
1½ level teaspoonfuls salt
Speck of pepper
2 level tablespoonfuls medium matzo meal
1 half egg shell of cold water
1 large egg
1 level tablespoonful ground almonds (optional but delicious)

Gefulte fish was originally a fish "forcemeat" made from a variety of freshwater fish, which was used to stuff the skin of a carp. The whole fish was then poached in a flavoured fish stock, which jellied when it was cold.

Today we make a similar mixture, but use mainly sea fish, and poach balls of this mixture directly in the stock. The same mixture can also be fried in the same way as fillets or steaks. I do not recommend using a mixture of less than 1½ lb. of fish, (weighed when filleted), as it is just not worth the trouble. However, both gefulte fish and chopped

181

fried fish keep extremely well, so this quantity is practical even for the small family.

Ask the fishmonger to fillet and skin the fish. When you get it home, wash it under cold water, drain it in a colander for half an hour, lightly sprinkled with salt. Cut it into chunks that will slide easily into the mincer, and remove as much of the white connective tissue as you can, or it will wind itself round the mincer cutter. Put the fish, the raw potato and the onion through the fine blade of the mincer. In a large bowl beat together the egg, the seasonings, the oil and the water, then stir in the matzo meal and almonds (if used). Now add the minced fish mixture and mix thoroughly with a fork (or use the whisk of the mixer at low speed), until all the ingredients are thoroughly blended without becoming packed together. At this stage the mixture should just be firm enough to form into patties with a wet hand. Try to make one; if it is too soft, add a little more meal; if it is too solid, add a little more water. Experience will soon tell you when the mixture is just right. At this point the mixture can be shaped and cooked, or it can be foil covered and left in the bottom of the refrigerator overnight, but it will then need to be left at room temperature for half an hour the next morning before it is formed into balls.

To Poach Gefulte Fish

The Fish Stock
1 cleaned hake or haddock head (ask the fishmonger to do this) with the skin and bones from the fish
1 medium onion, sliced
2 medium carrots, sliced
2 level teaspoonfuls sugar
2 level teaspoonfuls salt
Water to cover the bones

Put the fish head, the skin and the bones into a wide-based pan. Add the salt and cover with cold water. Bring slowly to the boil, cover and simmer for half an hour, while you are shaping the fish into balls the size of small apples. Remove the skin and bones, but leave in the head (which helps the stock to jelly when it is cold). Add the carrots, the onion and the sugar, and put the fish balls into the stock. Bring to the boil, reduce the light until the stock is barely simmering, then cover and simmer for $1\frac{1}{2}$ hours. Uncover and continue to simmer for a further half hour to reduce the stock. Lift out the fish balls and put them on to a platter at least 1 inch deep. Strain the stock over and round the fish and garnish it with the carrot. Cover and chill overnight.

The same amount of ingredients will make enough stock for up to 3 lb. of fish. Just add sufficient water to cover the fish. Many people, however, like to poach half the fish balls and fry the remainder, or all the fish may be fried, according to the recipe below.

Chopped Fried Fish

With wetted hands shape the gefulte fish mixture into balls the size of small apples, then flatten into patties and roll in a bowl full of crushed cornflake crumbs or fine dry bread-crumbs, patting the crumbs on evenly. Leave on a fish board. In a heavy fish-frying pan, put enough oil to come to a depth of 1 inch, and start to heat. When the oil is hot enough to brown a cube of bread in thirty seconds (375° F on an oil thermometer) carefully lower in the first batch of fish balls. They should just be submerged in the oil, with plenty of room between them for turning when necessary.

Allow the oil to bubble gently until the fish balls are a rich brown on both sides—about six minutes in all. Lift them out with a slotted spoon, and drain on crumpled tissue paper. When quite dry, arrange them on a platter and leave in a cool larder until required. If the whole batch of fish is fried, it will make ten fish balls, or thirty cocktail-size balls.

To Poach Salmon

A cut of salmon of any size (or separate steaks)
1 lemon sliced with the peel : squeeze of lemon juice in addition
6 peppercorns
2 level teaspoonfuls of salt
Sprinkle of white pepper
Buttered greaseproof paper

This method of "boiling" salmon results in tender, moist flesh. As the fish is left in the cooking liquor overnight, it is an especially convenient method to use if you are at work during the day, for you can cook the salmon while you are preparing an evening meal the day before, and it is ready to dish up with a salad twenty-four hours later.

Wash the fish thoroughly under cold running water to remove any blood or entrails. Lay it in a colander and sprinkle it with a little salt. After ten minutes, lay it on a large double sheet of buttered greaseproof paper and sprinkle the flesh with the juice of half a lemon. Tie up like a parcel with string or a loose rubber band to close it. Put it in a lidded pan, and add enough cold water to cover it, then add the salt, pepper, peppercorns and lemon slices. Put on the lid and bring slowly to the boil. This should take about half an hour. Boil for two minutes only, then turn out the light and leave the salmon covered in the pan, if possible overnight, or at least until the cooking liquor is quite cold. Just before serving, lift from the pan, drain well, and open the parcel. Skin and divide it into portions, then serve with mayonnaise.

Halibut in Egg and Lemon Sauce

4 halibut steaks (approximately 1½ lb. in all)
1 large onion, thinly sliced
6 level tablespoonfuls sugar, 2 level
teaspoonfuls salt, speck of white pepper
Water to cover the fish (approximately ¾ pint)

This delicious fish dish will keep for three or four days under refrigeration, and in any case tastes better the day after it has been made. If it is to be served as an entrée rather than a main course, the fish should be cut into six rather than four pieces, as halibut is a very substantial fish.

In a saucepan or lidded frying pan wide enough to hold all the fish in one layer, bring the water, the onion and the seasonings to the boil (adding the sugar at this stage greatly improves the taste of the fish, without noticeably sweetening it). Put in the washed and salted steaks, bring the liquid back to the boil, then lower the heat so that the liquid is barely bubbling. Partially cover the pan and simmer very gently for twenty minutes. Lift out the fish with a slotted spoon or fish slice, draining any liquid back into the pan. Place the fish in an oval entrée dish about 1½ inches in depth. Remove the skin but leave the bone. Leave to cool while you make the sauce.

Sauce
2 large eggs, 8 fl. oz. fish liquor
Juice of 2 lemons (3 fl. oz.)
1 level teaspoonful potato starch

After the fish has been removed, boil the fish liquor for three minutes to concentrate the flavour, then strain it and measure out 8 fl. oz. (a glassful). Beat the eggs thoroughly with a rotary whisk, then stir in the fish liquor and the potato flour (which has been mixed to a cream with the minimum of cold water). Put this liquid into a thick-bottomed saucepan and cook gently over low heat until the sauce thickens to the consistency of a coating custard —you will need to stir it constantly. Do not let it boil, or the eggs may curdle. Taste and add extra juice, if necessary, to make the sauce equally sweet and sour. Pour the sauce over the fish, coating it completely. Leave in a cool place overnight, covered with foil. Serve garnished with parsley.

Makes four generous helpings.

Vegetables

To Cook Fresh Green Vegetables

To conserve their colour and food value, all green vegetables should be cooked as rapidly as possible in the minimum of boiling water, then served as soon as they are barely tender.

Prepare the vegetables according to the variety (see below). Have ready a heavy-based saucepan with a tight-fitting lid, in which is boiling $\frac{1}{4}$ pint of water seasoned with 1 level teaspoonful of salt. Put in the prepared vegetables, bring the water back to the boil, put on the pan lid and then boil rapidly for ten to fifteen minutes, or until the vegetables feel barely tender when pierced with a slim knife. Pour off any liquid that is left and use it in soups and gravies, as it will be rich in mineral salts. Put the vegetables into a serving dish and top with a knob of butter (or margarine for a meat meal) and serve at once.

Preparation. Sprouts: Remove any discoloured outer leaves, and examine each sprout closely for maggots. If any are seen, discard the sprout. Make two little nicks in the stalk end (to hasten the cooking) then leave in water to cover, plus 1 level teaspoonful salt, for half an hour. Rinse well, and cook as above.

Cauliflower: Cut the flowerets free from the stalk end. Soak as above and cook.

Spring cabbage: Remove the coarse outer leaves and discard. Rinse the tender inner leaves under the cold tap, one at a time. Put on a chopping board and shred finely. Cook as above. When tender, drain well, put on board and chop till fine. Mix with a nut of butter or margarine.

White cabbage: Cut in quarters and remove the stalk. Cut each quarter into thin shreds and soak in salted water as for sprouts. Add 1 oz. of margarine to the cooking water, then proceed as above. When the cabbage is tender, strain, turn onto a board and chop until fine.

French beans : Remove strings, rinse under cold tap, cut in diagonal slices and cook as above.

Broad beans and peas : Shell and cook as above.

To Bake Potatoes

**1 medium potato per person
butter or margarine**

This method conserves all the nourishment which lies under the skin and is usually discarded with the potato peelings.

Set the oven at Gas No. 6 (400° F). Choose potatoes of an even size, so that they will be ready at the same time. Scrub thoroughly with a nylon pan scrub kept for the purpose, then remove any eyes with a potato peeler. Dry thoroughly, and prick all over with a fork (to stop the potato bursting).

Rub each potato with a butter or margarine wrapper to give it a light coating of fat. Arrange on a baking tin.

Cook for one to one and a half hours (depending on size) until the potato feels tender when it is gently squeezed.

To serve. Squeeze the skin to break it and allow some of the steam to escape from inside. This makes the potato floury and light. Serve in an uncovered dish to prevent the skin going soggy. Pass the butter, salt and a pepper mill. Soured cream flavoured with 2 teaspoonfuls of finely cut chives makes a delicious accompaniment.

Chips for Two

This is the simplest method of cooking chips for two.

**2 large potatoes (weighing ¾ lb. together)
A large heavy frying pan, filled with oil 1 inch
   deep**

Peel the potatoes, cut them into slices ⅜ inch thick, then cut the slices into strips ⅜ inch wide. Result : chips of equal width and depth (this is important for even cooking). If you are great chip eaters, you can, of course, invest in a chipper. Put the chips in cold water and leave for an hour—this preliminary soaking dissolves excess surface starch. Drain and dry thoroughly in a tea towel. Heat the oil over a moderate light for about five minutes until a chip sizzles gently when it is put in. Carefully put the remainder of the chips into the oil and cook at a steady but busy bubble for seven to ten minutes, or until they look a rich crisp brown. Lift out with a slotted spoon, drain briefly on crumpled tissue paper, and serve at once.

Serves two.

Fried Potatoes

1 lb. potatoes (boiled in their skins)
1 oz. butter
1 tablespoonful oil
   or
1 tablespoonful chicken fat
1 tablespoonful oil for a meat meal
Salt and black pepper

These are often more convenient to cook for two people than roast potatoes or chips. The potatoes should be fried slowly at first, so as to absorb the fat, and then more quickly just before serving, to make them crisp. Cold left-over potatoes can be used, but the finest results are achieved with potatoes cooked in their skins.

Scrub the potatoes, then cook them whole in their skins, covered with boiling salted water for twenty-five to forty minutes, depending on their size. Drain the potatoes, and return to the empty pan to dry off on a low light. Leave until cool enough to handle, then skin and cut into thick slices or cubes.

To fry. Put the oil and butter in a heavy frying pan. When the butter starts to foam, put in the potatoes and cook very gently, shaking the pan occasionally so that the potatoes absorb the fat rather than fry in it. This will take about fifteen minutes. When the potatoes are golden all over, increase the heat to make them crisp. Drain from the fat (there should be very little, if any, left), put in a dish and sprinkle with salt and black pepper.

To fry in chicken fat and oil. Heat the two fats together over moderate heat for five minutes, then put in the potatoes. They should sizzle slightly. Continue to cook as above.

Serves two.

Perfect Mashed Potatoes

1 lb. potatoes
1 level teaspoonful salt, speck of white pepper
1 oz. butter
4 tablespoonfuls hot milk

Mashed potatoes are made fluffy by whisking them over a low light with butter and hot milk (or margarine or chicken fat for a meat meal).

Peel the potatoes, cut them into quarters and put into a saucepan in which enough water is boiling to cover them. Add the salt, bring back to the boil, cover, then cook at a steady boil for fifteen minutes, or until a potato feels absolutely tender when pierced with a thin vegetable knife. (Do not boil potatoes too vigorously or they may become "soupy".) Take the pan to the sink, hold the lid at an angle to prevent the potatoes falling out, then drain off all the water. Return to the cooker and leave on a low

187

light until every drop of moisture has evaporated from the potatoes.

For a milk meal. Pour the milk down the side of the pan and cut the butter on top of the potatoes. When the milk is seen to be bubbling, beat it into the potatoes together with the butter, using a wire "balloon" whisk. Add a little more milk if the potatoes seem to be too dry. Continue to beat on a very low light until the mixture looks lighter in colour and fluffy in texture—about three minutes. Taste and add salt and pepper if necessary. Pile into a warm vegetable dish and serve as soon as possible. Mashed potatoes soon lose their Vitamin C content when kept hot.

For a meat meal. Proceed exactly as above, but omit the milk and substitute 1 rounded tablespoonful of chicken fat or 1 oz. of margarine for the butter.

Serves two.

Potato Latkes

2 large potatoes (1 breakfast cupful when grated)
1 large egg
½ level teaspoonful salt
1 level tablespoonful grated onion (may be omitted)
2 level tablespoonfuls self-raising flour

The secret of potato latkes is to drain off as much as possible of the starchy liquid that oozes out of the grated potatoes.

Grate the potatoes so finely that they are almost a pulp. Leave in a sieve to drain for ten minutes. (It does not matter if they turn brown.) Meanwhile, beat the egg until fluffy, then add the seasonings, the onion and the drained potatoes. Finally, fold in the flour.

In a heavy frying pan, put enough oil to come to a depth of half an inch. Heat until a little of the raw mixture sizzles when it is put into the fat. Put tablespoonfuls of the mixture into the hot fat, flattening each latke with the back of the spoon. Cook over moderate heat for five minutes, or until the underside is a rich brown, then turn and cook the other side. The latkes should be crunchy and crisp on the outside and creamy within. Drain on crumpled tissue paper and serve at once.

Serves two.

Roast Potatoes

1 lb. potatoes
Oil and margarine
Salt

If the potatoes are parboiled before roasting, rather than put in the oven raw, they develop a crisp yet tender crust and a deliciously soft inside.

Peel the potatoes and cut them (if large) into slices 1 inch thick. Put in a pan half-full of boiling water, add 1 level teaspoonful salt and bring slowly back to the boil. Cook until the potatoes are almost, but not quite, tender—they will feel slightly hard when pierced with a slim vegetable knife. This will take about fifteen to twenty minutes. Drain the potatoes, then return them to the empty pan and shake over a low light until they look absolutely dry. Meanwhile put in the oven a shallow roasting tin (just large enough to hold the potato slices in one layer) which has a thin layer of oil covering the bottom. The oven can be set at any moderate temperature (whichever is the most convenient for the main dish cooking at the same time). At Gas No. 3 (335° F) it will take the oil ten minutes to heat; at Gas No. 5 (375° F) it will take seven minutes. Put the tin of hot oil on the cooker, add a nut of margarine, then carefully lay the potatoes in it, and immediately turn them over so that they are coated with the hot fat. Sprinkle lightly with salt and return to the oven.

Cook at Gas No. 3 (335° F) for one and a quarter to one and a half hours.

Cook at Gas No. 5 (375° F) for one hour.

At either temperature, turn the potatoes at half-time.

Serves two.

Savoury Lokshen Pudding

4 oz. egg noodles
1 large egg
4 level tablespoonfuls rendered chicken fat, or margarine
2 level tablespoonfuls of grebenes
Salt and pepper

This can be served as a soup accompaniment, or in place of potatoes with the main course. The flavour is best when chicken fat is used as well as grebenes—the cracklings from the rendered fat.

Turn the oven to Gas No. 2 (315° F). Half fill an 8-inch diameter pan with cold water, add 1 level teaspoonful of salt and bring to the boil. Then add the lokshen, stir until the water comes back to the boil, half cover the pan and allow to boil steadily for eight minutes. (Do not cover tightly, or the water will froth over the side of the pan.) Taste a piece of lokshen. It should be "bite" tender. Turn into a metal sieve, but do not rinse under the cold tap, because the starch on the outside of the lokshen helps to "set" the pudding. Allow the lokshen to drain completely.

189

Put the chicken fat, or margarine, into a 2 pint casserole and leave in the oven for five minutes.

Meanwhile, beat the egg, add the grebenes, a pinch of salt and pepper, and the drained noodles. Take the hot dish out of the oven, swirl the fat round to coat the sides, then pour it onto the noodle mixture. Stir well, then spoon into the casserole. Bake for one and a half hours or until crispy on top and set within.

Lokshen kugel can be cooked in a Gas No. ¼ (200° F) oven overnight, but double the quantity must be used if the dish is not to be dry.

Salad Dressings

It is useful to have ready-mixed dressings in plastic containers always in stock in the refrigerator. It is then a matter of moments to make a variety of delicious salads, either from crisp greens or cooked or fresh vegetables.

French Dressing (To Store)

¼ pint corn or olive oil
3 tablespoonfuls wine or cider vinegar, or lemon juice
1 level teaspoonful salt
10 grinds of black pepper
Pinch of paprika
Pinch of sugar
Makes a cupful of dressing (enough for two servings on three occasions)

This is the basic dressing for mixed green salads. Add the herbs just before use, as they lose their colour if stored.

Place all the ingredients in a screw-top jar and shake until thickened—about two minutes.

Herb dressing. To a third of the dressing, add 2 teaspoonfuls of chopped herbs—basil, parsley, chives, tarragon or any combination of two or more of them. Use on a crisp green salad. Only enough dressing should be tossed with the greens to coat the leaves. Do this at the table.

Garlic dressing. To a third of the dressing, add a quarter of a clove of garlic, and leave for one hour before use. Discard the garlic before dressing the salad.

¼ pint mild olive oil
4 tablespoonfuls wine vinegar
2 tablespoonfuls lemon juice
1 peeled clove of garlic
2 level teaspoonfuls caster sugar
1 level teaspoonful made mustard
2 level teaspoonfuls chopped mixed herbs—such as chervil, parsley or chives
1 level teaspoonful salt, few grinds black pepper
1 level tablespoonful finely chopped onion

Sauce vinaigrette. A sharper dressing suitable for bland vegetables such as tomatoes, French beans, or artichoke hearts. This is the dressing to serve with avocado on the half shell or chilled artichokes, or to dress a hearty mixed salad such as Salade Niçoise.

Put the sugar, salt, onion, herbs and mustard into a screw-top jar and add the oil, vinegar and lemon juice. Shake vigorously for two to three minutes, until thickened. Leave for one hour before use. Serves six. If only a third of the

190

dressing is to be used (for two servings), add the herbs just before serving.

Blender Mayonnaise

1 whole egg, or two yolks (whichever is most convenient at the time)
1 tablespoonful lemon juice
2 level teaspoonfuls dry mustard
¼ pint corn oil, ¼ pint mild olive oil
1 level teaspoonful sugar
Speck of cayenne pepper
1 level teaspoonful salt
1 tablespoonful boiling water

If you have an electric blender or mixer, or a stout rotary whisk, I strongly recommend that you make your own mayonnaise. Either of the recipes below keeps well under refrigeration, and the flavour is superb.

Put the whole egg or the yolks into the blender, add the salt, pepper, sugar, mustard, and cayenne pepper, and blend at high speed for thirty seconds or until foamy. Add the lemon juice and blend for ten seconds. Uncover blender and add the ¼-pint of corn oil very slowly, trickling it in, with the blender at high speed. When all is in and the mayonnaise has thickened, add the olive oil and blend until it has been absorbed. Finally, add the boiling water to thin the mayonnaise to the consistency of thick cream. Makes ¾ pint. Store in the bottom of the refrigerator in a screw-top jar or plastic container. Do not freeze.

Whisked Mayonnaise

12 fl. oz. oil (all corn oil or half-and-half corn and olive oil)
2 egg yolks
1 level teaspoonful dry mustard
1 level teaspoonful French mustard
1 level teaspoonful each salt and sugar
Pinch of cayenne pepper
1 tablespoonful lemon juice
1 tablespoonful wine vinegar
1 tablespoonful boiling water

This must be more carefully made, as the oil must be added a drop at a time until the mayonnaise has started to thicken. The oil should be at room temperature. If it is too warm, the sauce may not thicken.

Beat the egg yolks until thick and creamy, then beat in all the seasonings and continue to beat. Add half the lemon juice. Now start dribbling the oil down the side of the mixing bowl, beating constantly, and adding more oil only when the previous addition has been absorbed. Once the mixture starts to thicken, the oil can be added more quickly, using the remaining lemon juice to thin the mixture down. When all the oil has been beaten in, whisk in the vinegar and the boiling water. Taste and add more seasonings if necessary. Store in a closed container in the bottom of the refrigerator. Makes rather more than ¾ pint of mayonnaise.

Charoset

3 oz. walnuts
¼ large cooking apple
2 level teaspoonfuls sugar
2 level teaspoonfuls cinnamon
Kosher wine to moisten the mixture

It is a pleasant tradition for the man of the house to make the "mortar" for the Seder table. This recipe cannot fail.

Use a "hackmesser" to chop the walnuts with the apple until both are very fine. Moisten with the kosher wine, and flavour with the cinnamon and sugar. The consistency should be that of mortar. Enough for a family of eight for two Sedarim.

Boiled Rice

Half a large cup of Patna rice
1 large cup of chicken stock (or water, plus a knob of chicken fat)
½ level teaspoonful salt

When time is short, it is often more convenient to cook rice rather than potatoes, as rice can go straight from packet to pan. This method uses packeted Patna rice, which has already been cleaned.

Bring liquid to boil with the salt, add rice, and stir until bubbling again. Cover tightly and simmer very gently for fifteen minutes. Turn off the heat and leave the pan covered in a warm place for a further ten minutes so that rice fluffs up in its own steam. Use as required, in any dish calling for boiled rice.

Serves two.

Risotto

Half a small onion, finely chopped
2 oz. mushrooms
3 chicken livers (optional)
1 tablespoonful chicken fat, 1 tablespoonful oil
  or
1 oz. margarine, 1 tablespoonful oil
1 teaspoonful tomato purée
1 crushed clove of garlic
6 oz. rice
I pint strong chicken stock
Pinch of salt
Few grinds of black pepper
Pinch of sugar

This is more savoury, and can be made into a main dish by the addition of left-over pieces of chicken, a few peas, and a few toasted almonds. This recipe will serve four. To make less is not worthwhile. Any left-over will keep under refrigeration for several days. It can then be reheated with a little extra stock.

Set the oven at Gas No. 4 (350°F). Put the chicken stock to heat in a small pan. Chop the onion and mushrooms finely, and slice the koshered livers (if used). In a heavy frying pan or heatproof casserole melt the fats and sauté the onion gently for five minutes, until soft and golden. Do not allow it to become crisp. Add the livers (if used) and the mushrooms and sauté for a further two minutes. Add the rice and stir well. Cook for three minutes, then pour on half the hot stock, and simmer until it has been absorbed. Now add the garlic, the purée and the seasonings, together with the remainder of the stock. Cover and transfer to the oven. Cook for eighteen minutes, by which time all the stock will have been absorbed and the grains of the rice will be separate and fluffy.

Serves two twice, or four at one meal.

Desserts

1 jam Swiss roll
1 can apricot halves in heavy syrup
1 packet kosher orange jelly
Juice of a lemon
1 tablespoonful whole fruit apricot jam
3 tablespoonfuls sherry, or apricot brandy or
    orange liqueur, such as Cointreau
$\frac{1}{4}$ pt. double cream, $\frac{1}{4}$ pt. single cream
1 level tablespoonful caster sugar
Decorations of glacè cherries, angelica and
    split, blanched almonds
Custard made with:
3 level tablespoonfuls custard powder
3 level tablespoonfuls sugar
1 pint milk

Chanucah Trifle

A trifle for Chanucah is a tradition in many Anglo-Jewish households. The trifle bowl should be deep and narrow rather than wide and shallow, so that each layer of mixture is deep enough to taste.

Put the jelly into a small, heavy saucepan, barely cover with hot water and heat gently, stirring all the time until dissolved. Pour into a glass measure, add the apricot jam, the lemon juice and enough syrup strained from the fruit to make up to a pint. Leave to cool. Slice the Swiss roll and arrange in the bottom of the trifle bowl. Top with the drained fruit, and then cover with the jelly. Leave to set. Make the custard according to the maker's directions.

Put into a bowl and cover with a piece of greasepaper wrung out in cold water—this prevents the formation of a skin. When the jelly has set, take the paper off the custard and whisk in the sherry, brandy or liqueur. Pour the custard over the jelly and leave the trifle to set once more. An hour before dinner, whisk the two creams together until thickened, then add the sugar and whisk again, until the mixture forms a peak when the beater is withdrawn. Do this beating by hand rather than with an electric mixer, for if cream is beaten too vigorously for too long it turns into butter.

Spoon or pipe the cream over the custard and decorate with the sliced cherries, angelica and blanched almonds. Put back in the refrigerator until required.

This will serve six to eight.

Cheese Blintzes

The tenderness of a blintze depends on cooking as thin a layer of batter as possible, as quickly as possible. To do this you will need a 6-inch frying pan with rounded sides so that the batter can be swirled round the pan, rather than tending to settle in a thick layer at the bottom.

The Batter
4 oz. plain flour
Pinch of salt
2 large eggs
8 fl. oz. of milk and water (half-and-half)

194

Sift the flour and salt into a bowl. Make a well in the centre and drop in the eggs and a third of the liquid. Gradually stir in the surrounding flour with a spoon, then add the second third of milk and water. Beat with a rotary beater, until the surface of the mixture is covered with tiny bubbles. Stir in the remaining milk and water, and leave in the refrigerator for an hour to allow the starch grains in the flour to soften.

Have ready a dish of butter and a saucer of oil. Take a 6-inch frying pan and put it over medium heat for three minutes. Drop in a teaspoonful of oil and rub it thoroughly round the sides and bottom of the hot pan, using a thick wedge of tissue paper.

Have the batter ready in a jug. Rub the tissue over the surface of the butter, then smear it very lightly over the pan. Immediately, pour in some batter and swirl it round, so that it coats the sides of the pan as well, then immediately pour it back into the jug. A thin layer of batter will be left in the pan. By the time the sides have curled away from the pan, the bottom will be brown and the top dry. Turn the pancake out onto a sheet of greaseproof paper covering a wooden board. Lightly re-butter the pan, and repeat the cooking process until all the pancakes have been made—there should be twelve pancakes. As each one stops steaming stack it on top of the others. Keep the heat moderate all the time.

The Filling
¾ lb. curd cheese
Pinch each of sugar and salt
2 tablespoonfuls top milk or single cream
Blend all the ingredients together

To stuff the blintzes. Lay each pancake on a board, brown side up. Spread a tablespoonful of the filling thinly over the bottom half, turn in the sides and roll up into a long thin roll. At this stage, the blintzes can be covered and refrigerated until required—overnight if necessary.

14

To serve. Put an ovenproof plate to heat in a low oven. In a large, heavy frying pan, gently melt 2 oz. of butter and a dessertspoonful of oil. The minute the butter stops foaming, put in the blintzes, joint upwards. Cook gently on the first side for three minutes or until golden brown, then turn and cook on the other side. Blintzes may be kept hot for ten minutes in a moderate oven, and then served plain or with a jug of ice-cold soured cream. Enough for six.

Fruit Salad

The basis of any fruit salad is a lemon syrup. When this is poured over any combination of cut-up fresh fruit, it draws out their natural juices, so that, after serveral hours, the fruit is immersed in a delicious fresh fruit syrup.

The Syrup
The juice of 1 large lemon
2 oz. sugar
Any juice that comes out of the fruit
  (especially the orange) as it is being prepared

The Fruit
4 large Jaffa oranges
¼ lb. black grapes
3 firm, ripe bananas
  or
3 large Jaffa oranges
1 small can of pineapple titbits (save the juice
  for other use)
Half a small melon, cut into balls
¼ lb. grapes

The combination of fruits can be varied according to the season. However, in making your choice, always include something juicy (like orange); something crisp (like apple, pineapple or fresh melon); something soft (like grapes, bananas, pears). A small can of pineapple titbits or fruit salad cocktail will enliven any fresh fruit salad. Also useful are small cans of blackcurrants, morello cherries, or loganberries. which will add tartness to an otherwise bland mixture. Bananas and grapes are always best added just before the fruit salad is served.

To prepare oranges, use a small, very sharp knife to cut the peel and pith off each orange as though it were an apple. Hold the fruit in the left hand, and, with the right, cut vertically between each two sections of pith, so that the orange flesh drops out. Put into a bowl. When all the orange sections have been removed in this way, take the "skeleton" of the orange and squeeze it in your palm, so that the remaining juice flows into a small pan. Add to the pan the sugar and lemon juice, and stir over a low light until the sugar has dissolved. Pour over the oranges and leave. At this point, also add the pineapple titbits and melon balls, or other fruit (if used). Half an hour before serving, add the bananas cut into slices and the grapes, halved and pipped. Stir well, then refrigerate until needed.

Flavour note. For variation, 1 tablespoonful of whole apricot jam, or 1 tablespoonful of raspberry jam can be added to the lemon syrup before it is poured over the fruit. The variations of a fruit salad are endless, and experiments will soon provide a dozen different combinations of fruit.

This amount serves four people generously.

Steamed Chanucah Pudding

Make this a month before Chanucah, and it will have time to deepen in colour and flavour. If you use a steamer to cook the pudding. make sure the water in the bottom never goes off the boil, and top it up as necessary with boiling water from the kettle. If the pudding is to be boiled, stand it on a trivet to lift it slightly off the bottom of the pan. Have enough boiling water in the pan to come one-third of the way up the basin. In both cases, the pan lid must be a tight fit.

Melt the margarine and sugar together over gentle heat. Sift the flour with the salt and spices. Now put all the ingredients into a large bowl and beat vigorously, either by hand or by machine, until thoroughly blended—about three minutes. Divide the mixture between two greased 2-pint pudding basins. Cover the top with a double thickness of greaseproof paper and then with a layer of foil. Steam or boil the puddings for six hours, or cook in the pressure cooker according to the makers' directions.

To store. When quite cold, take off the paper and foil lids and cover with a fresh piece of foil. Leave in a cool, dry cupboard. On the day the pudding is to be used, steam for a further three hours. These puddings will keep for months. Serve with wine sauce. Each pudding will serve six.

To make two 1½-lb. puddings
4 oz. margarine
4 oz. soft brown sugar
2 beaten eggs
Grated rind and juice of 1 orange
Grated rind of half a lemon
2 tablespoonfuls brandy
4 tablespoonfuls (⅛ pint) of Guinness or other stout
1 small apple, peeled, cored and grated
4 oz. fresh white bread crumbs
2 oz. blanched and chopped almonds or walnuts
2 oz. cut mixed peel
½ lb. currants
6 oz. sultanas
4 oz. raisins
4 oz. plain flour
Pinch each of salt, nutmeg and mixed spice

Wine Sauce

This sauce can be made long before it is to be served, left standing in warm water, and reheated over boiling water when needed.

Put the yolks and sugar into a basin or the top half of a double saucepan. Whisk together until the mixture is pale and thick and will fall in a continuous "ribbon" from the beater. Stir in the cornflour, the wine and the brandy. Stand the basin or pan over another half-full of boiling water, and whisk until the mixture thickens enough to coat

2 egg yolks
2 oz. caster sugar
1 level teaspoonful cornflour
8 fl. oz. kosher red wine or Israeli hock
1 tablespoonful brandy or orange-flavoured liqueur, such as Cointreau

197

the back of a wooden spoon. If a tarter flavour is preferred, add the juice of half a lemon. Serve with the pudding. Enough to serve six.

Sweet Lokshen Pudding

4 oz. broad lokshen (egg noodles)
1 large egg
2 oz. caster sugar
Pinch each of cinnamon and salt
Grated rind of half a lemon
2 tablespoonfuls seeded raisins, coarsely chopped
  or
2 tablespoonfuls currants which have been plumped in boiling water for five minutes
1 oz. margarine

A lokshen pudding can be varied with the dish that is used. In a narrow deep dish it will be more puddingy than when cooked in a shallower, wider dish, in which it will have a crisper top. In any case the dish used must have a 2-pint capacity. It can be reheated if covered with foil and left in a moderate oven (Gas No. 4, 350° F) for twenty minutes. A lokshen pudding can be left to cook overnight at Gas No. ¼, or at the lowest temperature setting of an electric oven, but this is only successful if the quantities given below are doubled.

Set the oven to Gas No. 2 (315° F). Half fill an 8-inch (diameter) pan with cold water, add 1 level teaspoonful of salt, and bring to the boil. Then add the lokshen, stir until the water comes back to the boil, half cover, and allow to boil steadily for eight minutes. (If the pan lid is on completely, the water may froth over the top.) Taste a piece; it should be "bite" tender. Turn into a metal sieve and hold under the cold water tap until the water runs clear—this means that any excess sticky starch has been washed away. Allow to drain completely.

Put the margarine into the baking dish and put into the hot oven to melt. Beat the egg until frothy, using a rotary egg-beater, then add the sugar, continuing to beat until thickened. Then stir in the seasonings and the raisins. Add the cooked noodles and stir well with a wooden spoon, until they are evenly coated with the egg mixture. Taste, and add a little more sugar if you feel it is necessary. As soon as the margarine has melted in the baking dish, take the dish from the oven, and swirl the margarine round inside so that it coats the sides. This makes the pudding deliciously crisp round the edges. Tip the margarine into the noodle mixture, stir and pour back into the dish. Bake near the bottom of the oven for one and a half hours, or until the inside is set and the top is crisp and brown.

Serves four people.

---

2 large baking apples
1 dessertspoonful lemon juice
2 tablespoonfuls water
1 oz. sugar
Topping
2 oz. flour
1 oz. porridge oats (1 heaped tablespoonful)
2 oz. butter (or margarine for a meat meal)
3 oz. soft brown sugar

Apple Crisp

A delicious combination of soft juicy fruit and crunchy topping. It can be prepared one day and baked the next.

Peel, core, and quarter the apples. Cut into slices an eighth of an inch thick. Arrange in a greased 1-pint casserole, about 2 inches in depth. Sprinkle with the lemon juice and water, and cover with the sugar. *For the topping,* mix together the flour, the porridge oats and the brown sugar in a large bowl, then gently rub in the margarine. Sprinkle this crumble over the apples, and pat it gently into a flat layer. Bake in a moderate oven (Gas No. 5, 375° F) for thirty minutes, until the top is a rich, crunchy brown. Serve plain, or with pouring cream or custard. Serves two to three.

Damson or Plum Crunch

This can be made in the same way as apple crisp. Arrange 1 lb. stewed fruit or a small can of fruit in the bottom of the casserole, and surround with juice to a depth of half an inch. Cover with topping, and bake in the same way as the apple crisp.

Apple Sponge

Use the same raw apple mixture as for the apple crisp, or left-over stewed fruit. In either case the topping is the same.

2 oz. butter (or margarine) soft enough to spread
2 oz. caster sugar
1 teaspoonful grated lemon rind
1 large egg
2½ oz. self-raising flour
1 tablespoonful water

Put all the ingredients into a bowl, and beat together until smooth and creamy—about two minutes. Spoon over the fruit and spread level. Bake in a quick moderate oven (Gas No. 5, 375° F) for thirty minutes, or until golden brown and firm to the touch. Serves two to four.

Biscuits

8 oz. plain flour
½ level teaspoonful baking powder
5 oz. butter
3 oz. caster sugar
About 2 tablespoonfuls of beaten egg
1 teaspoonful vanilla essence

The Topping
2 level tablespoonfuls caster sugar
2 level tablespoonfuls finely chopped almonds
½ level teaspoonful cinnamon

Jodekager (Jewish Cakes)

A delicious rolled butter biscuit of Danish origin which can be served as a treat on Shabbat or Yomtov. You will find the method easy once you have mastered the making of shortcrust pastry.

Sift the flour and baking powder into a large bowl. Cut the butter into 1-inch cubes, then gently rub into flour with the fingertips, until the mixture resembles coarse crumbs. Stir in the sugar and vanilla, and add enough of the egg to make a soft, but non-sticky, dough, Chill for an hour if possible, to make the dough easier to handle. When ready to roll out, set the oven at Gas No. 6 (400° F).

Lightly sprinkle a pastry board and rolling pin with flour. Put the dough on the board, tap the dough with the pin to flatten it, then roll out with short sharp strokes, turning the dough a quarter-turn clockwise after each few strokes, to prevent it sticking to the board. Do not, however turn the dough over, as this may toughen it. When the dough is an eighth of an inch thick, cut it into rounds or crescents, using a floured biscuit cutter. Lift with a spatula onto oiled biscuit trays. Paint the top with the remainder of the beaten egg. Mix the topping ingredients together, then sprinkle evenly on top of the biscuits.

Bake the biscuits for eight to nine minutes, or until golden brown. Do not overbake, for they burn easily.

Makes about three dozen biscuits.

Quick Kichlach (Biscuits)

2 eggs
¼ pint oil
2 teaspoonfuls vanilla essence
The grated rind of half a lemon
5 oz. caster sugar
8 oz. self-raising flour
Pinch of salt
Sugar, oil and nuts for decoration

The traditional kichel (biscuit) is made with oil, and rolled out on a sugared board, This is a tedious business. The two recipes below, one made with oil, and the other with butter, are much quicker to make. In one, the mixture is dropped from a teaspoon, in the other it is formed into balls between the palms of the hands. Both are delicious.

Set the oven at Gas No. 6 (400° F). Beat the eggs with a

large fork until frothy, then stir in the oil, the vanilla and the lemon rind. Next, blend in the sugar until the mixture starts to thicken. Sift the flour and the salt on top of this mixture and stir until blended. The mixture will be soft. Drop rounded teaspoonfuls of the mixture from the tip of a spoon on to lightly oiled baking sheets, leaving 2 inches between them. Dip the bottom of a tumbler first in a saucer of oil and then in a saucer of granulated sugar; then use it to flatten each biscuit in turn, recoating with oil and sugar when the glass starts to stick. Decorate each biscuit with chopped walnuts or almond nibs. Bake for ten minutes, or until golden brown. Remove from the tin using a flexible spatula, and leave to cool on a tray. Store in an airtight tin when quite cold.

Makes three dozen.

Gertrude's Kichlach

4 oz. melted butter
4 oz. caster sugar
1 large egg (beaten until frothy)
Grated rind of half a lemon
8 oz. self-raising flour
Granulated sugar for rolling

Set the oven at Gas No. 5 (375° F). Melt the butter very gently until it liquefies, but has not separated or boiled. Put in a mixing bowl and whisk with the sugar for two minutes until thickened, then beat in the egg followed by the lemon rind and the self-raising flour. Leave to firm up for ten minutes. Roll between the wetted palms into walnut-sized balls, then roll each ball in a saucer of granulated sugar. Arrange 2 inches apart on oiled baking tins. Bake for fifteen to eighteen minutes, or until golden brown.

Makes about thirty.

Vanilla Kipferl

4 oz. plain flour
2 oz. ground almonds
4 oz. butter
Generous 2 oz. of icing sugar
Pinch of salt
1 teaspoonful vanilla essence

A short and crunchy almond biscuit, which it is appropriate to make for Tu b'Shvat (New Year for Trees).

Cream the butter until soft, then beat in the icing sugar and salt. Stir in the essence, the almonds and the flour, and mix thoroughly until a dough is formed. Chill dough for half an hour. Set the oven at Gas No. 3 (325° F). Take teaspoonfuls of the dough and roll between your palm and the pastry board into a 3-inch long pencil, then curve in the ends to form a crescent. Place the biscuits on ungreased baking sheets.

Bake the biscuits for fifteen to eighteen minutes, until firm to the touch, but very pale gold in colour. Lift onto a cooling tray and leave for five minutes. Then roll one at a time in a basin of sifted icing sugar. Makes thirty biscuits. These keep extremely well if stored in an airtight tin.

Golden Buttons

A deliciously crunchy biscuit that is very quickly made.

3 oz. self-raising flour
Pinch of salt
3 oz. caster sugar
3 oz. rolled oats or porridge oats
1 level tablespoonful golden syrup
3 oz. butter
½ level teaspoonful bicarbonate of soda
1 tablespoonful cold milk

Set the oven at Gas No. 5 (375° F). Put the butter, syrup and sugar into a small pan, and heat gently until the sugar has dissolved. Do not allow to boil. Put the flour, salt and oats into a large bowl, then pour on the melted mixture. Put the bicarbonate into a cup and add the milk. Stir, and then pour onto the biscuit mixture. Stir well, Leave for ten to fifteen minutes for the mixture to stiffen—it should be like plasticine. Take walnut-sized pieces of the dough and roll into little balls between the palms. Place on greased baking trays, leaving 2 inches in between balls, as the biscuits spread in the oven. Bake for ten minutes or until golden brown. Take out of the oven and leave for five minutes, then lift off the baking trays with a spatula, and put on a wire cooling rack. When quite cold, store in a tin. Makes thirty.

Cakes

Cheese Cakes

There are as many kinds of cheese cake as there are Jewish cooks. However, the two recipes below are superb examples of the two main varieties—the Continental or American cheese cake, and the traditional Russian or Polish cheese cake. Both are very simple to make.

Traditional Cheese Cake

The Pastry
6 oz. plain flour
4 oz. butter
1 level tablespoonful icing sugar
Small pinch of salt
Grated rind of half a lemon, 1 teaspoonful lemon juice
The yolk of an egg with 1 dessertspoonful of water

Mix the flour, the sugar and the salt together in a bowl. Blend the egg yolk, the water and the lemon juice. Rub the butter gently into the flour mixture, until no lumps larger than a small pea appear on the surface when the bowl is shaken. Sprinkle the mixture with the liquid, and gather into a ball with the hand. The dough should be firm. Turn onto a lightly floured board and knead very gently until smooth and free of cracks. If possible, chill for half an hour, and then roll out until only one-eighth of an inch thick, to fit a 7-inch sandwich tin. Set the oven at Gas No. 6 (400° F).

The Filling
½ lb. curd cheese
1 egg, well beaten
1 tablespoonful currants (which have been plumped for five minutes in boiling water)
Rind and juice of half a lemon
1–2 oz. caster sugar (depending on sourness of cheese)
2 tablespoonfuls top milk or single cream

Mix all the filling ingredients together, then spoon into the unbaked cake. Roll out the pastry left-overs into long strips, and make a lattice work on top of the filling, sealing each strip of pastry to the edge of the flan tin with cold water. Beat up the left-over egg white until it is frothy, then paint it over the pastry and the top of the filling. Sprinkle lightly with granulated sugar. Bake for ten minutes, then turn the oven down to Gas No. 4 (350° F) and cook for another twenty-five minutes, or until the filling is set and golden.

American Cheese Cake

Enough thinly-sliced trifle sponges to cover the bottom of the tin to be used
1 lb. curd cheese
2 oz. caster sugar

This cake should be made the day before it is to be eaten, and refrigerated overnight. The sponge cake base is easy, and tastes delicious in combination with the creamy filling.

2 oz. melted butter
2 eggs (separated)
½ teaspoonful vanilla essence
1 level tablespoonful cornflour mixed to a cream with the top of a bottle of milk or 3 tablespoonfuls single cream

Topping
5 oz. carton soured cream
1 teaspoonful caster sugar
Pinch of cinnamon

4 oz. plain flour
1½ level teaspoonfuls baking powder
or
4 oz. self-raising flour
½ level teaspoonful baking powder
5 oz. caster sugar
3 tablespoonfuls oil
4 egg yolks
4 tablespoonfuls orange juice or cold water
Grated rind of 1 orange or grated rind of half a lemon
4 egg whites
¼ level teaspoonful cream of tartar

Set the oven at Gas No. 8 (450° F). Butter the bottom and sides of a 7-inch square tin or an 8-inch loose-bottomed tin. Arrange thinly sliced sponge all over the bottom.

Put all the ingredients (except the egg whites) into a bowl, and beat until smooth and fluffy. This is easiest with an electric mixer. Beat the whites until they hold stiff peaks, then beat in 2 teaspoonfuls caster sugar. Fold this meringue into the cheese mixture, then spoon into the sponge case and level with a spatula. Put the cake into the oven and *immediately* turn the temperature down to Gas No. 4 (350° F). Bake for twenty-five minutes, Open the oven and test the cake—it should feel firm to the touch for an inch all round the edge. If not, leave for another five minutes.

When the cake is ready, take it out and turn up the oven to Gas No. 7 (425° F). Stir the sugar into the soured cream, and then spread it evenly over the top of the warm cake. Sprinkle very lightly with the cinnamon. Put back into the oven for five minutes. Take out, and when quite cold, chill in the refrigerator, covered with foil.

Use a knife dipped in hot water to cut the cake into squares. This cheese cake will keep for several days in the refrigerator. The topping may be omitted, but the soured cream does set into a delicious creamy layer.

Chiffon Sponge Cake

This is a delicious cake, delicate in texture, yet moist to eat. It is perfect to serve with the cup of tea that breaks the fast after Yom Kippur.

Set the oven at Gas No. 3 (325° F). Have ready a large ring tin or a 9-inch wide, deep, round cake tin, or an 8-inch square, deep cake tin, but do *not* grease them. Into a medium mixing bowl put the sifted flour, the sugar, the baking powder and (if plain flour is used) a pinch of salt. Make a well in this mixture and add the oil, the unbeaten egg yolks, the water or orange juice, and the rind. Beat with a wooden spoon until smooth. Into a large bowl put the egg whites and the cream of tartar, and whisk them together until the meringue holds stiff peaks and is so solid that it will stay in the bowl even when it is turned upside down. Pour the yolk mixture onto this meringue, and use a metal spoon to cut and fold the two together until the mixture is evenly creamy in colour. Pour into the cake tin and bake for fifty-five minutes, or until firm to the touch. Leave the tin upside down on a cooling tray until it is quite cold. Then run a knife round the inside edges of the tin, and the cake will fall out.

Serve the cake plain, sifted with icing sugar, as an accompaniment to fruit or ice-cream; or split and fill it with fruit and cream.

Cut-And-Come-Again Cake

A superb cake recipe, which will keep tender and moist for a week in an airtight tin. It is delicious whether it is iced or left plain, save for a dusting of icing sugar.

3 oz butter
3 oz. white fat
7 oz. caster sugar
4 oz. plain flour and 4 oz. self-raising flour
3 large eggs
4 tablespoonfuls cold milk
1 teaspoonful vanilla essence

An hour beforehand, take your fats and eggs out of the refrigerator. *Turn on the oven* to Gas No. 4 (350° F). *Prepare your tin* by greasing it with oil on the bottom and sides, and lining the bottom (if it is square or round) with a piece of greased greaseproof paper cut to fit. (Lining is not necessary if a ring tin is used.) You can use an 8-inch square tin 2 inches deep, or a 9-inch diameter fluted ring tin, or a 7-inch round, loose-bottomed cake tin 3 inches deep. Sieve the two kinds of flour onto a square of greaseproof paper. Put the two fats in a large mixing bowl. If they are too hard to cream, put in your lit oven for *two minutes only* then remove; they must not melt at all or the cake texture will be spoilt.

Beat by hand using a wooden spoon, or with the mixer, until the two fats look like mayonnaise, then start adding the caster sugar a tablespoonful at a time, beating after each addition. Continue to beat until the mixture looks a very pale cream and has a fluffy, almost whipped cream texture. Beat in the essence. Break the eggs into a bowl and beat with a rotary whisk until the yolks and whites are thoroughly blended. Start adding to the creamed mixture a tablespoonful at a time, beating until fluffy again after each addition. Finally *stir* in the flour, alternately with the cold milk, in three separate portions. Use a metal spoon, so that no air is beaten out, Stir until the mixture looks smooth, and there is no sign of the flour.

To Make a Marble Cake

Use half the mixture to fill any of the tins, dropping it by spoonfuls with gaps in between, to leave room for the

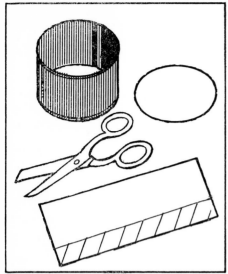

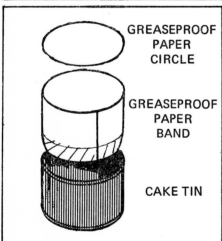

GREASEPROOF
PAPER
CIRCLE

GREASEPROOF
PAPER
BAND

CAKE TIN

chocolate half. To the remaining cake mixture, add 1 level tablespoonful of cocoa and 4 level tablespoonfuls of drinking chocolate. Stir well, then drop this mixture into the gaps left by the white portion. Gently smooth the top of the cake level.

Sultana Cake

Omit the vanilla essence and instead beat in the rind of half a lemon. Plump ½ lb. of sultanas by standing them in boiling water for five minutes then draining and dabbing dry with a tea towel. Stir into the cake mixture with the flour.

Coconut Cake

Fold 2 oz. desiccated coconut into the cake with the flour.

Almond Cake

Omit the vanilla essence and add eight drops of almond essence instead. Instead of 4 oz. of plain flour, fold in 2 oz. of plain flour and 2 oz. of ground almonds.

Madeira Cake

Leave the cake mixture plain, as in the basic recipe. Bake the cake in a 7-inch round cake tin. After half an hour of cooking time, open the oven, lay a 3-inch long sliver of orange or lemon peel over the cake and close the oven door again.

If you do not wish to ice the cakes, proceed as follows: before the cake is baked, paint the uncooked surface of the cake with milk, and scatter with a thin, even layer of caster sugar. (This is unnecessary in a ring tin, as the top of the cake will become the underside when it is cooked.)

To bake the cakes. In a square or ring tin, bake for one hour. In a round deep tin, bake for one hour, then reduce the heat to Gas No. 3 (325° F) for a further half hour.

To test whether done. Open the oven gently, and press the centre of the cake with the tip of the forefinger. If it is ready, the cake will spring back at once. If not, a faint impression will remain. The sides of the cake will have shrunk slightly from the sides of the tin.

When the cake is cooked, remove it from the oven and stand it in the tin on a metal cooling tray. Leave for five minutes. If it is in a ring tin, reverse the tin onto a second cooling tray. If it is a loose-bottomed tin, stand it on a canister of smaller circumference and gently ease down the sides. When the cake is quite cool, remove the loose bottom. If it is in a square, solid-bottomed tin, reverse onto a second cooling tray. When the cakes are quite cool, wrap in foil, and store in an airtight cake tin.

Fairy Cakes

2oz. white fat
2 oz. butter
5 oz. caster sugar
3 oz. plain flour and 3 oz. self-raising flour
2 large eggs
2 tablespoonfuls cold milk
Grated rind of half a lemon
$1\frac{1}{2}$ oz. halved glace cherries
1 oz. of slivered, blanched almonds

Use the basic method, with these ingredients.

Spoon the mixture into twenty-four paper cases standing on baking trays. Bake in a quick oven (Gas No. 5, 375° F) for fifteen to twenty minutes, or until golden brown and springy to the touch. Makes 24.

Lekach (Honey Cake)

4 tablespoonfuls oil
2 eggs
6. oz. self-raising flour
$\frac{1}{2}$ level teaspoonful bicarbonate of soda
$\frac{1}{2}$ level teaspoonful mixed spice
$\frac{1}{2}$ level teaspoonful cinnamon
$\frac{1}{2}$ level teaspoonful ginger
3 oz. caster sugar
$\frac{1}{2}$ lb. warm honey (stand it near the cooker for an hour)
2 oz. chopped walnuts or almonds
Juice and rind of a medium orange

Spice cakes sweetened with honey or syrup improve with keeping. This cake should be made four or five days before it is to be used. The orange juice makes a refreshing contrast to the sweetness of the honey.

Set oven at Gas No. 4 (350° F). Grease, then line, the bottom of an 8-inch square tin (2 inches in depth) with greased greaseproof paper. Whisk the oil and sugar until they begin to thicken, then whisk in the well-beaten eggs and the warm honey. Finally, stir in the flour (sifted with the bicarbonate of soda and the spices) alternately with the orange juice. Stir in the chopped nuts (sultanas may be substituted if preferred). Pour into the tin and bake for one hour, or until firm to the touch. Take out of the oven, and after five minutes turn out of the tin onto a cooling tray. Wash the tin and return the cooled cake, then cover tightly with foil. To serve, cut into diamonds and squares.

Wine Cake

1 lb. tin of golden syrup
Water to fill the empty tin
An 8 oz. glass filled with caster sugar
An 8 oz. glass filled with oil
3 eggs
1 lb. self-raising flour
2 level teaspoonfuls mixed spice
1 level teaspoonful ginger
1 level teaspoonful cinnamon
1 level teaspoonful baking powder
2 level teaspoonfuls bicarbonate of soda dissolved in 5 tablespoonfuls kosher wine

This is similar in texture to a honey cake, but is preferred by many people, as it is made with golden syrup. It is so moist that it can be eaten as soon as it is made, though it will keep well if required.

Set the oven at Gas No. 2 (315° F). Grease then line the bottom of a rectangular tin (approximately 12 inches × 9 inches × 2 inches), using greased greaseproof paper.

In a large pan put the syrup, water, sugar and oil, and heat until the sugar has dissolved, but do not allow the mixture to boil. Cool while you whisk three eggs until frothy, then stir in the syrup mixture. Finally, fold in the flour sifted with the spices, and the bicarbonate of soda dissolved in the wine.

Pour into the lined tin and bake for one and a half hours, or until the top feels firm to the touch. Take out of the tin after five minutes, and turn onto a cooling tray. Remove the paper. Wash the tin, then return the cake to it. Foil cover and store until needed.

To serve, cut in squares and diamonds.

Rich Fruit Cake

This is a rich, moist cake that is ideal to store and ice for special occasions, such as a wedding or a barmitzvah. It is equally delicious left plain. Unless one is especially interested in icing and has had some professional instruction, it is more satisfactory to bake the cake at home and have it iced by a confectioner.

10 oz. butter
10 oz. soft brown sugar
6 eggs
$\frac{1}{2}$ lb. currants
$\frac{1}{2}$ lb. seedless raisins
1 lb. sultanas
2 oz. cut-up angelica
2 oz. chopped glace pineapple
4 oz. chopped candied peel
4 oz. ground almonds
4 oz. halved glace cherries
Grated rind of half an orange and a lemon
2 level teaspoonfuls mixed spice
12 oz. plain flour
Pinch of salt
Pinch of bicarbonate of soda dissolved in
   2 teaspoonfuls of milk (this helps to darken
   the cake)

To make a successful fruit cake certain special points must be kept in mind:

(1) The richer the cake in fruit and eggs, the less artificial raising agent—such as baking powder, is needed. (This cake has none at all.)

(2) The richer the cake, the slower the oven and the longer the cooking time required.

(3) The longer the cooking time, the more protection is needed for the cake, to prevent it from drying out. Use well-oiled brown paper to line the cake tin, and leave a small container of boiling water in the bottom of the oven while the cake is baking, to keep it moist.

To prepare the currants, sultanas and raisins, even if pre-cleaned during manufacture, put in a bowl, cover with boiling water and leave for five minutes. Drain well, then dab dry on a tea towel. Or leave spread out on trays in cool (Gas No. 1, 300° F) oven for half an hour.

Set the oven at Gas No. 1 (300° F). Line the bottom and sides of an oiled 9-inch, loose-bottomed, deep cake tin with well-oiled brown paper (see illustration). Sift the flour with the salt and spices onto a square of greaseproof paper. Mix the fruit with the ground almonds and the grated peel. Cream the butter until like mayonnaise, then beat in the sugar until the mixture looks smooth and fluffy. Beat the eggs together until fluffy, then add a tablespoonful at a time to the creamed mixture, beating until smooth again after each addition. Add a teaspoonful of flour after each addition if the mixture looks as though it is about to curdle—that is, if it starts to separate and become "curdy". Curdled cake mixture does not hold the fruit well.

Finally, fold in the flour and spice, alternately with the almonds and fruit, then stir in the dissolved bicarbonate of soda. Spoon the cake mixture into the prepared tin, making a slight depression in the centre, so that the surface of the cake will be flat and even for icing. Bake for three to three and a half hours, or until a skewer comes out clean when the centre of the cake is pierced and there is no sizzling sound coming from the cake itself. Allow to cool completely before turning out onto a cooling tray. Two to three tablespoonfuls of brandy can be spooned over the warm cake while it is still in the tin.

Wrap in foil and store for one month, before it is iced or eaten.

Yomtov Chocolate Cake with Peppermint Icing

4 oz. caster sugar
4 oz. butter
2 eggs
5 oz. self-raising flour
3 oz. drinking chocolate
2 oz. ground almonds
½ teaspoonful vanilla essence
2 tablespoonfuls hot water
2 tablespoonfuls cold milk

This is a delicious cake to serve when the family comes for tea at Yomtov. It keeps moist and tender for a week.

Set the oven at Gas No. 4, 350° F. Oil, then line the bottom of a loose-bottomed 8-inch cake tin with oiled grease-paper. Have the butter at room temperature for an hour beforehand. Put into a bowl and beat with a wooden spoon until like mayonnaise. Add the caster sugar and continue to beat until fluffy and creamy. Add the vanilla. Beat in the eggs (beaten together until frothy) a tablespoonful at a time. Beat in the hot water. Sift the flour, the ground almonds and the drinking chocolate into a bowl. Add to the creamed mixture alternately with the cold milk. Spoon into the tin and level with a spatula. Bake for forty to fifty minutes, or until the top feels firm but spongy, when gently pressed with the forefinger. Leave for five minutes in the tin, then turn out onto a cooling tray and allow to go quite cold before it is iced.

Peppermint Icing

2 oz. plain dessert chocolate
1 oz. butter
Few drops of peppermint essence (available at the chemist)

Melt the butter in a basin standing in a pan of simmering water. Add the broken-up chocolate, and stir until smooth. Take away from the heat and add a few drops of peppermint essence. Pour immediately over the cake—it will set like chocolate as it cools. It can be left plain, or decorated while warm with coarsely chopped walnuts, or a decoration of blanched almonds and glacè cherry. If you like a really thick topping, double the quantities.

Pastry

1 packet prepared strudel paste
1 lb. cooking apples, peeled, cored and sliced
$\frac{1}{16}$ inch thick, mixed with 4 oz. sugar
3 oz. chopped, stoned raisins
1½ cups dry breadcrumbs, or fresh crumbs
  fried in half the butter
4 oz. melted butter (margarine for a meat meal)

8 oz. plain flour
Pinch of salt
5 oz. butter or 4 oz. margarine and 1 oz. white
  fat
1 whole egg and 1 tablespoonful of cold water,
  beaten together
1 teaspoonful vinegar
1 level tablespoonful icing sugar.

Apfel Strudel

A true stretched strudel dough is difficult to make, and can only be learned by watching an expert at work. However, it is possible for a new cook to make excellent strudel using a prepacked strudel dough. This is the recipe given below. Strudel should always be served warm. It can be reheated for ten minutes in a moderate oven (Gas No. 4, 350° F), before it is served.

On a table, put a damp, white tea towel, with the edge over-lapping the table. Do not open the strudel packet until you have everything ready. Open the packet carefully and unfold the strudel, which will be in two sheets. Lay a sheet on the damp cloth and brush it with butter (or margarine), then sprinkle with crumbs and a little sugar. Lay the second sheet of pastry on top, brush thickly with fat, and then with the remaining crumbs. If the crumbs are fried, use less butter to brush on. On the pastry half nearest to you, arrange the apple and raisin mixture. Dredge over a little more butter. Fold the pastry in at each end to cover apples, then lift the cloth and roll up the strudel into a roll. Roll on to a greased tray. Dredge with the remaining butter. Cover with greaseproof paper. Bake in a moderate oven (Gas No. 4, 350° F) for forty-five minutes, removing paper towards the end. Serves four generously, or makes six moderate portions.

Two-Crust Fruit Pie

In any pastry recipe it is the fat content that makes it tender, and an excess of flour that can make it tough. Too much water makes pastry hard, too little makes it crumbly and dry. So, perfect pastry has a high ratio of fat to flour (the fat never weighing less than half the weight of the flour), with only just enough liquid added to hold the dry ingredients together.

The ideal fat mixture for shortcrust is butter mixed with a

15

little white fat. However, if the pie is to be eaten after a meat meal, then margarine and white fat will give tender (if less tasty) results.

Fat must always be rubbed into the flour until no particles bigger than a small pea are visible when the bowl is shaken. This means, that as the fat melts in the oven heat, it can be quickly—and therefore crisply—absorbed by the surrounding flour.

A "light hand" with pastry is necessary when you get out the rolling pin. This must never be used like a steam roller to flatten the pastry, but should be wielded with short, sharp strokes, (with the main weight always on the forward push) so that the pastry is "persuaded" to flatten out. The use of egg is optional in pastry, but it does help to keep it fresh to eat on the second day.

I prefer to use plain flour for pastry, as the baking powder in self-raising tends to make the cooked crust stale. However, until you are an experienced pastry cook, you will get "lighter" results with a mixture of half plain and half self-raising flour.

Into a large mixing bowl, sift the flour, the salt and the icing sugar. Cut the fats used into 1-inch cubes, then rub gently into the flour mixture with the tips of the fingers of both hands. An electric mixer can be successfully used at slow speed, provided the whisk is used, as paddle-type beaters tend to crush the fat. When the fat has been rubbed in enough, the mixture will resemble coarse crumbs, with no particle larger than a small pea. Do not over-rub beyond this stage, or the mixture will become sticky and be unable to absorb the correct amount of liquid, and the baked pastry will be dry.

Beat together the yolk of the egg, the icy water and the vinegar. Sprinkle this liquid into the bowl, using your cupped hand to turn the mixture over and over, until all the particles are moistened but not wet—add a little more water if necessary. Gather the dampened mixture together, and lightly mould it into a ball. Turn it onto a pastry board sprinkled with a very light layer of flour. Knead it gently with your finger-tips to remove any cracks. Divide it into two portions, wrap each in foil and put in the refrigerator for half an hour at least. (At this stage it can be stored up to three days if required.)

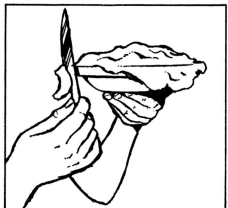

To finish the pie. Get ready a 10-inch pie plate or an 8-inch pie dish, 1 inch deep. Have the required filling ready in a bowl (see recipes below). Put one of the balls of pastry on a lightly floured pastry board. Lightly flour a rolling pin, and using short, sharp strokes, start rolling the pastry into a circle about 11 inches across. Keep making quarter turns of the pastry, so that the circle is kept even and it does not stick to the board. Do not turn the pastry over, as raw flour would then be rolled into both sides and the pastry would be toughened. Carefully ease the pastry circle onto the back of the rolling pin then lay it gently into position in the pie dish. Spoon in the filling.

Lift up the filled dish in one hand and, holding a sharp knife vertically with the other, cut off the overhanging pastry all the way round. Knead these remains into the second ball of pastry and roll that out in exactly the same way, to fit the top of the pie. With a pastry brush, dampen the edge of the bottom crust all the way round, then gently transfer the top crust via the rolling pin to fit on top. With the side of a finger press the two crusts together. Use a dull-bladed knife to nick the two crusts together all the way round, making "cuts" every eighth of an inch. Alternately you can "scallop" the two edges together with the fingers and thumb. Beat the white of the egg until it is frothy. Make six cuts in the centre of the top crust (to allow steam to escape), then paint the egg white evenly over the top. Scatter a thin layer of granulated sugar over the pie, and bake as directed below. (A sheet of foil on the shelf below is good insurance against any dripping, hot fruit juice.)

Perfect Apple Pie
The filling. Peel, quarter and core four large baking apples, then cut them into slices one-eighth of an inch thick. Put them into a bowl and mix with 4 oz. of granulated sugar, 2 level teaspoonfuls cornflour, 1 level teaspoonful cinnamon, and a grating of nutmeg. Two tablespoonfuls of raisins can also be added. Fill the pie with this mixture, mounding it into the centre. A pie dish 8 inches in circumference and 1 inch in depth is ideal. *Bake* in a hot oven (Gas No. 7, 425° F) for ten minutes, then reduce to moderate (Gas No. 5, 375° F) and bake for a further forty minutes, or until the pastry is a rich golden brown.

Bilberry Tart

Can be made with fresh or frozen fruit. Use a 10-inch flat pie plate.

The filling. Mix together ¾ lb. bilberries, four oz. sugar and the juice of half a lemon. Preheat the oven to Gas No. 6 (400° F). When the pie is put in, turn down to Gas No. 5 (375° F), and bake for thirty-five minutes.

Rhubarb Pie

Wash then cut the heel off each stick from 1 lb. of forced rhubarb, but do not peel the fruit. Cut into 1-inch lengths and put into a bowl with 6 oz. of granulated sugar and 2 level teaspoonfuls cornflour. Stir well, then spoon into the pie dish (use one 8 inches in diameter and 1 inch deep, as for an apple pie). Dot the surface of the fruit with ½ oz. of butter (or ½ oz. margarine for a meat meal) before putting on the top crust. Bake at Gas No. 7 (425° F) for ten minutes, then at Gas No. 5 (375° F) for a further thirty minutes.

Canned Pie Fillings

There are some excellent ready-to-use pie fillings on the market. However, most of them are improved by the juice of half a lemon stirred in gently before they are put into the pie dish.

All these pies will serve four to six people generously. It is really not practical to make less than the ½ lb. of pastry for which the recipe is given. However, if you really want to make a very small pie, buy a 7-inch pie tin, and use half the quantity of filling. Make the full amount of pastry, however, and use the remainder (you will probably have only a quarter of it left), to make half a dozen jam tarts. Roll the left-over pastry an eighth of an inch thick and cut into 2½-inch circles with a fluted cutter. Put in patty tins and cover with a teaspoonful of jam. Cover with a trellis of left-over pastry bits. Bake in a quick oven (Gas No. 7 425° F) for ten minutes and take out of the patty tins while warm, or they may stick.

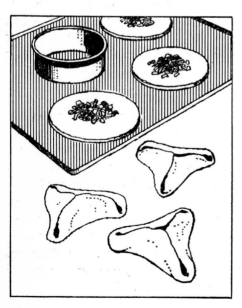

Hamantaschen

Like their corners, the varieties of Hamantaschen doughs number three—kichel, short pastry and yeast. Unless one is a dedicated yeast cook, it is more practicable to buy yeast dough Hamantaschen from the baker. The cakey, kichel dough is, however, easily made at home—it keeps fresh for weeks. And for those who like a crisp, only slightly sweetened pastry, I recommend a rich shortcrust mixture, crispened with icing sugar. With either, the filling is always the same.

Kichel Dough
10–12 oz. of flour (half plain and half self-raising)
5 oz. granulated sugar
4 fl. oz. oil
2 eggs
1 teaspoonful vanilla essence
Rind of half an orange

Whisk the eggs with a rotary beater, until they are thick, then whisk in the sugar, the oil, the vanilla and the orange rind. Finally, stir in enough of the measured flour to make a rollable dough.

Pastry Mixture
4 oz. plain flour
4 oz. self-raising flour
5 oz. butter
1 oz. icing sugar
1 egg yolk
1 dessertspoonful lemon juice
2 tablespoonfuls icy water

Sift the flour and icing sugar into a bowl. Gently rub the butter into the flour, until the mixture resembles coarse crumbs. Beat together the egg yolk, the lemon juice and the water. Add to the mixture gradually, mixing with your cupped hand until all the dry ingredients have been moistened—reserve a dessertspoonful of the liquid for glazing the Hamantaschen. Knead the dough lightly to remove any cracks, then wrap in foil, and chill for at least an hour.

To shape either kind of dough. Roll out the chilled dough an eighth of an inch thick, and cut into circles 3 inches in diameter, using a floured plain biscuit cutter and a floured pastry board. Put a spoonful of the selected filling onto the dough, then draw up the corners to make a Hamantasch shape. Brush with the remaining egg mixture.

To bake. Cook the *kichel dough* Hamantaschen in a moderate oven (Gas No. 4, 350° F) for half an hour, or until golden brown.

Cook the *pastry Hamantaschen* in a quick oven (Gas No. 6, 400° F) for fifteen minutes, or until golden brown and crunchy.

Fillings for Hamantaschen
Wine and Walnut Filling
4 oz. walnuts
4 oz. stoned dates
8-oz. packet of mixed dried fruits
1 tablespoonful Kiddush wine
2 tablespoonfuls of warmed golden syrup
Juice and grated rind of half a lemon
1 level teaspoonful cinnamon

Chop the walnuts and dates, and mix with all the remaining ingredients. (Left-over mixture can be stored in a screw-top jar in the refrigerator for several weeks. It can be used to fill little tart cases or pastry turnovers.)

15*

Poppy Seed Filling

1 breakfast cupful of poppy seeds
Half a cupful of milk
2 heaped tablespoonfuls honey
4 level tablespoonfuls raisins
1 level teaspoonful grated lemon rind

Apricot and Apple Filling

1 lb. apples, peeled, cored, quartered and
** thinly sliced**
Grated rind and juice of half a lemon
4 oz. sugar
1 tablespoonful apricot jam
Little butter for greasing pan

Prune Filling

½ lb. tenderised prunes
3 oz. raisins
2 oz. walnuts
Juice and rind of half a lemon
4 oz. sugar

The Pastry

6 oz. plain flour
6 oz. self-raising flour
8 oz. butter (or margarine if to be served after
** meat)**
3 oz. caster sugar
1 large egg
The grated rind and juice of half a lemon

The Filling

3 breakfast cupfuls of mixed dried fruit (this
** can be sultanas, raisins and currants, or**
** raisins, sliced glace cherries and chopped**
** dates)**
Raspberry or apricot jam
4 oz. granulated sugar mixed with
** ½ teaspoonful cinnamon**
2 grated apples (optional)

Pour boiling water over the seeds and leave until cool, then drain well. Either pound in a mortar, or with the end of a rolling pin, or put through a food mill. Put in a pan with the milk and honey, and cook until thick but still juicy, stirring well. Stir in the fruit and rind. Taste and add a little sugar if necessary. Use when cool.

Butter a heavy pan, and put in the lemon juice. Arrange the sliced apples and the sugar in layers, and top with the lemon rind and the jam. Bring to the boil, then reduce the heat until the mixture is simmering. Cover and cook for ten to fifteen minutes, stirring once. The apples should be tender, but not mushy. Allow to cool, then strain off any juice (use in a fruit salad), and use the apple mixture to fill the Hamantaschen.

Soak the prunes and raisins overnight, covered in strained, cold, left-over tea. Remove the prune stones. Chop or mince all the ingredients together.

Fruited Strudel (Made with a Rich Shortcrust Pastry)

This requires a light hand with the pastry, and a heavy hand with the filling! If possible, chill the dough for an hour before rolling, as it is then much easier to handle.

Mix the sugar and flours in a large bowl. Rub in the butter very gently until no lumps larger than a tiny pea appear when the bowl is shaken. Beat together the egg, the lemon juice and the rind. Sprinkle onto the flour mixture until it is evenly dampened, then gather together into a dough with your fingers. Divide into four balls, and chill for half an hour. Roll each ball of dough into a rectangle about 9 inches long and 4½ inches wide.

Plump all the dried fruit (other than the dates and cherries) by covering with boiling water, then drain after five minutes and dab dry. Mix all the dried fruit with the cinnamon and sugar. If apples are used, add them, together with an ounce of ground almonds, to absorb the juice. Spread each rectangle with jam, leave a ½-inch margin all round, and sprinkle thickly with the sugared fruit. Roll up each rectangle like a flattened Swiss roll, then carefully lay them on a greased tray, with the joint underneath. Mark lightly into slanting slices an inch wide, but do not cut right through the base of the strudel. Brush with milk and granulated sugar, or if preferred, with slightly beaten egg white and sugar. Bake in a moderate oven (Gas No. 4, 350° F) for forty-five minutes to one hour. The strudel should be a rich brown. Store in tins when quite cold, and cut through into slices just before serving.

Breads

1 lb. 2 oz. plain strong flour (ask the grocer for
  a bread flour)
2 level teaspoonfuls honey
2 level teaspoonfuls salt
2 level teaspoonfuls sugar
2 tablespoonfuls oil
1 egg
8 fl. oz. hot water (use a glass measure)
½ oz. fresh yeast

Challah Plait

The first time you bake bread, allow yourself plenty of time.
Either start the dough first thing on Friday morning, or
make it on Thursday afternoon and refrigerate it overnight
(see the instructions below). Make one loaf at first, until
you are confident of the way to handle the dough. Fresh
yeast will keep up to four days if foil-wrapped and refrigerated. It can be used as long as it looks pale and putty-like.
Discard it if it looks brown and granular.

Put 4 tablespoonfuls of the water into a little bowl, and
when it feels luke-warm, add the yeast and leave for five
minutes to dissolve. Pour the remaining hot water onto the
oil, sugar, salt and honey in a large mixing bowl. When it
feels luke-warm, stir in the dissolved yeast liquid and the
beaten egg (save a little for gilding the loaf). Now add half
the flour and beat with a wooden spoon or a paddle-type
mixer until the batter falls in "sheets" off the spoon. This
takes two to three minutes. Now stir in the remaining flour,
to form a soft dough. Leave for ten minutes. Tip out onto
a well-floured board, and using the floured heel of the
hand, knead until the dough looks smooth and silky and
does not stick to the board. Do not be afraid to add a little
extra flour if necessary. Put the dough into a large greased
plastic bag or into a 7-lb. biscuit tin kept for the purpose;
either way is equally satisfactory.

If the dough is to be refrigerated, put it away overnight. It
will rise slowly in the refrigerator and be ready to shape
next day. If to be made up the same day, leave near the
cooker (but away from direct heat) until the dough has
doubled in size, and springs back when an impression is
made with the forefinger. (About one and a half hours.)

Turn it onto the floured board, and knead it lightly with the
ball of the hand to distribute the large bubbles of gas evenly
throughout the dough. Cover with a tea towel on the board
and leave for a further five minutes.

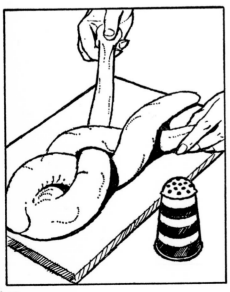

To shape the freshly risen dough or dough that has risen in the refrigerator, divide the dough into three. Roll each portion into a sausage 1½ inches in diameter. Have ready an oiled baking tray. Join the three sausages together at one end, then plait into a loaf shape. Lay on the greased tray, paint with the reserved egg, and scatter with poppy seeds, Leave for a further twenty minutes to rise again, then bake, first in a hot oven (Gas No. 7, 425° F) for ten minutes (to kill the yeast), and then for a further forty-five minutes at Gas No. 4 (350° F). When the bread is baked, it will sound hollow when the bottom is tapped.

Makes one large challah or two small ones.

Quick Streusel Kuchen

A sweet and fluffy kuchen with a crunchy topping. Serve it in wedges as a cake when it is fresh. After a few days, it can be sliced more thinly and buttered like a tea bread.

Turn the oven to Gas No. 5 (375° F). Grease the bottom and sides of a 9-inch diameter, deep, loose-bottomed, round cake tin, or one that is 8 inches square and approximately 2 inches deep.

The Cake
8 oz. self-raising flour, plus 1 level teaspoonful baking powder
3 oz. caster sugar
3 oz. butter
1 egg
¼ pint cold milk
1 rounded tablespoonful apricot jam or marmalade

The Streusel Topping
2 rounded tablespoonfuls plain or self-raising flour
2 heaped tablespoonfuls soft fine brown sugar (Barbados or "pieces")
1 oz. melted butter
1 level teaspoonful ground cinnamon

To make the cake. Sift the flour and baking powder into a large mixing bowl. Add the butter in 1-inch lumps, then gently rub in with the finger-tips until no lumps larger than a very small pea appear on the surface when the bowl is shaken. Stir in the sugar. Break the egg into a small bowl and add the milk. Beat with an egg whisk until frothy. Stir in the jam or marmalade. Pour the liquids onto the flour mixture, and stir with a wooden spoon until a soft thick batter is formed. Spoon into the tin, levelling the surface with a spatula.

To make the Streusel topping. In a small bowl, mix together the flour, brown sugar and cinnamon. Melt the butter gently in a small pan, then pour it onto the flour mixture. Mix with the tips of the fingers until a crumbly mixture is formed. Sprinkle evenly over the cake mixture. Put the cake in the oven slightly above the centre. Bake for forty minutes, or until the cake is springy to the touch and has shrunk from the sides of the tin. Allow to cool for five minutes, then remove from the tin as follows:

From a loose-bottomed tin. Run a knife gently round the

tin to loosen the cake. Stand the tin on a canister (such as a tea caddy), which is 2 inches smaller in diameter. Gently pull the cake tin sides down, leaving the cake balanced on the canister. Lift down on to a cooling tray. When cold, ease out the tin bottom.

From a square tin. If this has a loose bottom, proceed as above. If not, place the tin on a cooling tray for half an hour. Leave the Streusel in the tin, but cover it completely with foil. Cut squares off the cake as required.

Refrigerator Kuchen

This is a very simple yeast kuchen recipe. Chilling the dough after it has been mixed makes it easy to handle, and avoids the need for tedious kneading. The quantity makes a 2-lb. cinnamon fruit loaf and an 8-inch square Streusel kuchen—it is not practical to make it in smaller quantities. Yeast cakes develop the finest texture and flavour when the dough has been allowed to rise in a moist atmosphere of 80° F. This can be most easily achieved by placing the dough in a plastic bag and leaving it in the plate rack of a cooker, over a pan of gently steaming water. If you have no rack, put the dough in the airing cupboard.

1 lb. plain flour
1 level teaspoonful salt
1 oz. yeast
¼ pint warm milk
4 oz. butter
4 oz. caster sugar
2 eggs
Grated rind of half a lemon

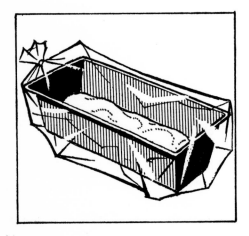

Heat the milk until bubbles form round the edge, then cool it to luke-warm—when there is no sensation either of heat or cold from a drop on the inside of the wrist. Put the milk into a basin with the yeast and salt, and leave to dissolve— about five minutes. Cream the butter, then beat in the sugar until fluffy. Add the beaten eggs a tablespoonful at a time. together with the lemon rind. Beat in half the flour, and beat for two minutes, then add the yeasty milk and enough of the remaining flour to make a dough that just leaves the sides of the bowl clean, but is too soft to handle. Beat until the dough looks shiny and silky (an electric mixer is best for the job). Tip the mixture into a polythene bag which has been rubbed with oil, close with a rubber band and leave in the refrigerator overnight.

To Make a Cinnamon Fruit Loaf

Take half the dough from the plastic bag, and roll it on a floured board into a rectangle measuring 6 inches × 15. (If the dough has become too cold to roll, leave it in the kitchen to soften for half an hour.) Spread it with a thin layer of soft butter (as though you were buttering bread) and sprinkle with 3 oz. of caster sugar mixed with half a level teaspoonful of ground cinnamon. Sprinkle with 2 tablespoonfuls of sultanas. Roll up lengthwise like a tight Swiss roll, and put joint side down into a greased 2-lb. loaf tin.

Put the tin into a large plastic bag (to prevent the surface of the dough from becoming dry). Leave in a warm kitchen or airing cupboard until the dough looks puffy and has half-filled the tin—this will take about an hour. Bake in a quick moderate oven (Gas No. 5, 375° F) for forty-five minutes, covering the loaf with a piece of foil if it has become a rich brown before the baking time is complete. Take out of the oven. Leave for five minutes on a cooling tray. then turn out of the tin. While still warm, brush with a mixture of 3 tablespoonfuls of sifted icing sugar mixed to a coating consistency with cold milk. When cold, slice and butter.

Streusel Kuchen

To make the Streusel, mix 2 heaped tablespoonfuls of soft brown sugar with 2 rounded tablespoonfuls of flour and half a level teaspoonful of cinnamon. Pour on 1 oz. of melted butter and mix to a crumbly consistency with the finger-tips.

Pat the remaining half of the chilled dough to fit an 8-inch square, greased cake tin (two inches in depth). Brush the surface with a little melted butter and sprinkle evenly with the Streusel. Allow to rise until puffy (about forty-five minutes). Bake in a quick moderate oven (Gas No. 5, 375° F) for forty minutes, or until a rich brown. Cut in squares to serve.

Kuchen should be stored in individual polythene bags in a bread tin or drawer, and not in an airtight cake tin, in which it might go mouldy.

The Dietary Laws As They Affect The Household

Which categories of food are we permitted?

(1) Meat and meat products: only of cud-chewing animals with cloven hooves.

(2) Poultry and poultry products: chickens, ducks, geese, capons, turkeys. Meat and poultry must be killed in the proper manner (*shechita*) and sold under recognised supervision. They must be koshered before cooking.

(3) Fish and fish products: only of fish with fins and scales.

(4) Eggs: those of permitted birds; but when they contain any blood, even the slightest spot, they may not be used.

(5) Vegetables and cereals: all kinds are permitted, but some vegetables must be carefully examined and cleaned before use.

(6) Milk and meat may not be cooked or eaten together.

(7) There must be a time-lapse after eating meat foods, before milk foods or beverages are taken. The generally accepted practice is to wait not less than three hours. When milk foods are followed by meat, the mouth should be cleaned between the courses by washing, and by chewing a hard substance such as bread.

The following shopping guide may be helpful:

The Butcher

Only *kosher* butcher and poultry shops licensed by a recognised communal authority, such as the Board for Shechita, and under the supervision of a recognised rabbinical authority, such as the Beth Din, are permitted to display the Registered Trade Mark of the National Council of Shechita Boards, and one should make sure that purchases of kosher meat and poultry are made only from these shops. Do not be misled by Jewish butchers, who display the word "Kosher" or a Magen David or exhibit kosher sausages for sale, but whose meat has not been prepared according to religious requirements.

The only warranty of kashrut is to buy from shops that display the Registered Trade Mark.

The Fishmonger

Much of the fish available comes within the kosher category, having fins and scales. Shellfish, however, are forbidden, as are also eel, turbot, sturgeon, etc. The roe of forbidden fish may not be eaten (e.g. caviare, which is sturgeon-roe).

Of course, poultry may not be bought from fishmongers (this may not apply to Israel, where communal arrangements are different).

The Baker

It is important to ensure that no non-kosher cooking fats or other forbidden ingredients have been used in the baking of bread, cake, or biscuits (sweet or otherwise). Also, milk loaves, not clearly marked, may unwittingly be used with meat meals. It is therefore essential to shop at a Jewish baker who is under proper kashrut supervision, such as that of the Beth Din and Kashrus Commission.

The Greengrocer

All vegetables and fruit may be used: various kinds, however, require careful examination for insects and maggots and should be stoned and washed before cooking or eating.

The Grocer

Eggs of permitted birds may be used, but any with even the smallest blood spot must be rejected. Eggs used for cooking should be broken, one at a time, into a glass, to ensure that they are free of blood spots or blood.

Cheese. Hard or processed cheese can be guaranteed as kosher only if sanctioned by a recognised rabbinical authority, as most of the ordinary cheeses are prepared with a rennet which may be a non-kosher meat product.

Fats. Purchase only kosher margarine and kosher cooking-fats which have a Beth Din seal and are, therefore, made with vegetable oils. These may be used for either meats or milk dishes.

Canned foods. Soups and meats should carry a Beth Din authorisation.

Fish must be of a permitted type, in vegetable oil only.

Fruit and vegetables are permitted if prepared in water and/or sugar solution only.

Fish and Meat Pastes. Unless these carry the label of a recognised rabbinical authority, they may not be used.

Dried fruits must be carefully examined to ensure that they are free of maggots, etc.

Frying and salad oils. Make sure these are of vegetable origin.

Cereals. All cereals may be used, but some, such as barley, rice, etc., should be carefully examined to ensure that they are free of webs or mites.

Some baby-cereals contain non-kosher bone-meal. Adults may not eat these, but they are permitted (for medical reasons) to infants, and separate bowls, spoons, etc., should be kept for use with baby foods of this kind.

Biscuits. Packets of biscuits in many varieties are obtainable bearing the Beth Din stamp. Without such a *hechsher* they may contain animal or other non-kosher ingredients.

Sundries such as jellies (including marshmallow and Turkish delight), ice-cream, ice-cream mixture, cake mixture. There are brands of all these products which bear the seal of the Beth Din and Kashrus Commission, but others are not permitted, as they probably contain animal fats or gelatine, which may be of non-kosher animal origin.

Frozen foods. Vegetables or fruits may be used, but must still be examined for insects. Only fish in the permissible category (uncooked) may be bought frozen.

Household cleansers. For cleaning cooking utensils only kosher soap and some scouring powders may be used. As detergents generally have a purely chemical content, most proprietary brands may be used.

Wines. Only kosher wines should be purchased, and the bottle should be clearly marked as kosher—כשר. The majority of kosher wines, sherries, etc., are produced in Israel, and the label indicates this very clearly. Wine has to be treated with special care from the time of production till the time of consumption, since it is used for sacred and ceremonial purposes in home and synagogue on many religious occasions.

Shopping is easier if you live in a district where kosher goods are readily available. If your have no local centre for Jewish shopping, however, you will still be able to make arrangements for a weekly or fortnightly delivery, as many retailers will be glad to send a regular supply ordered by telephone or letter. Orders are regularly sent by post or by rail to families resident in places which are comparatively remote from centres of Jewish population. There may sometimes be difficulties in obtaining the products you require, but, since the principle is so important, you should be resourceful enough to make a workable arrangement.

Some Useful Addresses

BETH DIN (Court of the Chief Rabbi)
Adler House,
Tavistock Square,
London WC1.   *Telephone:* 01-387 5772.

ASSOCIATION OF JEWISH WOMEN'S
ORGANISATIONS IN THE UNITED
KINGDOM
Room 4,
Woburn House,
Upper Woburn Place,
London WC.   *Telephone:* 01-387 7688.

JEWISH INSTITUTE OF FAMILY GUIDANCE,
LTD.
Mrs. R. C. Winegarten,
Hon. Secretary,
364 Finchley Road,
London NW3.

JEWISH MARRIAGE EDUCATION COUNCIL
529b Finchley Road,
London NW3.   *Telephone:* 01-794 5222.

LEEDS BETH DIN
98 Chapeltown Road,
Leeds 7.   *Telephone:* 0532 42297.

LIVERPOOL AND DISTRICT RABBINATE
Rabbi Z. Plitnick,
91 Dunbabin Road,
Liverpool 16.   *Telephone:* Childwall 4194.

MANCHESTER BETH DIN
149 Cheetham Hill Road,
Manchester 8.   *Telephone:* 061 DEA. 6961.

NEWCASTLE UPON TYNE SHECHITA
BOARD
H. M. Guttentag,
Hon. Secretary,
6 Lutterworth Road,
Sunderland.   *Telephone:* 6906.

GLASGOW RABBINICAL COURT
Falloch Road,
Glasgow S2.   *Telephone:* Battlefield 3704.

Other addresses of institutions can be found in
The Jewish Year Book (published by Vallentine,
Mitchell).

Royal Institute of British Architects
66 Portland Place,
London W1.

The Building Centre (located in the following
towns) :
   Belfast, Birmingham, Bristol, Cambridge,
   Coventry, Dublin, Glasgow, London, Manchester, Nottingham, Southampton, Stoke-
   on-Trent.
For addresses, consult your local telephone
directory.

The British Carpet Centre
Dorland House,
Regent Street,
London W1.

Consumer's Association (publishers of *Which ?*)
Subscription Department,
Caxton Hill,
Hertford.

The Consumer Council
3 Cornwall Terrace,
London NW1.

The British Electrical Development Association
Trafalgar Buildings,
1 Charing Cross,
London SW1.

The Gas Council
4-5 Grosvenor Place,
London SW1.

The Coal Utilisation Council
19 Rochester Row,
London SW1.

For further addresses of advice centres and manufacturers, I recommend *The Modern Home: Information Here,* by Robert and Christine Turner (published by Pelham Books).

For comprehensive guidance on household cleaning, I recommend *Keep it Clean,* by Lia Low (published by Bodley Head).

INDEX

INDEX